TARGETING CUSTOMERS

SECOND EDITION

How to Use Geodemographic and Lifestyle Data in Your Business

TARGETING CUSTOMERS

SECOND EDITION

How to Use Geodemographic and Lifestyle Data in Your Business

Peter Sleight
Target Market Consultancy

NTC PUBLICATIONS LTD

First edition published in 1993
This edition published in 1997 by
NTC Publications Limited
Farm Road
Henley-on-Thames
Oxfordshire RG9 1EJ
United Kingdom
Telephone: 01491 574671
Facsimile: 01491 571188

A CIP catalogue record for this book is
available from the British Library

ISBN 1-899314-78-4

Typeset in 12/14 pt Garamond
by NTC Publications Ltd
Printed and bound in Great Britain by
Biddles Ltd, King's Lynn

CONTENTS

ACKNOWLEDGEMENTS

I would like to thank all my friends in the business who have helped with this publication. It would be invidious to pick out names; they know who they are!

Readers wanting more information about the census should contact:

Census Customer Services
ONS Census Division
Segensworth Road
Titchfield
Hampshire PO15 5RR
Tel: 01329 813800

Or in Scotland:

Customer Services Population Statistics Branch
General Register Office for Scotland
Ladywell House
Ladywell Road
Edinburgh EH12 7TF
Tel: 0131 314 4254

Readers interested in the activities of the MRS Census Interest Group should contact:

MRS Census Interest Group
Market Research Society
15 Northburgh Street
London EC1V 0AH
Tel: 0171 490 4911

PREFACE TO THE SECOND EDITION

The first edition of *Targeting Customers* went to press in March 1993. In the four years since it was written much has changed in the geodemographic and lifestyle marketplace. Those changes are covered comprehensively in this second edition.

While the principles involved have not changed – so the chapters dealing with these principles have changed little – other chapters have been extensively rewritten and expanded. Three chapters have been added to cover geographical information systems (GIS), media applications, and 'geodemographics at work' which contains profiles of the main companies plus case histories to illustrate geodemographic data in use.

In short, we are seeing an industry still growing rapidly, still changing, and clearly destined to become a more important constituent of consumer marketing and retail applications.

HOW TO USE GEODEMOGRAPHIC AND LIFESTYLE DATA IN YOUR BUSINESS

The marketing world can be divided into two groups of people – those who have used geodemographics, and those who have not. Perhaps ambitiously, this report is written for *both* groups. It starts with the basics for those who are unfamiliar with the concepts and techniques, and it goes into sufficient detail so that (hopefully) all but the very experienced will find something new and useful.

The report has been written with *users* in mind. It is intended to impart sufficient knowledge for those who are new to the subject to be able to take a view about the relevance (or otherwise) of geodemographics to their business. If they decide to introduce geodemographics, or if it is already on the scene, this report should give them the information they need to talk intelligently about the subject with suppliers or colleagues.

The style is non-technical. There is a great deal of jargon in the geodemographic arena; this report sets out to explain the jargon, certainly not to use it. There are more technical articles and books on the subject, and reference is made to them in the text and in the Bibliography.

Finally, the report is written from a personal stance, and in my personal style (which is fairly conversational, as readers will soon discover). Hopefully the personal stance will add extra 'bite', rather than appear as bias; I have attempted an objective view, but inevitably some apparent bias may creep in when dealing with methodologies or industry controversies. I do not apologise for this, but welcome any debate that might be generated!

CHAPTER ONE

'WHY SHOULD I BE INTERESTED IN GEODEMOGRAPHICS AND LIFESTYLES?'

Introduction

It is astonishing how much the market analysis marketplace has changed in the four years since writing the first edition of this book. The market value has grown hugely (see the next section for details), and lifestyle data is now all pervasive. The big companies are more dominant than they were; there is a strong trend towards multi-national operations. A number of takeovers have changed the scene.

The other major event that occurred in the interim was the publication of the results of the 1991 census. This had the effect of changing all the geodemographic classifications; all the system authors rebuilt their systems to incorporate the new data, immediately consigning most of my appendices to history!

The geographical information systems (GIS) market has made major advances since 1993 too. There has been an explosion in desktop systems, Windows '95 has become the favourite operating system for the marketing and retail desktop GIS, and this is now the standard form of delivery system for geodemographics.

So, reason enough for a second edition; and further evidence of the growing importance of geodemographics and lifestyle data.

Market Overview

The estimate for the value of the geodemographics market in Britain was put at £25 million for 1992 in the first edition of this book (source: Dr. Vince Mitchell, Manchester School of Management at UMIST in *Logistics Information Management*, Vol. 5, No. 3, 1992). A more recent study, conducted by T.M.C. in 1995, put the market value for 1995 at *£54 million*. In the same study, the estimated turnover of the three major lifestyle database companies operating in the UK (CMT, ICD and NDL) was *£30 million* for 1995. The methodology involved asking all the companies in the geodemographic and lifestyle data supply industry for confidential turnover figures (and various breakdowns), which would then only be published in aggregate. The growth rates and expectations then current, projected a combined market value of approximately *£100 million* for 1996, geodemographics and lifestyle databases combined. This figu*re mere*ly represents the turnover *of the suppliers; it ignores users' in-house costs* of use and implementation.

These figures in themselves are perhaps reason enough to take geodemographics and lifestyles seriously. There are a growing number of end-users spending large sums of money on these data, software and techniques, and the market growth seems to be running at about 20 per cent per annum currently. However, if you are not currently a user of these techniques, it would be understandable if your response to these market figures went along the line of – 'Fine, but I've managed perfectly well without them so far; why should I change my mind?'

In my view, there are a number of reasons why geodemographics and lifestyles deserve attention (or reappraisal, as the case may be). I have set out these reasons in the course of this chapter. Before getting into the issues, let's start at the beginning by defining terms.

Definitions

There are a number of definitions of geodemographics. My favourite is – 'the analysis of people by where they *live*', or a snappier alternative, 'locality marketing'. The 'locality' aspect of geodemographics is its most fundamental feature, of which, much more later. As the name geodemographics implies, the technique involves a fusion of demographics with geography. The term is generally used with reference to neighbourhood classifications (and indeed, that is the only form in which the vast majority of commercial users will have encountered geodemographics), but it is possible to embrace a wider definition, which encompasses any use of demographic data within units of area (for example, households within postcode sectors, perhaps from the census of population). The units of geographical area can be whatever the user wants (within reason), but the standard unit of area in British geodemographics tends to be the census 'neighbourhood' of, on average, 150 households. Some systems operate at the level of the unit postcode (15 addresses on average). More about this in Chapter 3.

A working definition of lifestyle database companies might be – 'lifestyle database companies build large databases of individuals, sourced from "lifestyle questionnaires". They offer list rental and associated services'. So, an immediate difference – lifestyle databases deal in units of *individuals*, geodemographics deals in units of *neighbourhoods*.

The reader may wonder why I have 'lumped together' geodemographics and lifestyles, if they are different? Certainly, when the lifestyle database operators first appeared on the British scene (in the mid-late 1980s) there was a confrontational stance – 'geodemographics is dead, long live lifestyles' was the cry from some quarters, and indeed, some echoes of this still remain. However, in my view, both techniques inhabit the same marketplace; recent developments have seen a blurring of former distinctions, as lifestyle database companies adopt geodemographic techniques, and geodemographic companies utilise lifestyle data within their products. This convergence is now a well-established trend.

Market Classification and Segmentation

The 'traditional' discriminators applied to market classification and segmentation are, of course, age, sex and social grade. Age and sex go back forever, social grade has been with us since the 1950s. Where does geodemographics fit into the plethora of ways in which target markets may be classified and segmented?, I hear you ask. In my personal view, geodemographics fits *alongside* other methods, as appropriate to the task; I am not one of the geodemographic missionaries who wish to convert marketers from (say) IPA Social Grade to the geodemographic persuasion. Not to say that there are not criticisms of IPA Social Grade (A, B, C1, C2, D, E), but it has the merit of being *generally* understood by most marketing people, and generally used across many research studies. There is no merit in trying to substitute geodemographics; not least because there are a *number* of geodemographic systems. Which would you choose? What about the users of the other systems? Much better to *add* geodemographics as a discriminator, as and when you need it.

Let us consider other methods of classification and segmentation, such as psychographics and lifestyles. Psychographics, concerned with attitudes and beliefs, is familiar to marketing people usually via one of the 'typologies', such as Synergy's Social Value Groups, or Stanford Research Institute's VALS. This form of segmentation is particularly popular among advertising agencies because of the insight it can give into the motivations of core groups of consumers. However, having identified such a group, it is very difficult to find its constituent members 'on the ground'. Work with which I have been associated over the years has looked at relationships between psychographic typologies and geodemographics, and while it is unlikely that there would be a close correlation between the two (after all, psychographics clearly applies to *individuals*, geodemographics to *neighbourhoods*) nevertheless, there were some quite reasonable relationships between some of the clusters from each methodology. CCN's 'Psyche' classification was the only example of trying to apply a 'general purpose' psychographic typology to unit postcodes (but new developments are afoot – see Chapter 12 and Appendix 3). Again, in my view; geodemographics as well as, not instead of, psychographics. The reason for attempting to make such a link, if you were wondering, is the desire to link an 'above-the-line' target with a 'below-the-line' one, for mailing and/or sales promotional purposes.

'Lifestyles' can mean whatever you want it to mean, as you will have noticed. Sometimes it is used as though psychographics and lifestyles are interchangeable; on other occasions, lifestyles and lifestages are confused. For the sake of this report, 'lifestyle' is defined as the clues to a person's lifestyle that can be gained from the (mainly behavioural) questions such as those asked by the lifestyle database companies; interest, sports and hobbies, activities, etc., plus their family situation, occupation, income and basic demographics. Taken together, the answers to these questions provide a fairly full picture of the person and the life he or she leads. In some cases that picture is enhanced with 'harder' information such as car owned/driven and white and brown goods in the household, financial products and services held and used, even fmcg products and brands consumed. Lifestyle databases are covered in some detail in Chapter 4, and their relationship to geodemographics is described both there and elsewhere in this report.

The lifestyle databases hold the 'variables' outlined above (and many more) about the individuals appearing on them. Geodemographics contain the variables about the neighbourhoods in question, *within* the solution. The methodology that goes into the neighbourhood classification systems is explained in Chapter 3. At this stage, suffice it to say that familiar marketing variables such as age, some measure of class, family composition, household tenure, etc., are 'embedded' within the classifications. So, markets can be classified and segmented by geodemographics, and by the variables held on lifestyle databases. Indeed, different methods of segmentation (by attitudes, and by behaviour) have been employed by some of the lifestyle database operators, in addition to the more straightforward selection by combinations of the 'raw' variables held on the databases (for example, income, occupation, car ownership, or activities such as squash-playing or do-it-yourself). More about this in Chapter 4.

In summary, *geodemographic* segmentation is only one form of market segmentation, although a potentially very useful one, which can be employed as and when appropriate. Applications are covered later in the book.

Ease of Use

Both geodemographics and lifestyles are *easy* to *use* for classification and segmentation purposes. Geodemographics are simply attached via a person's postcode (whether customer, or research respondent); selections from a lifestyle database are straightforward. Admittedly, it may sometimes seem that a whole new language needs to be learned, in order to use geodemographics; actually, it is not at all difficult once the basics have been assimilated. However, it is a fair point, when newcomers to the technique are met with a barrage of jargon! I believe this is one area where the practitioners need to make more effort to speak in plain English, although it is a very easy trap to fall into, and I must confess my culpability in the past. Remembering back to my first 'indoctrination', I can still remember the way my eyes glazed over at the mention of iterative relocation; and even now, consultants tend to bandy about terms like 'spatial analysis', which, while being perfectly understandable to geography students, may put others in mind of rocket science! I wonder how many potential users have been put off at first contact.

The Locational Aspect

The fact that geodemographics has a *locational* element is, to me, its greatest strength. This quality means that once you have identified your target market in geodemographic terms, you then know *where* that market is located. And knowing that, you can establish the most cost effective means of *reaching* that market with your message. This does not automatically imply direct mail as the medium, although there is a prevailing view that geodemographics is a 'below-the-line' phenomenon. It is not. This association has probably done geodemographics no harm at all to date, given the inexorable rise of database marketing. I shall return to this subject shortly!

But first – to what extent was the 'locality marketing' aspect of geodemographics *revolutionary* when it burst on the marketing scene at the turn of the 1980s? From a personal point of view, I can report that it changed my thinking dramatically. My background had been fmcg marketing, mostly in the grocery market. We used television advertising extensively, and like most other fmcg manufacturing/marketing companies, ITV regions were the units of area that were used for planning and analysis purposes. We would study the demographics of ITV regions, true, and we would study brand and product penetration by these areas. And we used 'standard' demographics to describe our target markets, generally speaking.

Then along came geodemographics. The units of area shifted from one-twelfth of the country (on average) to one one-hundred-and-thirty-thousandth! (From a TV region to a census neighbourhood.) Using a neighbourhood classification system, we could distinguish 36 different types of census neighbourhood, and we could establish the relative importance of each of those types to our market. We could gain a much clearer picture of who was buying/using our brand, what sort of neighbourhood they lived in, and we could uncover a wealth of other information about other products they bought, newspapers they read, stores they used. (Virtually everything we might wish to know, in fact, other than their detailed TV viewing habits; that piece of the jigsaw had to wait another decade.)

But *knowing* this is all very interesting, I hear to you say; what can I *do* with this knowledge? Well, I can use it directly, to decide where to drop product samples, leaflets, coupons, etc. I can relate my knowledge about the location of my core target market to other types of geography, for example, sales territories, distribution regions or store catchment areas. I can relate it to the road network and traffic flows, when considering the locations of poster sites for my product. I can relate it to distribution areas of free newspapers, or I can *link* it (via the geodemographic linkage into syndicated research) into readership of newspapers or magazines. My geodemographic knowledge can permeate many aspects of marketing and operational planning, including research for new product development, customer satisfaction surveys, etc. If I operate via stores or branches, I can decide where to open or close branches, and base my decisions on *where* my customers live, work and shop. If I work for a bank or building society, I can decide where to place my ATMs, and understand the dynamics of my branch network. I can work towards *optimising* my communication; via branches, direct mail or telephone? I can do all these things by using geodemographics, but particularly because of its *locational* aspect.

Geodemographics provides a 'bottom-up' as well as a 'top-down' view of a market. Conceptually, it is best seen as a *map* (indeed, the computer mapping that often accompanies geodemographic analysis usually tends to illuminate the recipient's understanding). Look at small areas first, and understand the *patterns* before zooming out and taking a smaller-scale overview; that way, you can understand those patterns before you risk losing the detail by aggregating those smaller areas into regions, or the national situation. Like the 'spy in the sky' satellite, look down on a town, then within the town to the neighbourhoods that make it up; then the streets, finally the houses. Study the shopping and travel-to-work patterns; observe where the housewives go to shop for your brand, and your competitors' brands. Use geodemographic linkages into research to help to understand the patterns that you see, and/or use lifestyle databases for the same purpose. In understanding the patterns, learn how those patterns can be influenced by marketing action.

If this sounds rather far-fetched to those unfamiliar with geodemographic techniques, I sympathise. However, GIS are now fairly commonplace (see Chapter 8) and, given your own data, the scenario outlined above can be replicated on your own PC at relatively modest cost.

Direct Marketing, Geodemographics and Lifestyles

Much has been written about media fragmentation, the breaking down of former 'mass' markets, the growth of niche markets, the greater importance of targeting; apart from nodding to all that, I do not intend to repeat the detail of it here. The reason for raising the subject is to acknowledge the influence of these trends on the growth of both direct marketing on the one hand, and geodemographics on the other.

In talking about the growth of direct marketing, I am principally interested in its growth *out* of its origins in mail order, into a much wider marketing arena, until even fmcg companies have either embraced it or are at least investigating its relevance to them. One of its attractions, in these cost-conscious, cost-cutting times, is the measurability of direct marketing techniques. I believe that this same *measurability* has helped to fuel the growth of geodemographics; the technique is 'driven by numbers'. Once you have identified the geodemographic categories that are of interest to you, it is easy to establish how many households there are in those categories, both nationally and in any small area of interest. By analysing your own data, either from a customer database (if you have one) or via syndicated research, you can establish your *penetration* in each of the neighbourhood types of relevance to you. You can track your performance over time, by monitoring penetration or volume levels in these neighbourhood types. It is a far more sensitive measurement tool than 'standard' demographics could possible provide.

The dramatic increase in computing 'power per pound' has helped to fuel database marketing, including the lifestyle database growth – and also, geodemographics' expansion. Geodemographics was originally available as a bureau service from its agency suppliers; in the last seven or eight years it has moved increasingly into a PC environment, on users' desks. The ubiquity of PCs in marketing departments nowadays, and the much greater familiarity of marketing people with desk-top computing, has gone a long way to break down the 'technophobia' barriers that formerly existed. In tandem with this change, the authors of the PC geodemographic systems, initially launched 8–9 years ago, have rewritten the systems to be easier to use. Geodemographics is now far more accessible to end-users than it was.

The growing influence of direct marketing, particularly the concept of 'relationship marketing', has spurred the growth of customer databases. In some cases (notably the financial institutions), this has 'merely' required a change of focus from account-based computer systems, to *customer*-based databases. I should not make out that this has been easy! Many such organisations will attest to the fact that it has not; but at least they had their customers' names on computer in the first place. Other organisations did not have this luxury, and have had to capture customer names by other devices, such as capturing names of coupon redeemers, callers to helplines, or other promotional respondents. The lifestyle database companies have been able to help such companies, by identifying customers for them, and collecting much valuable information about them. By this means, and by providing extensive lists of 'lookalikes' for prospect mailing, the lifestyle database operators have made a major contribution to direct marketing in the UK. Geodemographics has played a significant role in direct marketing too; but let us now turn to its other major area of interest – that of *retail*, or quasi-retail, applications.

Retail 'versus' Manufacturer – Balance of Power

At the risk of stating the obvious (to retailers, anyway) a retailer is only immediately concerned with his prospective customers who have *access* to his stores or branches. I am referring to *geographical* access; hence the concept of the 'catchment area' – the geographical area from which store custom is drawn. It should be immediately apparent that geodemographics, in whatever form, should be very relevant to retailers, because not only does it provide a 'headcount' of the number of people potentially available to the store in question, but it also gives a breakdown of those people, in terms of age, sex, social class (or similar), car ownership, etc. If a neighbourhood classification is employed, it quantifies that aspect of the catchment area, by means of a profile. Crucially, however, by means of modelling techniques based on geodemographics, a measure of *potential* for the products or services sold by that retailer can be derived for the catchment area. This technique, outlined here but covered in some detail later, is used extensively by retailers, both in deciding where to open *new* stores or branches, and in evaluating the performance of *existing* outlets.

So geodemographics is potentially very useful to retailers, and many of them have recognised this potential and are using the technique. But what about manufacturers, who are selling to the public via retailers? In my experience (and as a generalisation of course, with some notable exceptions), manufacturers have not embraced geodemographics nearly as comprehensively as their retail customers. Perhaps the major exception to this general statement lies in the area of door-to-door distribution of coupons, leaflets and samples, where geodemographics is used extensively to determine which areas to cover, and which to ignore. This exercise is often performed in a quasi-retail fashion anyway, taking account of the catchment areas of the retailers concerned.

We could speculate on why it is that manufacturers (again, in general) have not made much use of geodemographic techniques. It may simply be that it is not a part of their company culture, or they cannot see it being particularly relevant to the way in which they do business. Certainly, given that retailers are responsible for the interface with the consumer, this might itself be a reason. But is not this fact in itself a problem? Development and protection of the brand franchise is the manufacturer's best method of ensuring future profitability (in the 'classical' scenario, at least), and increasingly, the cards are being stacked in favour of the retailer. Retailers have increasingly better systems of information; computerised stock control, EPOS – it is difficult for manufacturers to match their retail customers when it comes to information, and information (after all) is power.

The leading retailers are also among the leading exponents of geodemographic techniques. The importance of getting store location right has led them to invest very large sums in their own departments and systems which provide them with information on localised potential. They are spending some of this investment on ranging and merchandising analysis – ensuring that they are meeting *locality demand*. It is my belief that unless their branded suppliers also analyse local demand, and have that information available for discussion and negotiation with the retailers, then they run the risk of losing out. They simply will not have the data with which to argue the case. Or, to put the issue the other way around; if they can approach their retail customers with analyses that show how they can jointly maximise their opportunity, with targeted tailor-made activity (perhaps in selected catchment areas, where the analysis suggests they are not getting their 'share' of the available market), then they have a much better chance of retaining the initiative. So perhaps the analysis of local demand should be just as important to manufacturers as it is to retailers.

Summary

In this chapter I have set out to put across my view as to why geodemographics and lifestyle data should be of interest to virtually all marketing people whose ultimate customers are consumers.

As a method of customer classification and segmentation, I have suggested that geodemographics has a place *alongside* other methods (such as 'standard' demographics, including social grade, or psychographics). The particular strength of geodemographics lies in its *locational* capability; it is also very easy to use, requiring only customer or respondent postcodes. Lifestyle databases have made a very significant contribution to database marketing and direct mail; they enable companies without computerised customer records to acquire such data (enhanced with a wealth of other useful data), and they provide huge prospect lists for mailing customer 'lookalikes'.

I have recounted how geodemographics enabled fmcg marketers to move from units of area the size of TV regions, down to neighbourhoods; I have also commented that many such marketers have not yet made that move! I have explained the benefits, as I see them, of being able to model consumer behaviour at a small area level, and influence that behaviour both through local marketing activity, and by linking (via research) into national media, using geodemographics as the linking mechanism.

I have mentioned the use of geodemographic techniques by retailers and quasi-retailers; the fact that banks and building societies can both evaluate branch network strategies, and link other forms of communication (mail, telephone) using a common mechanism. I have shown how 'traditional' retailers use geodemographics to plan store locations, and to analyse local demand (for merchandise categories). And I have suggested that manufacturers, supplying consumers via these retailers, might take a leaf from their book!

Hopefully you will see something here that encourages you to read further. But finally, what's the bottom line?

I think you should consider using geodemographics and lifestyles because:

- these techniques will help to improve the quality of your market information;
- they will enable you to identify and locate your target customers;
- thus, they will make your business more efficient, and ultimately, more profitable!

Now, isn't that a worthwhile objective?

CHAPTER TWO

THE GROWTH OF GEODEMOGRAPHICS IN GREAT BRITAIN

Origins

The British geodemographics industry is large and growing fast, as outlined in the previous chapter. Although the vast majority of this business is done in the commercial sector, paradoxically its origin can be traced back to work done in the public sector in the mid-1970s, investigating social deprivation. Richard Webber, who figures large in the development of geodemographics in Britain, was then working at the Centre for Environmental Studies, investigating measures of deprivation in Liverpool. He used data from the 1966 census to build a ward-level classification that identified different types of deprived areas with different needs. Subsequently similar analyses were produced on a national basis; classifications of local authority districts, then parliamentary constituencies, then wards.

I think it is fair to say that the private sector were unaware of this work, and its potential usefulness for them, until it was exposed by John Bermingham, Ken Baker and Colin McDonald of BMRB at the Market Research Society conference in March 1979 – see References. Ken Baker had experimented with Webber's ward-based classification, using it as a sample frame for the Target Group Index (TGI). He discovered that when he cross-tabulated various product and media fields on the TGI with CRN codes (as they were then called) he found surprising levels of discrimination; for example CRN could distinguish between readers of the *Guardian* and *Telegraph* more effectively than the 'traditional' indicators such as social grade, age or education. So the Baker/Bermingham/McDonald paper at the 1979 MRS conference effectively brought this new technique into the marketing world, initially in the context of media research.

Also in 1979, CACI, who had been operating in Britain for a few years selling their 'SITE' system, recruited Richard Webber, who then developed his system for them. It was renamed ACORN (A Classification of Residential Neighbourhoods), was re-run at a census enumeration district (ED) level, and was linked into CACI's systems. I was at ABM as head of marketing at the time, and was introduced to Richard and CACI by John Billett, then media director of ABM. Between us and our departments, John and I experimented with the use of ACORN in many market areas, both on behalf of existing clients, and in new business presentations – of which there were many. Our start point was often cross-tabulations of TGI with ACORN, which was the way that many geodemographic users in Britain 'got into geodemographics'.

It is perhaps hard for more recent entrants to the market, who probably take it for granted, to realise just how revolutionary these developments seemed at the time.

Before continuing with the sequential development which started with CACI's acquisition of ACORN, it is perhaps worth mentioning that graduates of the Reader's Digest's direct marketing 'university' will point out that developments at the Reader's Digest had preceded those to which I have referred. Apparently, the use of census data in developing response models had taken place in 1973/74; while this was doubtless the case, this development was kept internal to the Digest, and did not spill over into the general marketing arena in the same way as did the

ACORN developments. Also, as it happens parallel developments were taking place in the US, where Claritas had produced their PRIZM classification system in the late 1970's. Just for the record, PRIZM is an acronym too – 'Potential Rating Index for Zip Markets'; and the first version was based on data from the 1970 US Census.

Early Growth

But back to CACI. In the early 1980s, CACI were developing various applications driven by ACORN. Some were concerned with retail, for example, catchment area analysis; others with direct marketing. The development that most assisted direct marketing (DM) applications was the linkage of ACORN census-based analysis to *postcodes*. Unit postcodes (on average, relating to about 15 addresses) could be located by a computer file variously named Postzon or Central Postcode Directory (CPD). This file had been prepared some years earlier for the Regional Highway Traffic Model, concerned with origins and destinations of vehicle journeys; now it provided the means to link postcodes (and thus addresses) with census geography. So, having classified census neighbourhoods, it was now possible to relate addresses to them; these might be addresses of customers or market research respondents. Thus, geodemographic profiling was born, and with it a means to *mail* customers or prospects in appropriate neighbourhood types.

CACI agreed with CCN to attach ACORN to CCN's computerised electoral roll (ER), in another 'milestone' development in the early 1980s. Thus a list of some 40 million names could be targeted by geodemographics (and frequently was!). This facility was exploited by the Direct Mail Sales Bureau (DMSB) from late 1982 onwards. The DMSB were very active in selling direct mail as a mainstream medium, principally to advertising agencies, which they did via a product called the Consumer Location System. This was based on ACORN/TGI cross-tabs, which were used to target electoral roll mailings. With the considerable benefit of hindsight, this activity probably did more than anything else to position geodemographics as a direct marketing/direct mailing tool (a positioning which has persisted ever since). It is also probable that the enthusiastic selling of electoral roll targeting (by CACI, the DMSB and others) in those early days led to unrealistic expectations in terms of the response rates that could be expected – with subsequent user unhappiness when response rates were disappointing. What was not generally realised at that time was the importance of mailing *responsiveness*; mailings sourced from rented lists of people who had been recruited by virtue of a mail-order purchase, would regularly out-perform the electoral roll, however well targeted by geodemographics. More about this later.

So the UK geodemographics industry was growing rapidly, but so far, CACI *was* the industry. ACORN was the only neighbourhood classification product (which it remained until mid-1985) and CACI was dedicated to making ACORN the 'thread' running through various marketing and marketing-related activities; customer profiling, area potential modelling, branch location, mailing, door-to-door distribution, market research analysis. In addition to TGI, ACORN was cross-tabbed with the National Readership Survey (NRS), most of the AGB consumer panels, even Taylor Nelson's 'Monitor' consumer typologies.

Market Fragmentation

CACI's monopoly did not last, largely due to personnel movement out of CACI and into new geodemographic operations. I was first to go! Having joined CACI in 1981, and having later been introduced to Gurmukh Singh, managing director of CAM, in mid-1982, I left CACI in the autumn of that year to help set up Pinpoint Analysis, which started trading in January 1983. Initially, Pinpoint concentrated on 'customised' projects (such as the Mills & Allen Poster Targeting System, launched in May 1983, and the Purnell KIDS targeting system, launched in autumn 1983). Part of Pinpoint's philosophy was that there were other aspects of geodemographics than 'just' neighbourhood classifications. 'KIDS' was a case in point; targeting households with high concentrations of children, using 'raw' census statistics.

IMS Geodemographics had announced their intention to launch into the market in April 1983, the team of Leon Leibman, Bob Hulks and Malcolm Winram. They intended to take on CACI and ACORN directly, with a neighbourhood classification sold on a price platform. IMS and Pinpoint agreed in principle to a co-operative venture, where Pinpoint would supply a postcoding front-end to IMS, and also supply computer mapping to enhance IMS' analyses; although there would be an element of competition 'in the middle' with census analysis, nevertheless the two companies were following different strategies. It might have worked – we'll never know, as in the event the IMS product was never launched. By the time this became clear it was 1984, and still no competitor had emerged for ACORN. So Pinpoint decided to develop a neighbourhood classification, and PiN was developed, tested, and launched in May 1985.

The mid-1980s saw a number of other developments which led to the fragmentation (and growth) of the geodemographics market. Mel Morris, managing director of SAMI, had joined CACI with a team of colleagues, establishing an office in Leamington Spa. They left again, en masse, in 1985 to form Sales Performance Analysis (SPA) which specialised in the use of geodemographics on PCs, mainly for sales territory organisation and retail applications.

Richard Webber left CACI in 1985 and joined CCN, where he developed their geodemographic capability and launched MOSAIC in late 1986. Richard took the opportunity with MOSAIC to add to the basic census data, other datasets available to CCN (principally from its credit referencing activities) such as credit applications by postcode, and county court judgements (CCJs) also by postcode. Thus MOSAIC broke new ground in its use of data.

Dr Stan Openshaw had been working in the geodemographic field for a number of years with his colleagues at Newcastle University. Stan has been responsible for a great deal of the basic research into geodemographics in this country, and has published many papers on the subject. One such, published in 1985, was entitled *Some New Classifications of Census Enumeration Districts in Britain: A Poor Man's ACORN* (jointly authored with Messrs Charlton and Wymer – see reference). This paper describes some of the extensive research carried out by Stan and others, and puts forward their proposed solution. The reason that this is relevant to the marketing community is that this same solution eventually came to the market in late 1986, as the SuperProfiles classification. Professors Batey and Brown of Liverpool University collaborated in the latter stages of development of

SuperProfiles, it was launched by O.E. McIntyre, and subsequently bought and marketed by CDMS.

The period late 1986/early 1987 was a time of vigorous expansion in the British geodemographics market. Not only did MOSAIC and SuperProfiles come to the marketplace, but Pinpoint launched FiNPiN at much the same time. FiNPiN was the first 'market specific' classification. It utilised data from the Financial Research Survey (FRS) in its construction, and the higher-level clusters were described in terms of financial activity. Indeed, it was the financial community that was the most active sector of the geodemographics user market at that time, following the structural changes brought about by the Financial Services Act. The 'head-to-head' pitches between ACORN (as the incumbent), FiNPiN, MOSAIC and SuperProfiles were legion; and the market expanded considerably as a result.

Desktop Developments

To date, the various geodemographic analyses, maps, etc., had been produced by the geodemographic agencies and provided to clients as reports in hard copy. Some clients could dial in to the geodemographic agencies on a bureau basis, and retrieve information on-line. But the next major development, which started in late 1987, was to make available PC-based systems so that users could conduct their own analyses, in-house. I mentioned earlier that Mel Morris and his team at SPA had been developing a system to run on PCs (they branded it 'The Marketing Machine'). In autumn of 1987, Richard Webber did a deal with SPA that effectively rebranded the product as MOSAIC Systems, and then put large resources behind its marketing – with considerable success. CACI and Pinpoint were both working on PC-based products too; CACI launched 'Insite' in 1988, and Pinpoint launched 'GEOPIN' at much the same time. While MOSAIC Systems and Insite were essentially geodemographic analysis systems with mapping 'bolted on', Pinpoint had taken a different approach, and wrote geodemographic applications to run on American ARC/INFO GIS software.

Pinpoint had taken a GIS approach because of Gurmukh Singh's strong interest in this technology. Gurmukh had sat on the Chorley Committee (the Committee of Enquiry for the Handling of Geographic Information) during 1986/87; the publication of the Chorley Report in mid-1987 raised the profile of GIS in the commercial sector, as well as reinforcing its importance in the public sector and the utilities, where it was already established. The importance of GIS in the marketing arena was foreshadowed by these events. I will return to this subject in Chapter 8; but briefly, GIS involves the attachment of data to *locations* and another of Gurmukh's earlier initiatives had addressed this issue in a revolutionary way.

The Locational Issue

Back in 1985, at the time of the launch of PiN, Pinpoint received considerable publicity because of its statements about the accuracy (or otherwise) of the locational data on which the link between census data and postcode data was based. Having acquired the file of digitised ED boundaries for the Greater London area from the former GLC, and by virtue of plotting the locations of postcodes at a large scale (using its sophisticated computer mapping software) Pinpoint discovered considerable discrepancies on the CPD file – the locations of postcodes. Its investigations showed that, in many cases, this was leading to an incorrect allocation of postcodes to census enumeration districts; the effect of this would be to distort customer profiles on the one hand, and to misdirect mailshots on the other. The problem was particularly acute in densely populated urban areas, where EDs were geographically small and tightly packed; particularly where (for example) 'up-market' EDs were adjacent to 'down-market' neighbourhoods.

The detail of this work was kept commercially confidential by Pinpoint, who corrected their own postcode/ED link files accordingly. In order to find the best solution to this problem, and more importantly, to produce the ideal 'building bricks' for GIS and geodemographics, the PAC project was born. PAC (Pinpoint Address Code) involved digitising the location of every address from very large-scale Ordnance Survey maps (1:1250 scale in urban areas – that's 50 inches to the mile!). The Ordnance Survey co-operated in this massive exercise, but the writing of the software and the physical digitisation was done by Pinpoint. PAC was initially launched in 1987, and a derivative, PRN – Pinpoint Road Network – followed.

Late 1980s to the Release of 1991 Census Data

In the late-1980s, other notable developments were, on the company front, the entry of Infolink to the geodemographic fray, with their DEFINE system; rather like MOSAIC, this system used credit activity and bad debt data in addition to census data, but unlike MOSAIC, DEFINE kept the two datasets separate. The credit-based data were used as an overlay to the census classifications.

On the personality front, Clive Humby, who had been running the market analysis division of CACI since the departures of Tony Bickford and Richard Webber, left with his wife Edwina Dunn to form Dunn-Humby Associates.

In other areas of the marketplace, the Unit for Retail Planning Information (URPI), which has been operating for many years and selling-on packaged census data since the mid-1980s, formed the Data Consultancy and branched out into low-priced GIS, using MapInfo. Market Profiles Limited, originally set up by Malcolm Winram and now run by John Taylor, supplied analyses using software and data under licence from several of the geodemographic agencies. Geomatrix, 'spawned' initially from CAD-CAM research at Sheffield University, developed its own GIS, branded Prospex. And at the University of Leeds, the work done by Prof. Alan Wilson and Dr. Martin Clarke and their colleagues in the geography department on gravity modelling found its commercial outlet in GMAP, in modelling for retailers. Other Academic Institutions made their mark in this commercial area; Reading University in retail location planning, Birkbeck College in GIS and census analysis, Durham University with the NOMIS data, and the Oxford Institute of Retail Management at Templeton College in retail location planning and the impact of (for example) the Metro Centre and Meadowhall.

The Launch of 1991 Census Data to Date

The output data from the 1991 census of population were published in the summer of 1993. Chapter 3 goes into some detail on the nature of census data; Chapter 13 indicates differences between 1991 data and the 1981 version. The remainder of this chapter deals with the main market developments since this summer 1993 'watershed' was crossed.

Twelve organisations signed up with the census offices to become census agencies. They were:

- CACI Limited
- CCN Marketing
- CDMS
- Capscan Limited
- Chadwyck-Healey Limited
- Claymore Services Limited
- Equifax Europe (UK) Limited
- GMAP Limited
- Infolink Decision Services Limited
- Pinpoint Analysis Limited
- SPA Marketing Systems Limited
- The Data Consultancy.

In the event, by no means all of these agencies elected to produce a neighbourhood classification; in fact, only six of them did so, and the number of available classifications changed little. Indeed, there was some market rationalisation. Pinpoint was first to the market with its new PiN and FiNPiN classifications (in September 1993), but within weeks, Pinpoint's geodemographic division had been taken over by CACI. Then CACI launched its updated ACORN, and CCN its updated MOSAIC, at almost the same time; CDMS came to the market with the new SuperProfiles, and Infolink with DEFINE. EuroDirect (which chose not to become a census agency, but rather a licensee) launched Neighbours & PROSPECTS. Later in 1994, Infolink launched PORTRAIT, based essentially on NDL lifestyle data; only for Infolink to be taken over one month later by Equifax. So Equifax effectively came to the UK classification market by incorporating Infolink's DEFINE and PORTRAIT in its product portfolio. More about these products appears in Chapter 3.

Meanwhile, one of the changes that had taken place in the lifestyle database arena had a knock-on effect on geodemographics. Two of the major players, CMT and NDL International, came together by acquisition to form the Calyx Group. Calyx launched a subsidiary (Marketing Information Consultancy, or MIC) to exploit geodemographic applications of its lifestyle data. And following this, NDL took a different view to the ongoing use of its data in the PORTRAIT product, effectively renegotiated its contract (now with Equifax), and as a result, PORTRAIT reverted to the Calyx Group.

Two more organisations joined the census agency line-up; GEOPLAN, and Business Geographics. However, both Pinpoint and Infolink had 'disappeared', as a result of acquisition and Claymore had relinquished its agency status, so the list actually reduced, to eleven census agencies.

The most recent development (as recent as mid-June 1996) saw the relaunch of Calyx Group subsidiary MIC as Claritas UK. This company launch was also the occasion for simultaneous launches of a desktop system (Catalyst) and neighbourhood classification (PRIZM). PRIZM is, in effect, a successor to PORTRAIT, using lifestyle data instead of census data to provide the demographic content of geodemographics. Six months after the launch, in January 1997, Calyx Group was renamed Claritas UK, and the former MIC is now Claritas Micromarketing.

In the last few years, other changes in the lifestyle database market have occurred. Two major new market entrants have appeared; CCN, with its 'Chorus' survey (so now CCN has a foot in each 'camp'), and Consumer Surveys with Lifestyle Focus. Meanwhile, two of the other large geodemographic agencies, CACI and Equifax, have also embraced lifestyle data; in both cases, licensed from ICD. All these developments are covered more fully in Chapters 3, 4 and 12.

Market Shares of the Geodemographics and Lifestyle Market

An end-user survey was conducted by T.M.C. in early 1995, in an attempt to fill a gap in market information. Topline details of, and results from, the survey appear in Appendix 7. Briefly, a postal questionnaire was mailed to a selection of readers of *Marketing* magazine (selection criteria are shown in the appendix). Respondents were asked a series of questions about awareness and usage of both geodemographic and lifestyle companies, and also about GIS and computer mapping.

Some of the highlights of the results were:

Usage of geodemographic suppliers in respondents' current organisation

CACI	40.4%
CCN	40.4%
Infolink	12.6%
Equifax	11.9%
CDMS	9.9%
Data Consultancy	5.3%
SPA	4.6%
Market Profiles/GEOPLAN	4.0%
Dunn-Humby	3.3%
EuroDirect	3.3%
GMAP	2.6%
Other	usage below 2.5%

Usage of lifestyle data suppliers in respondents' current organisation

ICD	19.9%
NDL	18.5%
CMT	11.9%

Applications addressed using geodemographic or lifestyle data

Targeting direct mail	55.6%
Market segmentation	47.0%
Customer database building	41.1%
Media analysis	34.4%
Retail location analysis	29.8%
Sales force organisation	13.2%
Other applications	12.6%

Note: Responses as a percentage of the total number of respondents.

Remember that this study was fielded in early 1995, so will be over two years out-of-date when this edition is published; but it is a market where hard data are notoriously difficult to obtain. See Appendix 7 for further detail, including relative strengths in PC analysis and mapping systems.

(Note: after this chapter was written CCN changed its name to Experian.)

GEODEMOGRAPHIC CLASSIFICATION SYSTEMS

Overview – Why Neighbourhood Classifications?

It is perfectly viable to use census data for marketing purposes *without* using the data in the form of a neighbourhood classification. For example, a particular demographic variable may be of key importance to the market in question; presence of children in household is one example. So, if you wished to find areas with the greatest concentration of households containing children, this would be straightforward, simply involving the *ranking* of areas on this one variable; census neighbourhoods could be ranked, or postcode sectors – any suitable unit of area.

So why have the neighbourhood classifications (ACORN, MOSAIC, etc.) become so pre-eminent? Why has this methodology virtually eclipsed all others in practice? The main reason, I believe, is the ability to *profile* which comes in train with a classification system. Both areas and customers can be profiled, and so (crucially) can market research surveys. The methodology by which neighbourhood classifications are constructed is described in this chapter, and so is the linking mechanism to addresses. This linkage enables addresses (of customers, or survey respondents) to have neighbourhood classifications attached. Once this has been achieved, the action of *profiling* is simply a *comparison* exercise.

Profiling can perhaps be illustrated with a simple (indeed, simplified) example. We'll use PiN, at the 12-fold 'group' level, and for illustration, we'll only use four of the 12 PiN types. (Yes, I know PiN is now consigned to history; but its use avoids any suggestion of favouritism!)

- A Rural
- C Upwardly mobile young families
- D Affluent households
- F Suburban middle-aged or older

The table below is fairly typical of the layout of profiles provided by geodemographics agencies. It is a customer profile for a fictional product:

Customer profile – product X: base – GB

PiN type	Profile count	Profile (%)	Base (%)	Index
A	150	7.5	5.1	147
C	1,040	52.0	14.1	369
D	750	37.5	10.0	375
F	60	3.0	17.0	18
Totals	**2,000**	**100**	**46.2**	

Note: This is slightly unrealistic, in that *all* the customers are in four of a total of twelve PiN types; nevertheless, it shows the principle of profiling clearly.

To explain the columns:

- 'Profile count' is a count of the customers in each of the PiN types. This will have been derived automatically by the profiling system, by analysing customer postcodes.

- 'Profile (%)' is the percentage represented by each PiN type of total customers; these numbers always add down to 100.

- 'Base (%)' is the percentage represented by each PiN type of the base area, in this case Great Britain. Most profiling systems allow the base to be specified.

- 'Index' is simply an expression of 'Profile (%)' divided by 'Base (%)', multiplied by 100. If the index = 100, this would indicate that the percentage of *customers* in that PiN type was exactly equal to the percentage of *population* in that PiN type, in GB – i.e. on the national average.

So, in this example, there are nearly one-and-one-half times as many PiN type 'A' customers (147 on the index) as one would 'expect'; there are three-and-three quarters as many PiN type 'D' customers (375 on the index) as there would be if the customers were quite typical of the population.

So that is the principle of geodemographic profiling – comparing the *penetration* of (say) customers within each PiN type, with the base area. The ways in which profiling is used will be described later.

Neighbourhood classifications are the result of multi-variate analysis techniques (many separate 'variables' go into their solution), so we are able to describe the neighbourhoods thus classified in terms of all the variables that were used to construct them. Typically, we can describe them in terms of 'housing' variables (size of houses, type of tenure, amenities, etc.); demographics of the people living there (age, profile, country of origin, family or household composition, qualifications) and socio-economics of the inhabitants (social class or socio-economic group, industry of occupation, etc.). Thus we have a very rich description of the type of neighbourhood concerned, for each neighbourhood type. This 'multi-faceted' picture of the classifications is enriched still further by relating them to industry research, to flesh out the behavioural characteristics of the people who live in each neighbourhood type.

How Neighbourhood Classifications are Constructed

I will deal in this section with the 'classic' methodology for producing neighbourhood classifications; the variations on this theme that have been employed by the authors of the systems currently on the market will be explained later in the chapter.

All the census-based neighbourhood classifications to date are the result of performing cluster analysis on census neighbourhoods. Most readers will probably be familiar with the concept of *cluster analysis*; in essence, it is a means of grouping together neighbourhoods that are similar to each other, and thus differentiating them from other neighbourhoods that are *less* similar. There are different types of cluster analysis, and many different algorithms; readers wishing to know more about this (and other multi-variate analysis techniques which regularly occur in a marketing context) could refer to a paper written jointly by Barry Leventhal and myself in the *Journal of Targeting, Measurement and Analysis for Marketing* (*JOTMAM* for short!), Vol. 1 No. 1 (and also Stan Openshaw's chapter in *An Introductory Guide to the 1991 Census* edited by Leventhal, Moy and Griffin).

The Nature of Census Data

The 'raw materials' which go into cluster analysis when producing neighbourhood classifications are the Small Area Statistics (SAS) from the census of population. These statistics are published for EDs, which average about 150 households each. There were approximately 130,000 EDs defined by the Office of Population Censuses and Surveys (OPCS) (N.B. in April 1996, OPCS was joined with CSO to form the Office for National Statistics) together with the General Register for Scotland (GRO(S)), in the 1991 census. These relate to England, Wales and Scotland. In fact, GRO(S) produced counts for 'Output Areas' (OAs), which are roughly one-third the size of EDs; but 'nested' them into EDs for comparability between 1981 and 1991.

A vast amount of data was published by OPCS and GRO(S) at the small area level. In the 1991 Census, no fewer that 9,000 'counts' were produced and published at the SAS level for each ED (or OA in Scotland). So theoretically, at the ED level, the matrix of data available for analysis is 130,000 areas (EDs) by 9,000 counts. What exactly is a 'count' in this context? How did the (relatively few) questions asked in the Census turn into such a vast data resource?

The SAS census output is produced as a series of tables. I will illustrate this with Table 12 from the SAS output for 1991, which has the considerable merit (for my purposes) of being one of the simpler such tables:

SAS Table 12: Residents in household with limiting long-term illness

Age	Total Persons	Males	Females
All Ages	*	*	*
0 – 15	*	*	*
16 – 29	*	*	*
30 – 44	*	*	*
45 – 59	*	*	*
60 – 64	*	*	*
65 – 74	*	*	*
75 and over	*	*	*

Source: OPCS/GRO(S) Crown Copyright.

The counts in this table – which are statistical counts relating to each individual ED – are represented by the *s; so this one simple table generates 24 counts. Some of them will be zeros, of course, and in total, very many of the counts in the total national SAS data matrix will be zeros.

It can be seen that the reason for the data volume within SAS is the *cross-tabulation* within these SAS tables, of the various facts collected from the census forms. The forms themselves ask fairly basic questions, covering the following topics for each household:

- name of head of household (N.B. this is *not* published)
- date of birth of each household member
- sex and marital status of each household member
- usual address one year ago (to track movement)
- family structure, i.e. relationships to head of household
- ethnic groups and country of birth
- long-term illness (asked in 1991 for the first time)
- employment
- occupation
- workplace
- name and business of employer
- number of hours worked per week
- educational and professional qualifications
- type of housing accommodation
- number of rooms in household
- amenities in household (e.g. inside wc, central heating)
- tenure (i.e. owner-occupied, etc.)
- cars/vans available to each household
- means of travel to work (e.g. car, train, bus, etc.).

The tables take these facts, *aggregated* to the total neighbourhood (ED) level, and express them in numerous combinations, for example, Table 2 gives age bands from 0 – 4 to 90 and over as columns, and cross-tabulates this with marital status in the rows, thus:

Total Persons	Males			Females		
	Total	Single, Widowed or Divorced	Married	Total	Single, Widowed or Divorced	Married

So a vast wealth of data is built up, applying both to the whole of the nation, but crucially from the point of view of geodemographics – applying to each census neighbourhood in the nation. To restate – these facts are published for each ED (averaging about 150 households) in the country, and these EDs form the 'building bricks' of geodemographics.

The 'Neighbourhood' Issue

There is one crucial point which must be grasped when using geodeomographics – these data are published about census *neighbourhoods*, and not about individuals. The reason for this is to protect personal privacy, and indeed, the people who work for ONS or GRO(S) must sign the Official Secrets Act and exercise great diligence in protecting privacy. When publishing the SAS output, the ONS/GRO(S) examine the data for each ED and either suppress or disguise any fact which might lead to the identification of any individual person or household. So privacy is jealously safeguarded; the other side of the coin is that the SAS data can *only* be used at a neighbourhood level, and targeting of individuals is not possible. Thus, to put the case slightly differently, we can know a vast amount about the neighbourhood within which an individual resides, but we can know nothing *specific* about the individual himself.

This is either a problem or an opportunity depending upon what you are trying to do. If you are planning to send a mailshot to an individual, geodemographics will tell you about the characteristics of his neighbourhood (and via techniques that will be explained later in this book, you can adduce a great deal about the propensity of that type of neighbourhood to be 'in the market for' the product in question). However, you cannot be certain that the individual shares the characteristics of the neighbourhood. Let us take an example – housing tenure. Say you have identified an ED of great potential for your product, which for the sake of illustration, is double glazing. Your research (and indeed your common sense!) tells you that householders who own, or are buying, their own home are better prospects than householders who are renting their home. The SAS statistics may tell you that 80 per cent of the households within your chosen ED are owner-occupied and 20 per cent are rented. If you mail that ED with your double-glazing proposition, 80 per cent of the mailings will plop through the letterboxes of owner-occupied properties, the other 20 per cent will be wasted. This is not necessarily the end of the world, of course, as all readers with experience of direct mail will realise, because a 20 per cent wastage on this one dimension is not too serious when a one per cent positive response leading to a sale is probably perfectly viable. But the point I am making is this; geodemographics on its own cannot identify which households within the ED are in your core target market, they can merely give the overall 'odds' in your favour. If, instead of mailing, you used your analysis to direct door-to-door salesmen to areas of best potential, you would possibly save a deal of wasted effort!

'Birds of a Feather'

Geodemographics relies for its validity on what is often expressed as the 'birds of a feather' phenomenon; people tend to live in neighbourhoods among people who are, generally speaking, similar to themselves. Our own experience tells us that this is true as a generalisation, although we can all think of those glorious exceptions to the rule! Most people with whom I have discussed this issue, when thinking about neighbourhoods with which they are familiar, agree that it fits their own experience. It is part of human nature to be more comfortable among people who share things in common, and this natural tendency is enforced by the likelihood of different types of housing stock to be clustered – from 'executive estates' at one extreme, to council estates at another; from inner-city 'bedsit land' to country cottages. Of course, one of the merits of geodemographics is that the base data themselves give the analyst a means to examine this hypothesis; the very detailed SAS data will show just how homogeneous (or heterogeneous) the EDs within a particular 'neighbourhood type' actually are. But I am running ahead of myself – I have not yet explained how this vast resource of raw data is transformed into neighbourhood types!

Just before I do, one more thought about the 'neighbourhood' issue. The assumption that one individual is necessarily typical of the neighbourhood in which he lives, is known by the geographers and social scientists who study such things, as the 'ecological fallacy'. For an explanation of this see *An Introductory Guide to the 1991 Census* (see References).

As with many aspects of geodemographics and associated techniques, the important thing is to keep a sense of proportion about what we are trying to do, and the pros and cons of the various ways we might do it. So I have pointed to the issue of the ecological fallacy so readers may be aware of it, as one of a series of *caveat emptors*; but let us not throw the baby out with the bath water. Geodemographics demonstrably works, there are many people who have used it effectively in their businesses. It is not perfect – a shortcoming it shares with many other aspects of marketing theory and practice – but if used properly, it is a considerable advance on what went before. We can guard against the downside risk of a single representative of a neighbourhood (say, a research respondent) not being typical of that neighbourhood, by using a sensibly-sized sample. See Chapter 6.

Producing a Neighbourhood Classification

First, take your raw materials ... the SAS data, as described above. The very first decision you need to make is which variables to use in your solution. In practice, most 'authors' of neighbourhood classifications have chosen similar variables, although some have used more variables than others. It is not surprising that similar variables would be chosen, particularly if the intention is to build a 'general purpose' classification system, because the objective is to find differences between neighbourhoods, and everyday experience tells us that differences will manifest themselves in extremes of, for example, house size, size of family, age of head of household, number of cars in household, type of housing tenure. Other differences will occur in variables such as ethnic origin, social class or socio-economic group (both derived from occupation of head of household), industry of employment, means of travel to work, attainment of academic and/or professional qualifications, etc.

For an example, Appendix 1 shows the 37 variables that were chosen to go into the ONS classification system (*The ONS Classification of Local and Health Authorities of Great Britain*, published by HMSO in 1996). This is a fairly typical list, other perhaps than the number of social classification variables used. The ONS used three 'breaks', some systems have used the full eighteen-fold SEG breakdown. More information on SEGs, social class and social grade can be found in Chapter 6 and Appendix 8.

So, you have chosen your 'input' variables; now your next decision is whether to reduce them via Principal Components Analysis (PCA), or not. Some of the systems have employed this technique, others have not (see later in this chapter). The reason for using PCA is simply expressed. In the type of 'sociological' variables we are dealing with, there are usually a number of variables which express a similar underlying 'theme' in the data. The 'themes' that will surface in this type of analysis are such things as wealth versus poverty, rural versus urban, 'young' areas versus 'old' areas (in terms of the ages of the inhabitants), etc. If you take a set of 'raw' census variables and put them straight into cluster analysis, you run the risk that the inter-correlation between variables – the extent to which certain variables are duplicating each other's effect – will cause 'noise' in the final result. As I said, the authors of the different systems each took a view on whether to go through this intermediate process or not; most did. Readers requiring more information could refer to the Sleight/Leventhal article in *JOTMAM* (referred to earlier), Stan Openshaw's chapter in the *Census User's Handbook* or, if requiring an excellent explanation of the multi-variate techniques which they may encounter in marketing and market research, the splendid (if dauntingly titled) book by Mick Alt, *Exploring Hyperspace*. References in appendices.

Let us assume that you have decided to use PCA. You need to extract the input variables which you have chosen, for each ED. This will give you a data matrix of n variables x 130,000 EDs – now run PCA on this matrix. The analysis will identify a number of 'components', or dummy variables, each comprising 'scores' on some of the original variables. These latter scores will help to interpret what each dummy variable 'means'. For example, from Pinpoint's experience in using PCA to devise its PiN classification system, the most prominent component was labelled the 'wealth indicator'. While not relating *directly* to 'wealth' – neither income nor net worth are collected on the UK census – in practice this component related to the 'trappings of wealth', such as large houses, owner-occupation, multiple car ownership, etc. One of the key aspects of PCA is that the dummy variables thus identified are uncorrelated with each other – they are each quite separate underlying themes, or dimensions, within the original data. These components are then put into cluster analysis.

As I mentioned previously, cluster analysis is a complex topic in its own right, and I have no desire to attempt any detailed discussion of the issues here (indeed, others are better qualified to do so). In outline, the statistician conducting the analysis will take the principal component scores for each ED from the previous PCA stage, and will run his chosen method of cluster analysis on them. He may try a number of runs, varying the total number of clusters (people who have not been involved in cluster analysis may be surprised to learn that the number of clusters is imposed on the solution, rather than emerging from it!) and testing the results, until an apparently 'acceptable' solution emerges. Knowing what represents an acceptable solution is very much a part of the skill involved in this process, because one of the fascinating properties of cluster analysis is that it will find patterns in *any* data thrown at it, even if the data are garbage! (In which case, the solution will inevitably be garbage too.) Having arrived at an apparently sensible solution, a very useful check on its apparent validity is to apply it to an area with which its author is familiar (such as his home area) and *map* the results. Does it confirm his prejudices about the neighbourhoods that he knows so well? If it does, it is probably viable! (More about how EDs are mapped in a little while.) In most cases the number of clusters will be aggregated to a higher level, or several higher levels, as appropriate – see comparison table, later in this chapter.

Having arrived at a cluster solution, the next task – and a very tricky one, at that – is to label the clusters. This involves adding those snappy, and necessarily concise, descriptions of the neighbourhood types that have emerged. The original census variables that went into the solutions will provide a clue here; what are the *particular* characteristics of the type in question that distinguishes it from the national average, and from its 'nearest neighbour' types? What are its predominant housing characteristics, tenure type, age profile, family composition? Is it urban or rural, lacking amenities and crowded, or car-rich and high-status? Do a high proportion of its occupants commute, work part-time, or are unemployed? Is there a high child-content, or is it full of childless couples, or retired people? A 'pen portrait' of each type can be built up in this way (supplemented by local knowledge, if this route has been followed). In the effort to find differences which can be exploited in the 'label', it is very easy to get over-excited by differences which, while striking in terms of indices against a national 'norm', are actually based on very small numbers within the neighbourhood type itself. Some of the system authors will provide a matrix of input variables by neighbourhood type, which shows both indices and GB counts for each variable used. This enables the user to establish the detailed census characteristics of each type.

Relating Addresses to Census Areas

I have described how census data are manipulated to produce a neighbourhood classification from 'raw' census variables at the ED level. As it stands the system might have classified all the EDs in the country, but it still cannot classify *addresses*. This is because 'census geography' and 'postal geography' do not coincide. Although this issue was addressed by the OPCS for the 1991 census (see later), and GRO(S) have based Scottish census geography on postal geography, this was a considerable problem for the census agencies dealing with 1981 census data.

First, let us examine the 'hierarchies' of the two different geographies in question:

UK Postal Geography

	Postcode Area	Postcode District	Postcode Sector	Postcode Unit
Number in UK	120	2,900	9,000	1,600,000
Households (average)	192,000	7,930	2,550	15
Illustration of a postcode (e.g. HP15 6QG)	Outward Code		Inward Code	
	HP	15	6	QG

The 'outward code' enables the Royal Mail to send the mail from its origin to the correct area for delivery; the 'inward code' is then used to sort the mail at the local delivery office.

In the postcode illustrated (HP15 6QG), HP is the postcode area, HP15 is the district, HP15 6 the sector, and HP15 6QG the full unit postcode, within a postman's walk.

For my purposes in this paper, this glimpse into the wonderful world of postcodes and postal geography is sufficient. Readers wishing to delve deeper should read *Postcodes: The New Geography* by Jonathan Raper, David Rhind and John Shepherd (see References).

GB Administrative/Census Areas 1991 Census

	Counties	Districts	Wards	Enumeration Districts (EDs)
England	46	366	8,985	106,866
Wales	8	37	945	6,330
Scotland †	9	56	1,003	12,701
Total GB	**63**	**459**	**10,933**	**125,897**
Households per (average)	347,577	47,707	2,003	174

Note: † **Differences in Scotland:** Regions not counties; pseudo sectors not wards; output areas (OAs) not enumeration districts (actually 38,254 OAs in Scotland, aggregated up to 'planning EDs' for comparison).

It will be seen that the smallest units of census geography (nationally) are EDs, with an average of about 175 households, unit postcodes contain about 15 households on average, so at the level of this theoretical average, there are some 11 or 12 unit postcodes within one ED. *But* – the boundaries are not common (other than in Scotland) – unit postcodes do not fit neatly into EDs. Nevertheless, to make geodemographics actionable, it is necessary to relate addresses (via their postcodes) to EDs. Having mentioned that the situation in Scotland is different, perhaps I should explain. GRO(S) have digitised the boundaries of all the unit postcodes in Scotland, and have built their OAs from aggregations of these unit postcodes. OAs also fit neatly into EDs in Scotland, so the overlap problem does not exist there – addresses can be correctly allocated to OAs, and thus, to EDs. (In 1991, Scottish Output Areas averaged just 53 households each!)

The situation in England and Wales is more complicated. I'll deal first with the nature of the problem in the last census decade, and then come to the 1991 scenario. The geodemographic systems based on 1981 census data had to allocate postcodes to EDs by a technique called 'proximity analysis'. Figure 1 shows a 'stylised' ED, with postcode boundaries, showing how postcodes fit into (or in some cases, overlap) the ED boundaries. This ED is fairly typical of a dense urban area. In practice, the geodemographic agencies did not have this detailed information available to them when constructing their neighbourhood classification systems, because at that time, neither ED boundaries nor postcode boundaries had been 'digitised' (captured on computer). So the agencies had to allocate postcodes to EDs by using the 'centroids' of each, as illustrated in Figure 2. Centroids are the geographical central points (roughly speaking!); the OPCS provide ED centroids on computer tape when they supply the SAS data to the agencies; the postcode centroids are supplied on the CPD (or Postzon) file. So the census agencies conducted proximity analysis, and allocated to each ED the postcodes whose centroids were nearest to that ED centroid. (Clear? – good!) I referred in Chapter 2 to the work that Pinpoint did in the mid-1980s in checking this linkage. Pinpoint were able to do this because they had acquired the 'digitised' boundaries of the EDs that had made up the boroughs in the former GLC, and plotted postcode centroids

Figure 1: 'Stylised' Relationship of Postcodes to an ED

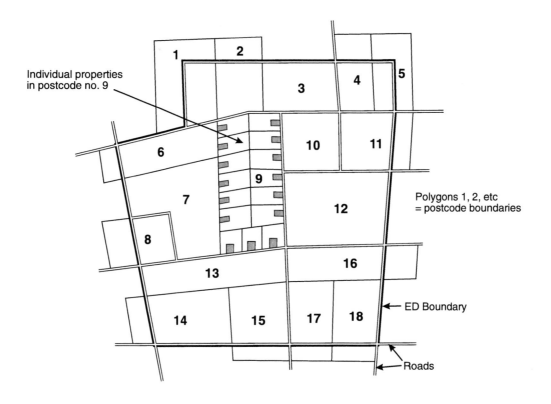

Figure 2: Centroids of Postcodes, and ED Boundary

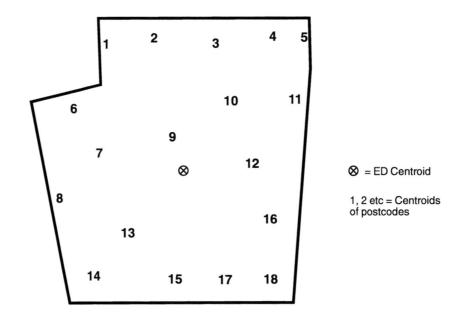

onto maps of these EDs, showing the discrepancies to which I referred, and thus embarking on the 'PAC' project. (See Leventhal and Sleight, *JMRS*, 1989)

Now, the 1991 Census – the OPCS have data-captured the postcode for each census return for the 1991 census, and produced a computer file linking EDs with postcodes; although postcodes still 'straddle' ED boundaries, this move has largely solved the problem that formerly existed. Anyway ... postcodes were allocated to EDs, so the linkage between census data and addresses could take place. Thus customer files, market research respondents, etc. can be 'coded' with geodemographic classifications, via their postcodes.

Use of Non-Census Data

The methodology outlined in this chapter has concentrated on the way that geodemographic classifications may be constructed from census data. In the early days of geodemographics, they were all made this way! (More or less.) However, I have also mentioned in Chapter 2 that there has been an increasing trend to the use of non-census data within classifications. This process started as long ago as 1986, when FiNPiN made use of FRS research data in its classification; and when MOSAIC incorporated non-census data (most notably financially-oriented data) within the classification. The non-census data within MOSAIC was added at a unit postcode level, so effectively MOSAIC operated at a postcode level. (The strength of the ED-level census data was nevertheless very evident within MOSAIC.)

When Infolink's DEFINE entered the market in 1989, like MOSAIC, financial data was utilised in addition to census data; but DEFINE used these data as an 'overlay' to the census-based classification. With the new census 'round' in 1993/94, the move to add non-census data accelerated. Table 1 (in the next section) indicates the non-census data used by the post 1991 neighbourhood classifications. The list had lengthened considerably, including (in total):

- credit 'activity' data (credit searches)
- CCJs
- ER indicators
- PAF data
- company directors (at home address)
- 'retail access', i.e. accessibility to retail centres
- TGI
- unemployment data
- insurance ratings within areas
- lifestyle data
- share ownership
- births and deaths within areas.

See the next section for details of the systems, and which system includes which data.

The most revolutionary data source is the use of lifestyle data within a neighbourhood classification system, essentially instead of census data. This has only become possible because of the huge volume of lifestyle data now available;

while household coverage is by no means total (Claritas claim 75 per cent coverage of UK households in summer 1997); it is nevertheless considerable.

The Current Neighbourhood Classification Systems

When the first edition of this book was written in spring 1993, there were six neighbourhood classification systems in general use in the British marketing community. (They were based on the 1981 census at that time – the list was ACORN, PiN and FiNPiN, SuperProfiles, MOSAIC, and DEFINE.)

Now there are seven 'general purpose', national classifications, plus two specialist financial classifications, and four 'regional' classifications (two for Scotland, two for Northern Ireland). In truth, it is surprising how little the line-up has changed, other than a few new companies involved and two former companies having been absorbed.

The seven general purpose national classifications are:

- ACORN, from CACI
- MOSAIC, from Experian (formerly CCN)
- SuperProfiles, from CDMS
- DEFINE, from Equifax (soon to be replaced by MicroVision)
- Neighbours & PROSPECTS, from EuroDirect
- PRIZM, from Claritas UK.

In addition, CACI has developed Financial*ACORN (the successor to FiNPiN) and Scottish*ACORN; CCN has developed Financial MOSAIC and Scottish MOSAIC. Now Northern Ireland has its own classifications – ACORN and MOSAIC.

The table on the following page (Geodemographic Classifications Post-1991) compares the national classifications on a number of criteria, and the remainder of the chapter describes these classifications in more detail.

ACORN

ACORN has a long history, its first version being produced (at a ward level) in 1978, based on 1971 census data. It was reworked in 1983, based on 1981 census data, this time at ED level; it was a very similar solution to the 1979 version. Its most recent manifestation is very different indeed from its predecessors, operating now at three levels (formerly two), and having as many as 54 'types' (formerly 38).

ACORN still utilises census data (exclusively) in its construction; this is really the only fact which is common to its predecessors. Other differences, apart from the number and hierarchy of output clusters, are methodological. The 1991 census based ACORN used PCA in its construction; its predecessors did not. And in another fundamental change, the 'national', GB ACORN was actually constructed from the amalgamation of three 'regional' products; one for Scotland, one for London, and a third from (England + Wales – London). Apparently this approach improved the product's discrimination markedly.

MOSAIC

MOSAIC was first launched in 1986, based on 1981 census data, plus (innovatively)

Geodemographic Classifications Post-1991

Organisation	Classification System	Number of Input Variables	Number of Clusters		Non-Census Data Used?
CACI	ACORN	79	(a)	6	No
			(b)	17	
			(c)	54	
Experian (formerly CCN)	MOSAIC	87	(a)	11	Credit data; CCJs; ER; PAF; company directors; retail access
			(b)	52	
CDMS	SuperProfiles	120 (+130)	(a)	10	Credit data; CCJs; TGI; ER
			(b)	40	
			(c)	160	
Equifax	DEFINE	146	(a)	10	Credit data; ER; unemployment stats; CCJs; insurance rating
			(b)	56	
			(c)	1,176	
	MicroVision	185	#(a)	11	*Lifestyle data; company directors; share ownership; electoral roll; CCJs; risk indices; unemployment stats
			(b)	52	
			(c)	200	
EuroDirect	Neighbours & PROSPECTS	48	(a)	9	No
			(b)	44	
Claritas UK	PRIZM	59 (+188)	(a)	4	*Lifestyle data; share ownership; company directors; unemployment stats; PAF; births & deaths
			(b)	19	
			(c)	72	

Notes: * MicroVision contains both census data and lifestyle data; PRIZM does not contain census data.
    # In MicroVision cluster numbers can be variable ('bespoke' solutions).
    'Number of input variables' refers to the variables that went into each classification. As was mentioned earlier in this chapter, the authors of the systems first decided which variables to use; the number chosen varied between 48 (for Neighbours & PROSPECTS) and 185 (for MicroVision).
    The table summarises the number of output clusters produced within each system; these are hierarchical. For example, ACORN can be used at any of three levels; the first (highest) divides the country into six groups, this level then splits into 17 groups at the next level down, which in turn splits into 54 'types' at the most detailed level. (The very high number of 'types' – 1,176 – in the most detailed level of DEFINE is the result of a 21-type 'overlay' being applied to a 50-type cluster solution; 21 x 56 = 1,176.)
    Finally, the table indicates whether non-census data were used, and if so, which types of data were utilised. More detail about the individual classifications are included in this chapter, and charts showing how they are clustered and 'labelled' are found in Appendix 2.

other datasets; credit search data, electoral roll-sourced indicators, CCJs, and information derived from the PAF file. The classification operated in an 11-group and 57-type structure; and at a unit postcode level. In fact, the census data was input at an ED level, and the other data were added at a postcode level.

The new, 1991 census based MOSAIC classification was basically very similar to its predecessor. The only significant change was a reduction in the number of types, from 57 to 52. Methodology was similar, apart from the use of a genetic algorithm to decide on variable weights in the cluster solution. Even more data sources were used; in addition to those in the previous version, new variables included presence of company directors (at home addresses), 'retail accessibility', and Experian's 'Stage' system for age-modelling from the ER.

SuperProfiles

The original SuperProfiles resulted in part from work done by Stan Openshaw and his colleagues at Newcastle University, who had conducted an ESRC-funded project on the optimisation of neighbourhood classifications. The classification that came to the market as SuperProfiles in 1986 also involved the University of Liverpool (Batey and Brown), 150 clusters in the detailed solution, then grouped into 37 'target markets' and 11 'lifestyles'. Census data (only) was used as input variables. CDMS bought the launch company in 1987.

The new version of SuperProfiles that was launched in early 1994 was conceptually similar, although in detail, considerable changes were made to the methodology (see Batey and Brown in *GIS for Business and Service Planning*, edited by Longley and Clarke). The main features of the changes were:

- the creation of a 'core classification' of 590 area types, based entirely on census data;
- use of additional census variables, and other non-census variables (from the ER, TGI data, CCJs and credit searches) to aid clustering and interpretation.

The new system retained a hierarchy similar to its predecessor; 160 detailed types (ranked by affluence), grouping to 40 'target markets' and ten 'lifestyles'. PCA was used in both new and old versions.

DEFINE

The first version of DEFINE was launched in 1989, based on 1981 census data. The second version, essentially similar in construction, was launched in early 1994. DEFINE is unusual, in that it's a 'two-tier' classification. The lower 'tier' is entirely census based; it's a 56-cluster solution, which aggregates to ten groups at the higher level. The higher 'tier' ('financialDEFINE') is an overlay, comprising a matrix of financial activity, credit risk, and a 'change indicator'. These measures involve analyses of credit searches, CCJs, and changes in the level of debt, for each UK postcode (i.e. unit postcode, average 15 addresses). So 21 financial 'types' are overlaid on 56 census types, to give a theoretical total of 1,176 neighbourhood types! DEFINE was built by Infolink, before that company was taken over by Equifax (November 1994).

Equifax are about to launch a new neighbourhood classification to replace

DEFINE. It will be branded MicroVision; an outline of its characteristics can be found in the profile of Equifax in Chapter 12. Its particular feature of interest will be that it utilises both census and lifestyle data, within the classification.

Neighbours & PROSPECTS

Neighbours & PROSPECTS was first developed in the early 1990s by EuroDirect Database Marketing Limited, initially on 1981 Census data. In its first manifestation it comprised 41 neighbourhood types, aggregated into 11 groups.

Neighbours & PROSPECTS was rebuilt on 1991 census data, and the new version has 44 types and 9 groups. The classification is built on census data, exclusively.

PRIZM

PRIZM was launched in June 1996 by Claritas Micromarketing, the newly-renamed subsidiary of Claritas UK (Claritas Micromarketing was formerly the Marketing Information Consultancy, launched in 1994 by CMT). PRIZM is unique among current neighbourhood classifications, in that it contains no census data, relying on lifestyle data for its demographics. In fact, it is the second 'GeoLifestyles' classification to have been developed in Britain; the first, PORTRAIT, was launched by Infolink in 1994, but after various 'political' events, it was withdrawn at the time of the PRIZM launch.

PRIZM is constructed from the Claritas 'Lifestyle Census' data, i.e. the aggregated CMT/NDL databases, deduped. Thus it is able to use 'lifestyle' variables (such as income, ownership of financial products, hobbies and interests) in its solution. As indicated in Table 1, 59 variables went into the cluster solution, and a further 188 variables were used to describe the resultant clusters. In addition to lifestyle variables *per se*, other data sources used in the solution included company directors (at home addresses), shareholders, unemployment statistics, births and deaths, and house names from PAF. The classification can be used at three levels; at the most detailed level, there are 72 types, which are aggregated to 19 groups (termed 'lifestage/income groups', as they are combined from two higher-level aggregations; into four lifestage groups, and five income groups). The full code which identifies the detailed types contains the lifestage and income indicators. See Appendix 2 for the detail of this.

Claritas coped with the fact that the 'Lifestyle Census', although huge, only covered 70 per cent of British households (as against the census of population 98 per cent) by adopting a system of small area weighting and imputation. PCA was used as part of the methodology of analysis and clustering.

Comments and Further Reading

In addition to these 'commercial' classifications, another post 1991 census innovation is the production of a local authority district and ward-based classification by ONS themselves. This can be acquired inexpensively from ONS; see contact details in the Acknowledgements. Some details of this system may be found in Appendix 1. The first part of this Appendix, 'Specification of variables', gives some insight into the variable choice faced by classification 'authors'.

If the comparison above seems to beg the question: 'which system is best?' –

this is a fair point. However, as with many apparently simple questions, it does not have a simple answer. To my knowledge, apart from the system suppliers (whose answers might be considered to show some bias, whether fairly or not!), there has been little independent work in this area. One exception is Barry Leventhal's paper for the February 1993 MRS conference, written in December 1992; Barry tested a number of neighbourhood classifications on common market research surveys, and found no clear 'winner', rather 'horses for courses'. Some classifications were best on certain products, others better on others. This accords with my experience, and other anecdotal evidence. (See References for details of Barry Leventhal's paper.)

Readers wishing to know more about the census should read the excellent publication *An Introductory Guide to the 1991 Census*, edited by Barry Leventhal, Corrine Moy and James Griffin, also published by NTC Publications. One issue covered in the *Guide* which I have not mentioned here is the fact that some of the SAS tables published by OPCS/GRO(S) are so-called '10 per cent' tables. These are the tabulations of census questions which were relatively hard to code (such as occupation), where the OPCS took a one in ten sample of household returns for each ED. These '10 per cent' tables perhaps need to have a 'health warning' applied to them: in the average 1981 ED, the 10 per cent statistics related to some 15 households, and it is clear that due caution should be applied. This consideration is likely to apply more to 'advanced' users than the beginner or 'average' user.

CHAPTER FOUR

THE GROWTH OF LIFESTYLE DATABASES

Market Development

The lifestyle database market in the UK has changed dramatically in the last few years. Since writing the first edition of this book four years ago, the market has been transformed. At that time, there were three sizeable companies operating in the market CMT, ICD and NDL. Since then, the total 'critical mass' of lifestyle data has grown hugely, to the point where it is now used extensively in geodemographic applications. All three above-mentioned companies have changed ownership, and they have been joined in the market by a further three companies; Consumer Data, Consumer Surveys Ltd, and CCN/Experian – the latter now collecting its own lifestyle data, having formerly had an arrangement to utilise CMT data.

Origins

Lifestyle databases originated in the US, and the practice spread to Britain in the mid-1980s.

As a working definition, lifestyle database companies build large databases of individuals, sourced from 'lifestyle questionnaires'. They offer list rental and associated services. The first major initiative in Britain came when NDL (National Demographics and Lifestyles) set up an office here in 1985. NDL, which had been operating in the US for some ten years, brought its methodology to Britain; it specialised in 'extended' guarantee cards for consumer durables manufacturers.

CMT (Computerised Marketing Technologies) arrived in Britain in 1987, also from an American base. CMT had a very different emphasis from NDL – it concentrated on fmcg products, mainly grocery, sponsored either by manufacturers or retailers.

The third company to get involved in lifestyle databases was International Communications and Data (ICD). It started on this activity with a first 'wave' of questionnaire distribution in 1988, having been operating under its previous name of Publishing Holdings for some years prior to that.

Appendix 5 details the addresses of the lifestyle database companies currently operating in the UK.

In the last few years, the ownership of the three 'majors' operating in the UK market has changed. First, the British subsidiary of CMT was acquired by a consortium headed by R.L. Polk of the US, which also had a majority shareholding in NDL. The British subsidiary of NDL then came together with CMT within the Calyx Group – although the two companies continued to operate as separate organisations. Then VNU – the Dutch publishing and information group – purchased Calyx, and put it together with its American subsidiary Claritas (the author of the first US neighbourhood classification, PRIZM). Calyx changed its name to Claritas UK in early 1997.

ICD was also acquired, in this case by US-based printing and direct marketing services company R.R. Donnelley and Sons, and now reports in to Donnelley's Metromail subsidiary.

How NDL Operates

When NDL first arrived in the UK and set up a British subsidiary, it used a bureau to build and hold the databases which it was constructing for its clients. NDL recruited an initially small number of durables manufacturers and distributors, and persuaded them to participate in a database-building exercise. Once having reached a 'critical mass', NDL took the database in-house.

NDL undertook the data-capture and database building for its clients; the clients agreed to pack 'extended guarantee cards' with their products. In addition to the details normally collected for ownership registration (name and address, product purchased and date of purchase), additional questionnaire information is solicited, and this is divided into two parts. One part is sponsored by the manufacturer in question, and asks for additional details about the product purchased:

- whether received as a gift;
- if so, for what occasion;
- where purchased (names of major stockists);
- how first learned about this product (i.e. advertisement etc.);
- factors influencing choice;
- whether replacement, additional, or first purchase.

The answers to these questions are used by the manufacturer for tracking sales, monitoring customer satisfaction, and establishing other useful facts about its customers.

The third part of the questionnaire, together with the name and address, forms the 'Lifestyle Database', and is made available to other clients of NDL for list rental. (There is an opt-out box for those consumers not wishing such additional mailings, and apparently some 20 per cent of consumers decide to opt out.)

The questions routinely asked in the third, lifestyle part of the questionnaire include:

- gender of person completing questionnaire;
- date of birth;
- marital status;
- occupation (of self and spouse);
- ages of children living at home;
- family income band;
- credit/charge cards regularly used;
- housing tenure;
- how long at present address;
- leisure interests and activities (currently 59, including hobbies, pursuits, sports and interests, from Eating Out to Watching Sports on TV);
- three favourite activities (self and spouse);
- car ownership (own or company car);
- make and model of car, age of car.

Clearly, if the consumer has filled in all this information completely and accurately it will give a very comprehensive insight into many aspects of that person and the associated household, which may be used for marketing purposes. This is true whether the objective is to mail this person/household, or to use the information for profiling or modelling purposes.

The questions on leisure interests and activities are particularly comprehensive (and potentially useful) as they cover both active and sedentary sports, hobbies such as gardening, car maintenance and DIY, activities such as eating out, going to the pub and slimming (the latter being separate activities!), different types of holidays, charitable interests, financial products, cultural and religious activities, interest in home computing, computer games and videos, and smoking (pipe, cigar or cigarettes).

This considerable volume of data is stored on a database, which in NDL's case has now assumed huge proportions. By the end of 1996, NDL had received some 30 million lifestyle questionnaires, of which 11 million are 'current' (i.e. latest); 85% of NDL respondents have responded more than once. This huge database is available for mailing selections (N.B. only those who have not ticked the opt out box, of course). Clients can choose selections by demographics, or by any of the other variables collected. This database is called The Lifestyle Selector, and datacards are produced regularly to show the number of selections available for each variable. For example, in the June 1997 datacard, NDL could offer 5,886,292 gardeners, and 1,481,903 golfers. Depending on NDL's client's business, this type of selection could be of direct interest (plant catalogues or golfing items, for example), but a development that was introduced some years ago was the Customer Profile Analysis (CPA). This involves NDL clients supplying a computer file of their customers to NDL, and NDL matching a percentage of those customers on its database, then using scoring techniques to rank prospect names from the Lifestyle Selector database in order of their similarity to the client's customers. A list selection is then made from the top of the ranking, to the volume required. Like geodemographic profiling, this technique works on the basis of finding prospects as similar as possible to existing customers; unlike geodemographics, lifestyle database profiling works on *individual* characteristics, not *neighbourhood* characteristics.

Another form of profiling practised by NDL (and its lifestyle database competitors) is that of 'data tagging'. As in CPA, the client provides a computer file of customers and NDL looks for *matches* on its Lifestyle Selector database. Apparently match rates can vary from five per cent to 20 per cent of the customer file (or up to 60 per cent if NDL use the Lifestyle Census for matching). Then the additional facts held on the Lifestyle Database can be added to the customer file, adding considerably to the client company's knowledge of its customers.

NDL's operation – known as Consumerlink to the general public – has experimented with the alternative method of recruitment practised by its rivals, that of distributing questionnaires with the promise of 'free coupons for your favourite products', with some additional questions over and above those asked on the extended guarantee cards. It is not known how significant has been this additional source, although it is felt unlikely to radically affect NDL's main data collection methodology. Apart from the product registration incentive *per se*, there is usually a prize draw incentive for product purchasers to return the completed questionnaire.

One useful facility which forms a part of NDL's profiling products is the 'Z score', which identifies the significance of each variable by taking account of the volume occurrence of the variable, as well as its index score. This prevents the user getting excited about high indices where the absolute penetration is low.

How CMT Operates

CMT (Computerised Marketing Technologies) has been operating in Britain for about ten years now. Its lifestyle database is branded 'Behaviourbank', and is built by a rather different technique from that used by NDL. CMT distributes regular 'waves' of questionnaires, branded the National Shoppers' Survey, via magazine inserts or door-to-door distribution. It encourages consumers to complete and return these questionnaires by means of a reward pack of money-off coupons and other offers. CMT encourages the main shopper of the household to complete the questionnaire and indeed, many of the questions are about household products and brands bought.

Naturally enough, the questionnaire has some similarities with NDL's questionnaire, although CMT's is considerably longer. It starts with name and address of the respondent (plus spouse's first name), and questions about housing:

- Tenure (own, rent-private or council)?

- How long at present address?

- Type of home (flat, semi, etc)?

- If owned, was it bought from council?

- Planning to move in next year? If so, when?

Clearly this latter question could provide valuable mailing opportunities to providers of products and services relevant to a new home. Respondents wishing to opt out of this type of opportunity, will find an opt-out box to tick.

Additional encouragement to complete and return the questionnaire is provided in the form of a free prize draw. The majority of the questions concern regularity of product purchase and brands bought; such questions may be sponsored by manufacturers, who will then have exclusive rights to the questions or sections they have sponsored. This gives them a potentially very valuable opportunity to 'tailor' follow-up mailings very precisely; for example, relatively low-value coupons to loyal users of their brand (to reinforce such loyalty) but higher-value coupons to users of competitive brands, to encourage brand switching. This aspect of competitive marketing is strongly promoted by CMT as a reason for using their services, and about 50 per cent of questions are sponsored.

There is a grocery retailer section, where respondents are asked to specify which stores they use for food and grocery shopping – a comprehensive list is supplied – they are asked to indicate the store in which they do their main shopping too. They are also asked to indicate how much they spend on grocery shopping per week, in their main store and elsewhere. (These answers are used in the CMT Storescan product – see later in this chapter.) Finally, respondents are asked their reason for doing their main shopping wherever they do (distance/convenience, car parking, prices, etc.), and how far is the store from their home.

There are extensive questions relating to motoring, for example:

- Who drives a car in your household?
- Number of drivers in your household?
- Number of cars in your household?
- Where do you keep your car(s)?
- Which motoring organisation are you a member of?
- When does your current motor insurance expire?
- What percentage no claims bonus do you have?
- What do you use your car(s) for?
- Has anyone who drives your car had:
  - an accident in the last three years?
  - a licence endorsement in the last five years?
- If you have a company car, can you choose the make/model?

It is obvious how useful some of these answers could be to firms selling cars, motor insurance, motoring accessories, garages, or other car-related products or services. The questionnaire goes on to ask details, both of main car and second car, if owned, about:

- make of car;
- model and cc;
- type/registration letter;
- main driver;
- car ownership (private/company);
- annual mileage;
- year it was purchased;
- bought new/used;
- plans to change car.

Also valuable information for car manufacturers!

The questionnaire has other useful demographic details, such as:

- occupation of adults in the home;
- employment type (self-employed, business owner, etc.);
- university graduate or not;
- dates of birth, respondent and spouse;
- number of people in home;
- age and sex of children living at home;
- annual family income.

It also asks about number of telephones in home, charitable cause contributed to (by type), type of contribution to charity (in the street, at door, by covenant, etc.); newspaper(s) regularly read by the family and products bought through the mail in the last 12 months. So, very useful data for charities, media information for any client participant, and mail order propensity for DM use. Respondents are asked how many dogs and cats are owned, their ages, and in the case of dogs, their size!

Ownership of main consumer durables is queried (CD player, computer, dishwasher, freezer, microwave, TV, satellite TV, video, washer-dryer); there is a detailed section on holiday habits (in terms of type of holiday taken, type of accommodation used, winter holiday habits, number of package holidays in last five years, weekend breaks); habits such as entering contests, prize draws, competitions or lotteries, and betting habits (pools, bingo, horseracing) are also queried, and an extremely detailed set of questions appears on financial products and services owned and used. Finally, there is a lifestyle section, similar to that in the NDL questionnaire; CMT's version lists 59 leisure interests and activities, and asks for four favourite activities each for spouse and self to be nominated.

From this listing of questions included, it is clear what a wealth of information is held on the Behaviourbank database, and the use that could be made of these data by marketers, both directly, and as raw material for profiling and modelling. There are currently some 6.5 million records on Behaviourbank available for rental (therefore net of sponsor-owned data), all of which are at most three years old. CMT mail respondents after they have been on the database for one year, and update their information; they go to great lengths to 'refresh' the data, enclosing 'bounceback' questionnaires with reward packs.

In terms of profiling, CMT's practice is similar to that of NDL. CMT's Customer File Analysis (similar to NDL's CPA) looks for exact matches between respondents on Behaviourbank and the client's customer file. Then the wealth of information from Behaviourbank is profiled, to provide much additional insight about the characteristics and interests of these customers. Also like NDL, CMT will conduct a similar response analysis for the client, taking a file of respondents to a mailing, matching them to the Behaviourbank database, and using the resultant analysis to provide a ranked list of 'lookalike' prospects for further mailing.

As well as regression, CMT has introduced a CHAID scoring model. CHAID stands for Chi-Squared Automatic Interaction Detector (sounds heavy! If you wish to know more, see the *JOTMAM* Vol. 1, No. 1, reference in Chapter 2 and references). It is a scoring technique which produces a 'tree diagram', identifying which variables are the best predictors of response to a mailing. Of crucial importance is the fact that this technique takes account of *interactions* between variables; this contrasts with the much more commonly used regression technique, which cannot cope with interactions. CMT can demonstrate examples where the use of CHAID on its data has provided clients with valuable insights which may not have been manifested without its use.

CMT segments its offer to the marketplace by means of a number of market sector offerings, namely, CharityBank, MediaBank, FinanceBank and CarBank. It also provides clients with insert opportunities within its mailings, and has other products which will be covered later in this chapter.

Another interesting aspect of CMT's business is that it has a large retailer sector in its client base, in addition to its manufacturer and charity clients. Indeed, a number of major retailers have distributed sponsored questionnaires, and benefited from the resultant data.

Claritas UK

As mentioned earlier in this chapter, NDL and CMT came together within the Calyx Group, which was acquired by VNU and more recently rebranded Claritas UK. Claritas is not only the holding company for NDL and CMT; it also owns Claritas Micromarketing, the geodemographic consultancy, which was originally launched by CMT under the branding of MIC (Marketing Information Consultancy).

The biggest benefit to Claritas of having both CMT and NDL within the group is the opportunity it provides to *combine* the data from both operators. This has been done, and the resultant data file (which has a deduplicated total of some 17 million households, or 75 per cent of all GB households) is marketed as the Lifestyle Census. This is obviously a very powerful resource, and has been exploited in various ways:

- as a 'link file' to market research (for example, TN AGB and BMRB – see Chapter 10);

- as an input to Claritas' PRIZM neighbourhood classification (see Chapter 3);

- direct use in targeting, for example, Claritas' Postcode Aggregated Data (PAD) file;

- as raw material for Claritas' FIND income profile product.

The geodemographic applications of lifestyle data will be covered later in this chapter.

As a Group, Claritas UK is a major player within the UK geodemographics and lifestyles marketplace. Its constituent lifestyle companies, CMT and NDL were already substantial before coming together within Claritas. And Claritas Micromarketing – while the most recent player to join the UK geodemographics market – has the data, skills and resource to make a considerable impact. The UK Group had collected a total of 40 million lifestyle questionnaires by the end of 1996 (some are now 'expired', of course), and targeted over 200 million pieces of direct mail in 1996 alone. Claritas is very well established in the US, having launched PRIZM there in 1978; it is using the Calyx acquisition as a springboard into mainland Europe. CMT had already started a French operation some years ago, then in 1976, VNU acquired IFMS in Germany. IFMS had collated its own data and developed its own units of area to build a very successful geodemographic company, specialising in the financial services sector. In addition to these French and German operations, Claritas has initiatives in Austria, Switzerland and The Netherlands.

Claritas' strategy is to put in place the data and tools to allow marketing people to *integrate* their customer and market information, their communications planning, and their market analysis. As a key plank in this strategy, Claritas have forged links with market research organisations; not just at the level of cross-tabulations of survey data, but also at the level of individual matching of market research respondents with the same individuals on the Lifestyle Census. The section at the end of Chapter 10 (Market Research Meets Database Marketing) explains more about this. Another technique utilised by Claritas to link in market research data is called 'PRIZM Grids' – it was 'imported' from Claritas UK's American sister company, SPECTRA. This involves constructing a grid with 'best' neighbourhood types on one dimension, and *individual* characteristics, usually sourced from market research, on the other. This enables very tight targeting indeed. In the UK manifestation, it can be applied by using the Lifestyle Census. A product called Spectra Advantage is just being released (mid-1997) which borrows from Claritas' US sister company. It uses PRIZM grids and a further refinement of the approach is to supply an analyst, on-site at the client's premises, to conduct the analyses and to integrate them with the client's own data.

September 1997, will see the launch of 'The Lifestyle Universe' from Claritas UK. It is a lifestyle database consisting of 12 demographics and over 50 lifestyles covering 22 million households – virtually all households in GB. It is being built from the 45 million lifestyle questionnaires held by Claritas, which cover 75 per cent of households. The remaining 25 per cent is being derived using data fusion techniques which include additional data such as the ER, share registers, Claritas' PAD file, etc.

Claritas Micromarketing

Claritas Micromarketing started life as the MIC, a subsidiary of CMT, in 1994. Its original role was to market lifestyle data in geodemographic applications. CMT and NDL had already come together within the Calyx Group, so MIC had access to the combined files of the two companies, branded the Lifestyle Census. Its first derived product was FIND, which provided incoming profiling at unit postcode level. MIC went on to develop the PRIZM neighbourhood classification system, and the CATALYST desktop analysis/mapping system; the latter were launched in June 1996, at the same time that MIC changed its name to Claritas. Claritas Micromarketing adopted an unusual strategy, compared with its direct competitors. It decided to concentrate its efforts on key clients; to make them a specific proposition, in terms of data access and closeness of relationship with Claritas. It was less concerned with selling data, although data sales could be made through intermediaries. Thus, the preferred role was that of strategic partner, not just supplying data, but helping the client to get the most out of it.

Geodemographic Products from the Claritas Group

As I have stated earlier in this chapter, list rental has been the core business of lifestyle database companies, including CMT and NDL. CMT have also developed a substantial business with StoreScan – see below – and NDL had started to venture into geographical analysis with 'Lifestyle Market Location' and its data interest in PORTRAIT. However, the formation of the Calyx Group and subsequent developments have tended to focus non-list-rental activities on Claritas Micromarketing. In summary, their products are:

- The Lifestyle Census; combined CMT/NDL databases, giving up to 300 characteristics for 17 million households.

- FIND income profiles for unit postcodes; gives average/median income, spread, and rank for each postcode.

- PRIZM neighbourhood classification, built from lifestyle and other data; includes income ranking and age ranking.

- Postcode Aggregated Data File (PAD); counts for each variable on the Lifestyle Census at unit postcode level.

- CATALYST desktop analysis/mapping system, allowing users to manipulate their own data with any of the above products, plus perform GIS/retail analysis functions. Also used for StoreScan (see below).

StoreScan is operated by the fmcg marketing division of CMT. It utilises CMT's National Shoppers' Survey (NSS) lifestyle data, and serves both fmcg manufacturers and fmcg retailers.

CATALYST provides the analysis/mapping platform for StoreScan, which enables users to look at the NSS data geographically – for example, by store catchment. The wealth of brand and product usage data in the NSS is used within StoreScan to establish for CMT's clients exactly how they compete, at a single store level. Manufacturers might wish to study category management or promotional 'battleplans'; retailers to determine store-by-store competitive strategy. The NSS data are held at postcode sector level, and the (one million plus) records are weighted to reflect the universe. The supply points, in the sense of store locations, are also included within StoreScan. The grocery market was the first to be analysed, as long ago as 1989 (in those days, CMT were collaborating with CCN, and used MOSAIC Systems software for analysis). A very recent development is market-specific versions of StoreScan:

- LiquorScan (for the spirits market – incorporates volumetric information);
- MediScan (for the pharmaceutical market, mainly OTC);
- BeerScan (for the brewery trade – managed house data has been incorporated).

The former joint CCN/CMT product, then branded 'Checkout', was able to look at grocery superstore market share by postcode sector within trading areas; since the CCN/CMT collaboration ceased, CMT include this analysis within StoreScan, and CCN/Experian now provide similar analyses using their own Chorus lifestyle data.

How ICD Operates

ICD had formerly been trading as Publishing Holdings, under which name it had assembled the British Investors' Database (BID). This was a very enterprising initiative to data-capture the names and addresses of shareholders, sourced from share registers. The huge privatisation issues of the late 1980s formed the bulk of the raw material for the BID, which was subsequently promoted very successfully as a mailing list.

ICD saw the opportunity inherent in lifestyle databases, and started to collect data for this purpose in 1988. Its survey was called 'Facts of Living' and was distributed (in similar fashion to CMT's NSS) via magazine inserts. A very similar questionnaire called 'Contactstream' used to be mailed to 750,000 consumers every quarter; personally addressed, with names either rented from mail-responsive lists, or selected from the ER. In 1996, this individually-addressed questionnaire activity went up several gears when ICD rebranded the survey as the National Lifestyle Survey and mailed the whole ER (in excess of 20 million households) with its questionnaire, in September of that year. This exercise was repeated in June 1997, and ICD plan to repeat it again in February 1998. The June mailing broke new ground, in that it was accompanied by TV advertising which urged consumers to fill in and return the questionnaires. A sign of ICD's determination to get the response level up (and possibly, of the funding available following their acquisition by Metromail). Certainly, the numbers of questionnaire responses have been growing fast in recent years; from a claimed 5.1 million individuals in 1995, to a claimed 8.6 million after the first national survey (i.e. late 1996). ICD achieved about a ten per cent response to their first national mailing – some 2 million questionnaires returned. They expect a 17 per cent response to the mid-1997 national mailing; which, if achieved, will give them 3.4 million households and 5.6 million individuals from that one mailing alone. They plan two national mailings in 1998, with an estimated total response of 11.2 million individuals. ICD's data collection department goes by the name of the Consumer Research Bureau. As with CMT, many of the questions on the questionnaire are sponsored, therefore these specific answers can be exclusive to the sponsoring company; but, also like CMT, the basic demographics, lifestyle and lead-to-purchase questions are available for list rental to all clients of ICD.

The ICD questionnaire is very extensive; the recent National Survey questionnaire is indicative. It starts with a letter to the would-be respondent (remember, it is personally-addressed) explaining the background to the request. It is presented as a research questionnaire, and indeed, the sub-heading of the letter page is 'An invitation to take part in an important national survey with an entry into a prize draw'. There is an opt-out box at the end of the questionnaire. The questions cover:

- *Marital status*/spouse's name. (Thereafter, tick boxes for both self and partner).

- *Holiday and travel* section: taken in the last three years or considering, by destination and holiday type (includes how booked, likely spend per person, business flying, travel insurance.)

- *Leisure* section, including the lifestyle questions – 17 leisure activities plus 17 sporting activities; pairs of boxes, for self and spouse. Includes media habits (newspapers usually read, number of hours of TV watched per day, satellite/cable TV owned or considering, number of TV sets – and how good is Channel 5 reception! Subscription magazines taken, including a long list of special interest magazines to which the respondent might consider subscribing). Also, other leisure activities, such as eating out, type of musical interest, National Trust membership, and collectibles of interest.

- Motoring section, including:
    number of cars in household;
    private/company/new/used;
    what make? tick box or write in;
    model and type, engine size;
    registration letter;
    when anticipating replacement;
    questions about likely replacement, and how it will be financed;

questions about motor insurance and renewal date;
annual mileage, membership of motoring organisations;
questions about motorbike, caravan, etc.

- *Health* section, including questions on private medical insurance; 'hospital treatment following accident or industrial disease', and opportunity to try for compensation (these questions sponsored, of course!); a list of medical complaints, with tick boxes; questions about mobility, spectacles, sensitive teeth, and finally 'are you seriously concerned about ... losing weight? giving up smoking?'

- *Money and investments*: fairly comprehensive section, covering accounts held with banks and building societies, how long current account held and whether considering a change; where mortgage held, would you consider direct banking, credit/charge cards held. Questions about credit card habits and intentions, perceived need for a personal loan, investments or financial provisions made or under consideration; how prepared to buy financial services over the telephone, maturity date for TESSAs, interest in PEPs, and issues concerned with financial advice.

- *'Your home'*: a long section, which asks questions about most aspects of one's home; type of house, number of bedrooms, tenure, when built, how long living there, any plans to move, issues with regard to mortgage, approximate value of home. Then questions about building insurance, home improvements (double glazing etc) – have, or considering, type of central heating, supplier of LPG (if used). Ownership of specified electrical appliances (or considering purchase), questions about mobile phones, international calls, quarterly utility bills; a question about willingness to change utility suppliers (and a rating of satisfaction with current electricity supplier). Questions about contents insurance, mechanical breakdown insurance for household appliances, PC at home, PC equipment, and subscription to an on-line/Internet service.

(This reads like a catalogue, I realise! but I believe it is valuable to give a 'flavour' of the contents of the lifestyle databases, so the reader may compare them, and appreciate the wealth of data collected and its possibilities.)

- *Shopping*: a lengthy section, much of it sponsored, which asks a comprehensive set of questions about fmcg products/brands purchased. It starts with a question about store used (20 named candidates) for food and grocery shopping, and asks for first and second most-used stores to be specified; also weekly expenditure at the supermarket. Apart from groceries, the section includes questions on tobacco products, beer, and spirits.

- *Mail order*: an initial question about use of mail order in last two years, then a question on type of goods which respondent has bought, or would consider buying, by mail or telephone. List of 38 catalogues – 'do you/your partner shop regularly by mail order from?' Questions regarding outsize shopping, and about Christmas hampers.

- *General information*: basic demographics about everyone in the household, including dates of birth. Occupation, family income, additional questions about current and previous work, owning or starting a business. Cats and dogs in home; financial provisions for retirement, 'would you consider' – insuring against redundancy/legal expenses, and (not connected!) – becoming a member of a political party (specified).

- *Charitable concerns*: questions about donations (by type), 'would you consider supporting any of the following charitable concerns' (by type of charity); then list of named charities (sponsored questions). 'Would you consider a charitable bequest?' – and finally – 'do you/your partner regularly attend any of the following places of worship?'

The final section asks for a choice of prize, should the respondent win a runner's up prize; and asks whether the respondent has seen the Consumer Research Bureau TV commercial.

So, a very comprehensive questionnaire, providing a wealth of information for sponsors or for list rental clients.

ICD's main business is in list rental and sponsorship; they also build customer and prospect databases for clients, 'populated' by questionnaire responses. In the case of general demographic, lifestyle, and lead-to-purchase data (i.e. other than that specifically sponsored, therefore exclusive), ICD also supply these data to CACI and Equifax.

When ICD was acquired by R.R. Donnelley in 1995, it came together with DATA *by Design* (which had been bought by Donnelley in 1993, having been originally set up by PPHN, the direct marketing agency, in 1990). DATA *by Design* conducts statistical analysis and builds models; while the two companies were initially kept separate, DATA *by Design* was then merged into ICD in 1996. This led to a number of analytical products being developed by DATA *by Design* on ICD's lifestyle database (for example, FACTS '96, Reflector, Translife – see later in this chapter). ICD is divided into functional divisions – ICD Surveys, ICD List Rental, DATA *by Design*, and ICD Value-added Services (the latter being responsible for data supply to CACI, Equifax, Continental Research, etc). Apart from the huge national mailings (some questions being sponsored, of course), ICD Surveys also conducts customised survey work for individual clients, which leads to customer and prospect database building. The client provides the distribution means, for example, an insert in the packaging of product or publication, a handout at the checkout, or a survey distributed with a service. This service is branded ICD Data Ventures.

In summary, the products and services available from ICD are:

- List rental, both from the Lifestyle Database, and the British Investor Database (note – ICD's lively trade press advertising is quick to exploit fresh data 'waves', for example, lead-to-purchase data, and currently in mid-1997, 'windfall' building society savers benefiting from conversions to plc status).

- Sponsored questions on lifestyle surveys.

- Profiling a client file against ICD's Lifestyle Database, using DATA *by Design*'s profiling products:

□ FACTS '96 (which uses regression modelling and a 'power curve' approach to select prospects from the Lifestyle Database)

□ Reflector (which uses the same approach, this time to highlight differences between high value and low value customers)

□ Translife (which uses a combination of client's transactional data, and data 'tagged' from ICD's Lifestyle Database).

– Data enhancement or data tagging – overlaying variables from the Lifestyle Database on to matched records from client files; specific Enhancer products have been developed for some markets, for example, finance, retail, mail order, publishing. Statistical inference can be used to predict variables, for those customer records where matches cannot be made.

– Building customer databases for clients via branded questionnaires.

ICD does not itself get involved in geodemographics; although it licenses its data to CACI, CCN and Equifax, who use ICD's data as a part of their geodemographic offerings. I gather that this situation will change in 1998 with the launch of some lifestyle/geodemographics products by ICD.

How Consumerdata Operates

Consumerdata specialises in customer satisfaction surveys within the travel industry. It claims to be the European market leader in this area, currently working with nine of the top twelve UK tour operators. Have you ever filled in a questionnaire on your return flight from holiday? If so, you'll know that the questionnaire is comprehensive, and similar in concept to those operated by the lifestyle database companies.

Consumerdata is a part of the Cadogan Group, which was set up in late 1992 as a 'full service database marketing company'. It started by purchasing the market research, data analysis and data-preparation side of UIS Ltd; then in 1993, acquired the CCS Division of the Lewis Group plc, which brought with it database design/build and address management facilities.

In summary, Consumerdata's services include:

– questionnaire design;

– scanning data capture or manual data-entry;

– database design, build and management;

– market research and analytical services;

– brochure management and agent performance systems.

Concentrating on the travel industry, Consumerdata claims to have surveyed 20–25 per cent of all UK package holiday takers in 1996.

How Consumer Surveys Limited Operates

Consumer Surveys Limited (CSL) started to operate in 1995. CSL is a wholly-owned subsidiary of the Dudley Jenkins Group, the largest independently-owned listbroking company. CSL's consumer-facing name is The Centre for Consumer Interests, and it takes a very direct approach to collecting data. The cover of its lifestyle questionnaire asks the householder 'What do you want from YOUR post?', and invites him/her to complete the survey as a way of influencing the direct mail that is received; '...help you to get the advertising mail you actually want'. Effectively, by completing and returning the questionnaire, the consumer is 'opting in'; unlike most such lifestyle questionnaires, where it is necessary to tick an opt-out box if direct mail is not wanted.

Like most of the lifestyle databases, CSL uses a prize draw as an incentive; however, unlike the others, CSL also offers £9-worth of Beefeater restaurant vouchers, free with the questionnaire (i.e. you can use them even if you do not complete the questionnaire). There were 182 questions on the 1996 questionnaire – more than CMT or NDL, but slightly less than ICD. The questionnaires are delivered via door-to-door distribution; CSL claim to have received 3 million completed questionnaires within their first year of operation.

How Experian (formerly CCN) Operates

The preceding chapters have mentioned CCN's place in the UK geodemographic market (and Chapter 12 contains more information, including the fact that the company changed its name to Experian in June 1997). After the severance of CCN's relationship with CMT – covered later in this chapter – CCN started to collect its own lifestyle data, through its Chorus initiative.

The Chorus strategy is different from that employed by (for example) CMT or ICD, in that Chorus employs mainly 'tailored' surveys for specific clients or distributors; Experian identifies markets in demand, and either surveys these itself, or with partners. Distribution methods vary from door-to-door, to ER-based direct mail, to inserts in the national or regional press or magazines; but in many cases, a specific client or distributor is sponsoring the survey. Like the other lifestyle database operators, Experian has an agreement to utilise the 'general' demographic and lifestyle information, while sponsors retain their specific information. One by-product of the Chorus strategy is that its volumes are not as large as those of the big players; in late 1996, the Chorus file was approximately one million; it has reached one and a half million in mid-1997, and is projected at two million in March 1998. Thus, recency of the data is very good – but the rollout capacity is limited.

Some high-profile 'collaborators' with Chorus, who received trade press publicity when their involvement was announced, were the *Daily Telegraph*, with its large readers' database; and EMAP Magazines, where the majority of EMAP's 90 consumer magazines carried the reader questionnaires. Clearly, such activity provides the publication with both a valuable database, and extra insight into its readers' lifestyles.

The Checkout product, which resulted from the former collaboration between CCN and CMT, was replaced in CCN's portfolio by a similar product based on Chorus data. Checkout had formerly used CMT data to analyse market share by supermarket operator within postcode sectors. Experian has not (so far) used its own lifestyle data in any other geodemographic applications.

Other Issues

As was said at the outset, the main business of the lifestyle database companies was (and still is) list rental. Before they reached their current volumes, they found it helpful to 'extend the lists' to generate greater volumes of cold mailing prospects.

The first to adopt this strategy was ICD, who acquired a copy of the ER in 1989. They linked their existing data (investor information from the British Investors' Database, lifestyle information from the Facts of Living survey) to the ER and they branded the new product the 'National Consumer Database'. NDL addressed the same issue in 1991, with its launch of 'The Lifestyle Network'. Like ICD, it acquired a copy of the ER, and merged it with its 'Lifestyle Selector' database. Unlike ICD, NDL collaborated with a geodemographic agency (Infolink), and used Infolink's DEFINE neighbourhood classification system to add modelling power to its database. So, both lifestyle database operators were modelling from the hard data which they had collected, to impute characteristics to those addresses where hard data were lacking.

ICD stopped using the ER in 1995, and now just market the names and addresses which they have collected (although their Enhancer product still uses imputation techniques on client files). At a Group level, Claritas UK has been working on its combined file, the Lifestyle Census, to enhance it by adding data for the 25 per cent of households where it does not hold lifestyle data. As reported earlier in this chapter, it will launch the resultant product (The Lifestyle Universe) in September 1997. The 'missing data' are being modelled from the ER, share registers, PAD data, etc. This will almost certainly be the most comprehensive attempt to date to build a file of consumer characteristics to cover the entire household population.

Looking back at other products that were current in the previous edition of this book, the ones which are now most notable by their absence are those that resulted from the former collaboration between CCN and CMT – Checkout, and Persona. Checkout was mentioned in the section dealing with geodemographic products from Claritas; lifestyle data from CMT regarding grocery superstore used were analysed geographically by CCN, and provided to clients on CCN's MOSAIC Systems. This enabled 'share of trade' data by superstore operator to be studied at postcode sector level. After CCN and CMT's collaboration ended in 1994, CMT 'absorbed' this product into their StoreScan service, and CCN produced a similar product from its own Chorus lifestyle data.

'Persona' was an interesting product; 'behaviourgraphics' rather than geodemographics *per se*. A set of variables from CMT's Behaviourbank was subjected to cluster analysis, and 20 behavioural types were identified (they were given evocative names such as 'Young Affluentials', 'Golf Clubs and Volvos', 'Trinkets and Treasures' and 'Pubs, Pools and Bingo'). The initial clustering was conducted on CMT's Behaviourbank lifestyle database, so on *individual* respondents; and CMT offered Persona as an individual selection criterion. However, CCN's version was actually 'Geo-Persona', and operated at a pseudo-ED (Enumeration District) level – pseudo EDs were classified according to respondents therein, or modelled from other data. Clearly, this was a much 'looser' link than CMT's individual version. Nevertheless, Persona was a casualty of the severance of the CCN/CMT relationship.

Another issue, where much progress has been made in the last few years, is the relationship between lifestyle databases and market research. I made the point in the first edition of this book that the market research industry would need to decide whether lifestyle databases are a problem or an opportunity. Sensibly, some of the big market research players have decided the latter; the last section of Chapter 10 outlines initiatives involving Taylor Nelson AGB and its Superpanel service, and BMRB and its TGI survey. Another high profile link between the two disciplines is from Continental Research, with its 'Million+Panel' services. This utilises the ICD lifestyle database, or more specifically, a subset which has been taken by Continental Research, weighted to be representative of the UK, and then used in two ways; for recruiting minority samples for further research, and for producing national reports on some of the markets addressed by ICD's database.

In conclusion, the lifestyle database sector has never been more buoyant; all the current players are very active, with volumes continuing to grow. One could speculate that Claritas, with some 75 per cent of British households on its Lifestyle Census, may be approaching its threshold. On the other hand, one might have speculated in similar vein some years ago, when volumes were considerably less.

CHAPTER FIVE

NON-CENSUS DATA
USED IN GEODEMOGRAPHICS

Introduction

Chapter 3 has given several clues to the type of data that can be used in geodemographics. Reference was made to the incorporation within one or more of the systems, of a number of types of non-census data; credit-related data, PAF, ER data, market research data. This chapter elaborates on the brief descriptions of some of these data already provided, and goes on to show how (in particular) the electoral roll and market research data have been used in geodemographics.

Credit-Related Data

Two companies dominate the UK credit referencing industry; Experian (formerly CCN) and Equifax. Experian is part of the Great Universal Stores (GUS) Group, and has also been in the geodemographics market since 1986. Equifax Europe is owned by Equifax in the US, which is very big in the US credit referencing market, and also owned NDS, one of the largest operators in the US geodemographics industry. Equifax took over the Wescot operation in the UK, formerly owned by Next/Grattan. Equifax then took over Infolink in late-1994, thus acquiring both Infolink's credit referencing business, and its geodemographic classifications, PORTRAIT and DEFINE.

Both these companies operate credit referencing bureaux. This enables their clients to link in to the bureau's central computer to check the credit status of members of the public. The bureaux compile huge national databases, usually based on the PAF file, with ER information added, and then records of the credit 'history' of (consumer) customers of their clients. For example, Experian handles the credit records for customer files of the GUS-owned mail-order companies; so they can track applications for credit, acceptances/refusals, defaults on payment, etc. All credit lenders will use a service of this sort, in order to protect themselves (as best they can) against fraud or default. Banks, building societies, credit card companies, finance house, retailers and mail order companies, all use this service. The bureaux form 'closed user groups' of lenders who are prepared to pool their data for the common good. As a result, the bureaux build up 'histories' for very many individuals who apply for and use credit. They supplement this transactional information with data from the Lord Chancellor's Office. This Office supplies details of CCJs against individuals for non-payment of debts (and also, the subsequent 'satisfactions', when the debtor pays his creditor). CCJs are 'flagged' on these individuals' records by the credit bureaux, as a warning to would-be lenders.

Individual credit 'histories' and the presence or absence of CCJs have both been used by two of the geodemographic agencies (Experian and Infolink, the former as an integral part of the MOSAIC classification, the latter as an overlay to the census-based classification. In both cases, the data in question are summed to a unit postcode level (an average of 15 addresses), thus 'anonymising' it and avoiding invasion of individual privacy. Households with CCJs are simply counted up within postcodes, and expressed as a penetration of the total. In the case of credit application data, the numbers of credit searches within each postcode are logged and used as a 'credit activity indicator'; this gives a proxy for the degree to which the inhabitants of each postcode are active purchasers. It is clear that these data are both useful in their own right, and also as enhancements to neighbourhood classification systems.

The Postcode Address File (PAF)

The GB postcode system was described in outline in Chapter 3 – but little was said about PAF. PAF is the official Royal Mail file of all the addresses in England, Scotland, Wales and Northern Ireland. It contains some 24 million 'delivery points' (mostly domestic, of course, but all company addresses are also included). There are about 170,000 'large users', which are almost invariably businesses, the criterion being addresses in receipt of 25 or more items of mail per day. As its name implies, PAF has postcodes attached to all addresses, indeed the addresses are ordered by postcode, within 'postal geography' (see Chapter 3).

PAF can be supplied on magnetic tape or on CD-ROM, and unsurprisingly, this latter medium has become very popular. The Postzon file (which supplies the grid reference of each postcode) can be supplied in association with the PAF file and it is this which supplies the 'key' which links to GIS and geodemographic applications. PAF is often used as the 'core' of large customer databases, to which all the customer information can be attached. PAF is an essential ingredient of geodemographics.

The Electoral Roll (ER)

The ER, or register of electors, has been used for mailing purposes for many years. It is collected by local authorities, obviously in order that people eligible to vote in local or national elections can do so and are duly recorded; but the local authorities are also obliged to supply their own rolls, either on paper or on magnetic media, to legitimate purchasers, and these data are then permitted by law to be used for direct mailing purposes (and other legitimate purposes, such as credit referencing, as described earlier in this chapter). A recent development has been for ER data to be provided to purchasers on CD-ROM, usually enhanced with the seller's neighbourhood classification. EuroDirect was the first to offer this product; Equifax, Experian, Capscan, Data Discoveries and GB Information Management have joined the fray.

Approximately 44 million names appear on the ER. While the figures fluctuate from year to year, in round terms it can be assumed that about 95 per cent of those eligible to vote appear on the register. The shortfall tends to be concentrated in inner-city areas; again, in broad terms, a similar profile to those 'missed' from the 1991 Census.

Apart from the obvious value of the ER as a huge mailing list, segmentable by geodemographics, there are other characteristics which provide additional opportunities for segmentation. For example, organisations which have been collating the ER for a number of years, can set up their computer systems to 'recognise' changes of name at an address from one year to the next, and can also record the converse; people who have been at the *same* address for 'x' years. Both pieces of information are useful, the former to mail 'movers' with offers applicable to occupants of a new home, the latter as a 'stability indicator' – which improves the score on a credit 'scorecard'! When children in the household reach the age of 17, the head of household is asked to record this fact on the return, so that they will appear on the register in time for their eighteenth birthday – from which date they are legally entitled to vote. This information is captured by the bureaux which compile the ER electronically; these young people are called 'attainers' (because they have attained the age of 18). This subset of the ER is valuable in its own right (attainers may well be mailed offers relating to financial services) but it also enables the bureaux to record the ages of these people within the household, and so long as they remain in that household, their ages will be known and thus available for selection.

Another important segmentation criterion is *household composition*. Of course, it is impossible to know presence of children below the age of 'attainment' from the ER source, but in the case of attainers and other adults, the clues are there. Households containing a single adult are easy; so (apparently) are households with two adults with the same surname, one male, one female. They will probably be assumed to be husband and wife, although they might be brother and sister, father and daughter, etc. The bureaux develop 'rules' which make assumptions about likely relationships. Most of the time they are probably right, but it is clear that embarrassing mistakes could occur when these assumed relationships are 'translated' into direct mail messages! The growth of co-habitation has not helped the 'modellers' – yet another opportunity to get it wrong – but on the other hand, families with male plus female, same surname, with one or more 'attainer', same surname – would provide a very high probability of a correctly-interpreted family composition.

So to summarise the ER-based variables that can be used for mailing segmentation, they are:

- household composition
- young voters
- recent movers
- length of residency.

As you will no doubt recall from personal experience, the ER is updated on an annual cycle. The forms go out from local authorities in August/September each year, with a requirement for return by 30 October 30. The provisional 'draft' register is available for inspection from end-November onwards; then the bureaux start to receive final data from mid-February, and can then update their own databases from that point. They expect to have received all the local authority data by end-March, and complete their updates by May/June. This should be borne in mind when considering, for example, 'recent movers'; in fact, these people will have moved at some time between October one year and October the next, and this information may only be available to the marketplace some six months later than that. I make this point not in an attempt to question the usefulness of the ER and its additional 'indicators', far from it; merely to observe that the user needs to appreciate the nature of the beast in order to use it sensibly. This same comment could equally apply to the whole of the targeting marketplace.

Name-Based Indicators

There is one other piece of information which can be gleaned from the ER; the *first names* of the adults and attainers present. CACI has made use of this information in its 'MONICA' system, which models likely age-band from 'given' name. To take CACI's own quoted examples of names frequently occurring within its four age-bands:

- Youngest (18 – 24 years), e.g. Michelle, Sharon, Kevin, Gary;
- Maturing (25 – 44 years), e.g. Pamela, Janet, Philip, Brian;
- Mature Family (45 – 64 years), e.g. Sylvia, Brenda, Kenneth, Raymond;
- Retired (65+ years), e.g. Hilda, Ethel, Percy, Herbert

Clearly, these 'rules' cannot be rigidly applied because there will always be exceptions; but CACI has several techniques to improve its accuracy. The first is to look at the name of the 'partner' within household, if there is one; this combination of names apparently improves the certainty of age-band. The other technique is to incorporate both MONICA and the 'household composition' information, also derived from the ER as described above, into CACI's 'Household*ACORN' product. In this case, the ACORN neighbourhood characteristics are overlaid on the ER-based characteristics, thus pushing ER segmentation to its ultimate manifestation. More about this in Chapter 10. Experian has developed a similar product called 'Stages'.

NDL has also produced a name-based segmentation system on its 'Lifestyle Selector' lifestyle database. NDL call it ANNA; in concept it is similar to MONICA, but in NDL's case it is derived from analysis of the individuals on the company's extensive database, where both first name *and* age are present. NDL can then use the ANNA model on other lists to predict age from given name.

Other Miscellaneous Data

Chapter 2 listed the types of non-census data now utilised in neighbourhood classifications. Apart from the types of data mentioned elsewhere in this chapter, there is another category of miscellaneous datasets which have been used by various system authors within their classifications:

- Company directors (at home address); sourced from one of the proprietary directories, original source likely to be Companies House. Proxy for affluence.

- Share ownership; similarly, sourced from a proprietary directory, originally from share registers. Suggests a positive attitude towards investment!

- Insurance ratings (within postcode sectors); sourced from an insurance company. Gives a measure of relative risk.

- Unemployment data (within postcode sectors); from ONS records. Gives additional clues to nature of areas.

- Retail access (to retail centres); sourced from a proprietary analysis.

Additionally, the use of lifestyle data within classifications had already been covered in Chapters 2, 3 and 4.

Market Research Data

Market research links have always been very important to UK geodemographics. Indeed, as I mentioned in Chapter 2, the commercial introduction of geodemographics into the marketing and media mainstream resulted from cross-tabulation work on BMRB's TGI. Since that time, TGI has remained as a key linkage for geodemographics; indeed, most of the major neighbourhood classification systems are available for cross-tabulation of TGI.

Perhaps I should explain what I mean by 'cross-tabulation', although users of market research will be familiar with the concept. To take a typical TGI cross-tab, for example cinema-going cross-tabbed by PiN, a very simple extract from a page of cross-tabs might be:

		Number of Respondents	Cinema-Going	
			All	Heavy
PiNPOINT	25 level	786	417	88
PiN types	'000s	1,421	779	174
Type Dh	Vert. (%)	3.14	4.01	3.92
	Horz. (%)	100.00	54.82	12.24
	Index	100	128	125

Source: BMRB

The 'number of respondents'/'PiNPOINT 25 level' row is the 'raw' number of respondents; thus there were 786 TGI respondents in this PiN type. Of these, 417 say they go to the cinema 'at all', and 88 are 'heavy' cinema-goers (on TGI's definition). The next row down grosses these numbers up for the population (more about this shortly), so some 779,000 adults go to the cinema 'at all' during the year in question.

The next row down ('Vert. (%)' – vertical percentage) is important to this cross-tab, because it shows the *penetration* of cinema-goers in this PiN type, as against all adults in this PiN type. You will see that 3.14 per cent of adults fall within this PiN type nationally, but 4.01 per cent of cinema-goers are in this PiN type; this leads to the index figures in the last row, which shows an index of 128 for cinema-going in PiN type h. (This is derived by dividing 4.01 by 3.14 and multiplying by 100.) The other row ('Horz. (%)' – horizontal percentage) shows that 54.82 per cent of adults in this PiN type (779,000 of 1,421,000) are cinema-goers.

So one can derive a wealth of information from this small fraction of a cross-tab page from TGI. In fact, something like 3,000 brands in 200 fmcg product fields are covered by the TGI, plus more than 450 other brands in financial services, cars, retail, holidays, etc. The unique feature of TGI is that it also covers media usage; readership of some 220 newspapers and magazines, weight of viewing of commercial TV channels and radio, and exposure to outdoor media and cinema. The sample is 25,000 adults each year; a carefully-balanced sample that can be grossed up to the national situation with some confidence.

The reason for covering the TGI in this relative detail (within the context of this chapter) is two-fold; first, its importance to the geodemographics 'industry', and second, to provide a fairly typical illustration of how other survey research is used by geodemographers and client end-users. In a nutshell, as (hopefully) illustrated by the example above, geodemographic cross-tabs are used to derive *profiles* of product or media usage; the *penetration* of (say) cinema-going within each neighbourhood type. Often, the profile will then be presented in a format similar to that illustrated in Chapter 3. TGI has been the source of countless geodemographic cross-tabs since 1979, not least because BMRB has made it very easy for users to access this facility. The latest development in this regard is the 'Choices' software, which enables a user of a PC-based geodemographic system to interface directly with TGI data.

But I must not seem to suggest that TGI is the only option! A number of other major syndicated research sources can be cross-tabbed with geodemographics. Marketing people will generally want to use whichever research source they use as 'currency' in their marketplace; for many fmcg marketers, this will mean consumer panel data, either AGB or ACNielsen. Recent developments in technology have improved the consumer panel 'product' considerably; providing respondents with hand-held scanners, for daily scanning of grocery purchases, is a good case in point. Both AGB's Superpanel and ACNielsen's Homescan use this methodology, which allows not only very fast reporting, but also a much less 'clustered' sample. This improves the quality of the results, particularly in terms of source of purchase, where the formerly clustered samples might show distortions depending on their geographical relationship with supermarket catchment areas. Anyway, both Superpanel and Homescan can be cross-tabbed by selected geodemographic systems, which brings a different dimension to geodemographic analysis for clients of these services. They can study the geodemographics of (for example) loyal users of brand A versus brand B, 'promiscuous' users of both, early trialists of a new product, purchasers of brand A from retailer C, etc., thus exploiting the strengths of this research methodology. I will return to what they might *do* with these analyses later in this book.

As I mentioned earlier, other major industry surveys may be cross-tabbed with geodemographics. Readers operating within the clothing and footwear market will doubtless be familiar with the TMS survey, conducted by the TMS Partnership. TMS interviews some 80,000 adults per annum for this survey, asking detailed questions about all purchases of clothing and footwear; purchases for children in household are also covered. These data can be cross-tabbed by most of the neighbourhood classification systems.

In the financial services marketplace, the FRS is operated by NOP; in excess of 60,000 adults per annum are interviewed about all aspects of financial activity. This ranges from bank and building society accounts held, through usage of credit, debit, store and charge cards, to shareholdings, National Savings and insurance products. Again, this can be cross-tabbed by most of the classifications. More recently, MORI Financial Services (MFS) has started up in competition with FRS, and I understand that MFS allows cross-tabs by several of the classifications.

The beer market survey, fielded annually by PAS, is the basis of the 'Indicator' area modelling service, marketed by Stats MR, Indicator uses geodemographics to model potential for different types of beer within residential areas, and thus, within catchment areas of pubs. In other markets, the Home Audit, formerly run by AGB, but subsequently taken over by GfK, provides geodemographic cross-tabs on an *ad hoc* basis in the DIY, home improvement and durables markets.

Finally, syndicated media research sources. TGI has already been mentioned, of course; in addition, NRS and BARB are available for geodemographic cross-tabulation. The NRS interviews a sample of some 30,000 adults per annum, collecting information on readership of around 250 titles. Additionally, information is collected on ownership of consumer durables and some other 'product' information, such as holiday taking; plus exposure to the media. These 'product' questions provide useful material for geodemographic cross-tabs; in addition, of course, to the readership data. The NRS is responsible for the IPA social grading system (A, B, C1, C2, D, E).

The Broadcasters' Audience Research Board (BARB) is a panel of approximately 4,500 households, whose television viewing is monitored via 'peoplemeters' attached to their TV sets and video recorders. BARB data is the 'currency' for television media planning and buying. As recently as 1991, BARB data became available for geodemographic analysis. Other media industry research sources (e.g. JICREG for Regional Press, RAJAR for Commercial Radio) have geodemographic linkages. See Chapter 11.

These are the main sources of syndicated research which can be cross-tabulated by geodemographics. Usage of the results of such cross-tabulation will be covered in subsequent chapters. Of course, *any* piece of research with an adequate sample size can be analysed by geodemographics; postcodes of respondents give the 'key'.

CHAPTER SIX

USING GEODEMOGRAPHIC
AND LIFESTYLE DATA

Introduction

Essentially, the main use of both geodemographic and lifestyle data is for identifying and describing your customers, and then finding more prospective customers like them. This implies *profiling*. The basics of geodemographic profiling were covered in Chapter 3, but more will be said on this subject below; it will be compared with profiling your customers against a lifestyle database. The basic questions we want to answer are:

- Who are your customers?
- What are they like?
- What are their:
    - □ *individual* characteristics? (lifestyle data)
    - □ *neighbourhood* characteristics? (geodemographics)
- Where do they live?
- What other products/services do they buy?
- Where can we find more like them?

Profiling

The *Concise Oxford English Dictionary* defines a profile as 'a representation by a graph or chart of information (esp. on certain characteristics) recorded in a quantified form'. So a customer profile is a means of *representing* (say) a customer file by a chart of the characteristics of those customers; and by inference, it involves comparing them with some 'universe', which might be the overall population profile of GB. In practice, we can profile by any variables that are available to us; for example, any information we may have collected from our customers, or can derive from the information they have provided (age, sex, income, etc.). We may profile by what we might term 'standard marketing variables' – the types of discriminators that will normally be collected in market research exercises, or that may be derived from the census.

A few points about this; first, we will always need a 'base' to profile against, so if we want to produce a customer profile by 'standard marketing variables', we need to know the *national* figures for each variable (to take the same examples as those given above, the *national* profiles of age, sex and income) so we can see how our customers vary. A second point, already mentioned in Chapter 3, is that income is *not* among the many variables published in the Census, and the national figures would need to be derived from a source such as the Family Expenditure Survey (FES) – also conducted by ONS, who administers the census. Third, when it comes to socio-economic classification, there are differences between the government 'social class' and the marketing world's 'social grade'. The average user of geodemographic data does not need to worry overmuch about government social class, nor indeed about socio-economic groups (SEGs) which are produced as part of the census output, other than to note, perhaps, that SEGs can be grouped in a way that approximates to NRS social grade; all this detail has been included in the appendices, for those who are interested. Social grade, which has been around since the 1950s as a classification system, uses the occupation of head of household to classify all the members of the household into the familiar A, B, C1, C2, D, E social grades. The national figures (which can be used as a base for profiling) are collected every year on the NRS; see appendices for descriptions, and distribution of adult population by social grade. The crucial aspect in terms of the issues under discussion here, is that information on occupation of head of household is necessary before a customer file could be classified by social grade (and this is a considerable administrative exercise); compare this with geodemographic classification in the following section.

Geodemographic Profiling

The basics of geodemographic profiling were explained in Chapter 3. Each inhabitant of a census ED is taken to be representative of that census neighbourhood; the link from ED to address is the postcode, thus all we need to profile a customer file by geodemographics are the *postcodes* of customers. Then the profiling is simply a comparison of the *penetrations* of customers in each neighbourhood type, against the *penetrations* of these neighbourhood types within the base area. See the example in Chapter 3. Given the locational aspect of geodemographics, the base area can be defined with great flexibility. Often, the GB profile will be the 'default option'; but the base can be any relevant geographic area (standard region, store catchment area, TV region, etc.), or it could be related back to customers in some way. A prime example of the latter is to profile 'subsets' of the customer file, using the overall customer file as a base. To explain; we may have derived our geodemographic profile of the complete customer file, and established the neighbourhood types that are most significant. However, we can also *segment* our customer file in terms of (say), products purchased, or monetary value, and we want to establish whether there are any *differences* between these subsets of customers, and the complete customer file. If we profile each customer subset, using the profile of the overall customer file as a base, this will serve to accentuate the differences.

Within the overall customer profile, even for the same product, there are likely to be distinct sub-markets which are using the product for different reasons, with different intensities, or even for different purposes (depending upon the type of product, of course!). Market research may be a necessary pre-requisite for discovering and exploring these sub-markets but having done so, they can be quantified and located via geodemographics. This requires a geodemographic cross-tab of the research (explained in Chapter 5), which is simply achieved via the postcodes of the research respondents. Concentrating on relevant sub-markets is often the name of the game – geodemographics can help.

Lifestyle Database Profiling

Geodemographic profiles are profiles of the *neighbourhoods* within which customers or respondents live; profiling a customer file against a lifestyle database involves finding *individual matches* of customers on the file, who are also on the database. Depending on the quality of the addresses on the customer file, and the size of the lifestyle database, something like a ten per cent match of customers might be expected. The point of the exercise is to *add* to the customer file, all the additional information held on the lifestyle database about those customers; this information then provides the customer profile. The profile information will no doubt be useful in its own right; it puts 'flesh on the bones' of existing customer information – but it is usually conducted to provide a 'template' for the selection of lookalikes from the lifestyle database, for prospect mailing purposes.

Comments on Profiling

Readers may wonder just how accurate these profiling methods might be. On one dimension, the larger the numbers involved, the better; this issue is covered in the next section. However, given adequate sample sizes, what about the methodology itself? It is reassuring to be able to 'check' the profiles that have been derived against some independent source, such as market research. In the case of geodemographics, this should be straightforward; cross-tab an industry survey on the same product field by the same geodemographic classifier, and compare the results. In the case of lifestyle database profiling, again a research source can be compared, but in this case, choose some variables that are common to both the research and the lifestyle database (for example, variables like age, household tenure, car ownership, industry of occupation; generally, whatever is available as a cross-tab on the research, because the chances are those variables will also be present on the lifestyle database). If the profiles are similar, this will suggest that the 'matches' on the lifestyle database are reasonably representative of the universe.

An additional point to watch out for, is the importance of *indices*. Both geodemographic and lifestyle database profiles tend to use indices of penetration as guides for the neighbourhood types (geodemographics) or variables (lifestyles). With the average being 100, the highest indices will often seem to denote the neighbourhood types or variables to 'go for'. However, there is a trap here for the unwary. Sometimes the characteristics which produce the highest indices actually have a very low penetration. To take an example from geodemographics, suppose the table 'PiN Profile (Extract)' on the following page is an extract from a customer profile of product 'y'.

Looking at the last column (the 'Index' column), we can see that PiN type 20 has an index of 562 (i.e. over five times the average), and is clearly a key target for product 'y'. PiN type 21 is second highest on this dimension (within this extract, anyway) with an index of 390.

However, if we now look at the first column ('Profile Count'), which is actually the number of customers within each PiN type, we see that it is actually PiN type 21 which contains more customers (182 versus type 20's 31). And PiN type 19 has even more (314); so a high index must not be looked at in isolation. The lifestyle database equivalent of this issue is a similar situation where a particular variable shows a high index within a profile, but is actually a low penetration variable. The lifestyle database companies provide 'Z scores' as a part of the profile, to indicate each variable's overall significance, and to prevent clients misinterpreting the importance of high indices alone.

PiN Profile (Extract)

Profile: Product 'y' Customers   **Base:** GB households

	Profile count	Profile (%)	Base (%)	Index
D. Affluent households				
19. Wealthy	314	16.2	7.3	220
20. Exclusive residential areas	31	1.6	0.3	562
21. Most affluent residential areas	182	9.4	2.4	390
E. Older people in small houses				
22. Council flats with pensions	12	0.6	2.2	28
23. Comfortable retirement areas	51	2.6	2.3	114

Notes: For the explanation, refer to Chapter 3. This is just a small extract from the overall profile: five PiN types are shown, from the total of 60.

Cell Sizes and Levels of Aggregation

When dealing with geodemographic profiles the issue of statistical validity often arises. The simple rule of thumb, when deciding on the number of customer records to profile, is to aim for 10,000 records to give a good, robust profile. If you have less records than that, use all of them; if you have considerably more, then consider taking a 'one in n' sample to give 10,000 records. To take a very simple example; if you have a customer file containing 100,000 records, then there is no point putting them all through the profiling system as the result will not differ appreciably from a profile based on a representative sample of 10,000. So in this case, 'n' = 10, and every tenth record will be taken to give the 10,000 sample.

The important issue is to ensure that there are sufficient records in the file to be profiled, to adequately 'populate' each cell in the profile. In other words, the customers in each of the neighbourhood types should be sufficient to be reliable. This is as much a matter of experience and 'feel' as of any hard and fast rules. The system authors should be able to advise on this. As the 'minimum' rule of thumb, for a classification system operating at around the 40 – 60 cluster level, fewer than 5,000 records is probably undesirable. The results will be indicative rather than conclusive.

The route to take when faced with small numbers for profiling is to *aggregate*. All the 1991-based systems have at least two levels of solution; if you have insufficient records to profile at the most detailed level, then use the 'group' level, and profile at the 10 – 12 level. Suddenly the results will be far more robust. One of the comforting things about geodemographic methodology is that the numbers in each cell, the observations and the base used will be explicitly stated as part of the output, so you know where you stand. It is also good practice, observed by most of the practitioners, to 'flag' unreliable cells (i.e. where the numbers are small, and should be treated with caution) in cross-tabulations.

Just because a classification system may have a large number of clusters, there is no need to use it at this 'maximum solution' unless the *application* demands it. So, for mailing applications, by all means use the solution at its finest degree of discrimination, because for the price of a postage stamp, the Royal Mail will deliver each letter. On the other hand, if you propose to use door-to-door delivery, whether Post Office HDS or one of the commercial distributors, such a 'fine' solution will be overkill, because the distribution will usually be organised and carried out at a postcode sector level, where a target expressed at a 'group' level is likely to be good enough. In practice, if a postcode sector ranking is carried out, this can utilise a profile at whatever level the input data can stand, and will optimise against that profile. But if you are targeting against a few specific neighbourhood types, 'group' level will probably be best. The delivery mechanism tends to determine whether the targeting is 'inclusive' (group level) or 'exclusive' (finer, type level).

Strengths and Weaknesses of Geodemographics

The ability of geodemographics to *link* easily to both customer data and research data, is undoubtedly one of the strengths of the technique. As I have stated several times before, only a postcode is needed to attach a geodemographic code; once you know the neighbourhood classification, the research survey or customer database link will give a 'propensity' figure for that neighbourhood type (that is, the likelihood to be 'in the market for' the product or service in question). It would be an overclaim to say that the propensity figure is an *absolute*, in reality it is an indication, a probability. However, let's not underclaim, either! The probability is directly usable in planning marketing activity. As all practitioners in marketing will appreciate, it is by no means a perfect world, much of marketing is to do with improving the odds in your favour. Targeting via geodemographics achieves this.

Another major strength of geodemographics is its *locational* aspect. Having established (say) the FiNPiN types of greatest potential for PEPs, we can see how the distribution of these types relates to our branch network. The assessment of area potential based on geodemographics is arguably its most useful application.

The *universal coverage* of (census-based) geodemographics is a major strength. Putting aside, briefly, the fact that the census data still in use at this point in time is now six years old (this will surface again shortly as a weakness!), at the date of the census virtually 100 per cent of GB households are covered; they all fill in the same detail, and the resultant data is a mine of very valuable information for every neighbourhood in the country. So, while still reasonably 'fresh' the census data are invaluable as a base for modelling and for understanding the precise demographics of these very small areas, nationwide. However successful the lifestyle database operators become in building this representation, it is very unlikely that they could achieve anything approaching this coverage. (The issue of blending the best of census and lifestyles is covered later in this chapter, and elsewhere.)

Finally, geodemographics can form a *'common thread'* running through the targeting definition of various marketing, operational and media applications. I have repeated (probably *ad nauseam*) the ease of use aspect of geodemographics – given an address with a postcode, whether customer or research respondent, a neighbourhood classification may be simply attached. This leads to the ability to have this common definition attached to many different 'tools' and areas:

- customer database;
- mailing list (i.e. rented list);
- door-to-door targeting;
- U&A research;
- syndicated research;
- retail catchment analysis;
- sales territory analysis;
- media research.

Indeed, there is now geodemographic linkage to virtually all syndicated media research surveys; NRS (press and magazines, plus exposure to other media, for example, TV and cinema); TGI (press, TV, radio, cinema, posters); BARB (TV audience measurement); RAJAR (radio); Newspaper Society (via Press Ad and JICREG) for regional press.

Thus, a common target market definition can run through all these, and can be quantified in any geographical area.

Weaknesses of geodemographics include the updating problem, already mentioned. The census takes place on a ten-yearly cycle, and on the last few occasions, has taken two years from collection to publication of data. While there are methods for updating (see later in this chapter), it is impossible to update *all* the census-based variables that go into neighbourhood classifications, so strictly speaking, these classifications cannot be updated between censuses. Clearly, the longer the elapsed time since census date, the less reliable are the ED-based data on which geodemographics are founded. It is worth making a few comments about this, however. The first is that many areas change very slowly, in reality. We can all think of the heroic exceptions to this statement, of course; areas that become 'gentrified', or areas that are razed to the ground and rebuilt as very different neighbourhoods. Nevertheless, in the vast majority of cases there in little change from one census to another, in the *type* of area. The second point is directly related to this. People sometimes ask me 'how many of the people who lived in a certain census ED in 1991, still live there?'. The answer may very well be 'none of them!' – but that is not the point. Geodemographics classifies the *area*, and even if the inhabitants present on census night 1991 have moved on, they may well have been replaced by people much like they were when *they* moved in. We can all think of types of neighbourhoods that relate to lifestages (such as bedsits, starter homes, young family homes, mature family homes, etc.), where the area remains fairly constant although its inhabitants move on. Nevertheless, updating the base data is a problem with geodemographics.

Given that the base census data will change with each census, necessarily the census-based geodemographic classifiers will need to change too. It is unrealistic to think that the classification would stay exactly the same from one census to another (that would smack of 'fiddling'!), so there will be discontinuity at the changeover; as one classification system is replaced with another, the work of profiling, linking, potential estimation, etc., will need to be redone. Whether this is regarded as a weakness, or merely a necessary upgrading and improvement, is a matter of opinion.

Finally, the fact that geodemographic classifiers are *neighbourhood* classifiers, rather than individual classifiers, is a weakness in applications like direct mail targeting. This issue is discussed in Chapter 10. It is only a weakness *relative to* some other targeting methods, and direct mail targeting by geodemographics still has a place in the market. But it is clearly less precise to mail households in a neighbourhood, about whom you can model a probability, than to mail an individual about whom you know something for certain. More later.

The 'neighbourhood' aspect is *not* a weakness in retail, or area analysis, applications – far from it. Indeed, this is an application where the 'balance of power' between geodemographics and lifestyles is reversed.

Strengths and Weaknesses of Lifestyle Databases

The main strength of the lifestyle databases is that they hold large lists of consumers about whom a great deal is known, and these people (provided they have not 'opted out' of mailings) therefore make good prospects for direct mail. The individuals on the database can be mailed on the basis of hard fact (such as, their demographics, hobbies and interests, car ownership, brand preference, etc.) and even some indication of mailing responsiveness (that is, whether they have bought previously by mail-order). This is clearly a more reliable basis on which to target them than their neighbourhood characteristics, as noted above.

Another strength of lifestyle data is its currency; it is not generally used if it is more than three years old, and the responses are 'flagged' with their date of receipt, so it is possible to use very up-to-date names and addresses, if required. Depending on which operator is involved and its methodology, the response data will be refreshed once per annum or more frequently. Clearly, this strength runs counter to the geodemographic weakness (namely the updating problem) and this is an area where the two techniques can complement each other.

This leads neatly on to the use of lifestyle data in 'geodemographic' mode, that is in area analysis applications. At the time of writing the first edition of this book, the NDL database had reached sufficient critical mass to be used at postcode sector level for area profiling. Since then, two neighbourhood classifications (PORTRAIT and PRIZM) have been built from lifestyle data, and a third (MicroVision) has been built from a combination of lifestyle and census data. This is, in part, a reflection of the growth of the biggest lifestyle databases over the last four years. It is also a reflection of methodological advances (in imputation techniques) and, in the case of Equifax's MicroVision, a preparedness to use *both* lifestyle data *and* census data in the solution. The best of both worlds? To me, the ideal solution to this problem is the use of census data (ideally, reasonably 'fresh') to weight and balance the sample back to the universe. Both datasets can complement each other, to the benefit of the solution. The census data play to their strength of 'universality', the lifestyle data to theirs – currency and depth of information.

Updates

As discussed, lifestyle databases have an update facility as a part of their *modus operandi*, and it is planned that this facility will be used to update those geodemographic systems built on these data. However, the 'classic' geodemographic systems have been regularly updated since the mid-eighties, using mainly public domain data. In truth, the updating is restricted to key variables such as total households and population, plus age and sex; given that the other input variables to the census-based classification systems are not collected between censuses, the classifications themselves cannot be 'updated' in their entirety until a new census is taken. MOSAIC is the exception, in that the non-census data that forms a part of MOSAIC (from ER and credit sources) *can* be updated. However, in reality this is only a partial update; the census component of MOSAIC suffers the same problem in this regard as the other systems.

One of the key sources for updates has tended to be the ONS mid-year estimates of population and households. Valuable although these are, they are produced at the level of local authority districts (LADs) only; these areas average some 45,000 households each, so are not fine enough for usual geodemographic applications. So the geodemographic agencies tend to run their own analyses, either disaggregating ONS figures, or taking base census data and applying births, marriages and deaths. The trickiest aspect of such analysis is *migration* between areas, which is incompletely documented (NHS records of patient movement between doctors' panels are available, but not ideal). Migration statistics are published by ONS as part of the census output, although these data relate to the year before the census only (based on a question about change of address during that period). The ER is often used to try to get a 'fix' on migration; it is a good source, so long as the data have been carefully input to the agencies' systems, but suffers some shortfall, particularly in inner-city areas. As is often the case, the best solution is probably to take all these inputs and use them to model the patterns, utilising today's relatively cheap computer power.

Degree of Discrimination

When considering geodemographics as a classification and segmentation system, one of the questions which often arises is the *degree of discrimination* inherent in geodemographics, compared with other classification systems. Part of the answer relates to the number of 'divisions' available in the classification system in question; obviously, the more divisions, the greater the potential degree of discrimination. As an example of this, it is clear that using the 160 clusters in the most detailed level of Super Profiles, will allow much greater discrimination than using (say) the six-fold breakdown of social grade. However, in practical terms this assumes a very large sample for analysis, or the 160-fold breakdown will result in very small data cells unless this is the case. On applications such as segmentation of large customer databases, or mailing minority targets, the very fine discrimination of geodemographics at its most detailed level is valuable. On smaller datasets, not so, and the aggregated 'groups' need to be used.

The other part of the answer goes back to the 'neighbourhood' issue. As a neighbourhood-based classification, geodemographics is intrinsically different from an individual-based classification such as social grade (perhaps more correctly, social grade is a 'household-based' classification, based as it is on occupation of head of household!). In practice, an individually-based classifier will usually outperform a neighbourhood-based classifier, other things being equal (it is a classic example of 'what is known versus what is modelled'). In his very interesting paper at the 1993 MRS conference (see references), Barry Leventhal showed the result of some analyses which he had conducted, based on FRS data cross-tabbed by the leading geodemographic classification systems, and also by social grade and 'lifestage'. Social grade and lifestage usually outperformed the geodemographic systems (the latter tested at their 'course', group level for comparability), although this was not always the case. The analysis of geodemographics at the 'fine', type level showed the best-performing neighbourhood types outperforming social grade or lifestage as discriminators – so for targeting key minority market sectors, geodemographics proved to be the best solution. And yes!, Barry did test the geodemographics available on FRS (ACORN, PiN, FiNPiN and MOSAIC) against each other; he found no clear winner, as different classifications performed 'best' on different financial products. The paper is well worth studying for those interested in this issue, but be warned – Barry has presented the results 'anonymously', without identifying which classification is which. (See References.)

In practical terms, a would-be user can easily discover whether geodemographics 'works well' as a discriminator in his market (and can also test *which* geodemographic system 'works best') by profiling some relevant data and examining the results. This could be a sample of customer data, or perhaps a syndicated market research source. Are the 'peaks and troughs' of the histogram which usually accompanies the profile, interesting or not? Crudely speaking, a 'spiky' pattern shows good discrimination, a relatively 'flat' pattern, does not. Once again, note the caveat about cell sizes (covered earlier in this chapter) when appraising the results. Barry Leventhal's paper, referred to earlier, suggests some statistical tests that may be applied to compare the discrimination of different systems in a rather more rigorous way.

Readers may notice that there has been little mention of lifestyle data in this chapter, other than in the context of lifestyle database profiling, and the strengths and weaknesses of lifestyle data. The reason for this is that lifestyle data cannot be considered as a classification or segmentation system *per se*, although clearly some classification data are collected on the lifestyle databases, and various forms of segmentation can be conducted on them. There is more discussion of 'how to use' lifestyle data in Chapter 10 and some mention of retail applications in Chapter 9.

Conclusions

Once users have familiarised themselves with geodemographic concepts and methodology, their application is really quite straightforward. At first sight, the systems may seem daunting; there seems to be a new language to learn and a different way of doing things to be accommodated. But in reality, it is mainly commonsense. In my belief, the crucial aspect is to develop an understanding of the data and the underlying assumptions; if you have read this far, you should know enough already! The next chapters discuss the *application* of geodemographic and lifestyle data to market analysis, retail and direct marketing, and even if you are mainly interested in one application only, I recommend you read all of them to get a more rounded view.

By using geodemographics, we are essentially 'playing the numbers game'; *quantifying* the targeting task, *quantifying* potential within areas. Thus we can bring greater cost-effectiveness to our marketing activities – and improve the odds in our favour.

CHAPTER SEVEN

MARKET ANALYSIS

Introduction

'Market Analysis' is clearly a very broad subject; unsurprisingly in the context of this report, I am dealing here with market analysis using geodemographic data. To put it slightly differently, I am dealing with *area* analysis, with a view to measuring the *potential* within areas for the product or service in question. This assumes an information base (whether a market research source, or a customer database) upon which the area potential model can be based. This a prime application for geodemographics, and conceptually it is obvious why this should be so; if we can envisage areas in a mapping sense, and we can identify different neighbourhood types, each with a different (but measurable) propensity to buy or use our product or service, then what I am addressing in this chapter is the quantification of that propensity, or potential.

Area Profiling

The analysis of area characteristics is very straightforward, using one of the proprietary area analysis systems from the geodemographic agencies. At its simplest, the agency will have pre-specified which of the 'raw' variables you will get from your analysis; you simply define the area, 'press the button', and the analysis spews out. The agency has taken the decision about which variables are contained in the analysis, generally speaking. Usually, from 60 – 132 variables are 'pre-processed' by the agency. Typically, they will include variables such as:

- total population
- total households
- age groups of population
- tenure of housing
- housing amenities
- house size (number of rooms)
- car ownership
- family composition
- means of travel to work
- industry of employment
- level of unemployment
- working women (full-time/part-time)
- social class or socio-economic group
- country of origin.

Thus, such an analysis would give a clear indication of the number and type of households and population within the area in question, and a good means of comparing population profiles between areas. Depending upon the product or service in question, some variables would be of key importance in terms of indicating level of potential. But so far I have only dealt with profiling areas by 'raw' census variables; as Chapter 3 explained, there are often advantages in using 'processed' census variables, notably neighbourhood classifications. In the case of area profiling, the particular advantage lies in the *linkage* this can give into area potential modelling. I am not saying that area profiling using a classification system is 'better than' profiling using basic demographics; I am saying 'horses for courses', and in many cases it will be useful to profile by both methods.

The next issue is – how to define the area concerned. And linked into that – what *units of area* shall we use for analysis? Before the advent of the 'clever' computer analysis systems, areas tended to be defined by means of the 'administrative geography' by which census data are output; counties, local authority district, or wards (see Chapter 3). This was fine so far as it went, but it was very inflexible. Not a problem for central or local government, of course, because those were boundaries that they used anyway; but for commercial organisations, administrative boundaries were unwieldy. The gap was filled by Plumbley Bricks, which I recall from my formative years in the business, as relatively small geographical areas which came complete with population estimates, and were used to build sales territories. The advent of 'postal geography', introduced in the 1960s but only readily available in mapped form much later, has now become the predominant form of geography in commercial usage. It is convenient to use as any postcoded address can readily be assigned to its 'hierarchy' of postal sectors, districts and areas (see Chapter 3). Specifically, *postcode sectors* have become an extremely popular set of units; at an average of 2,500 households, they are manageable in size and tend to follow 'sensible' boundaries, such as main roads, rivers, etc. Thus, they can be easily aggregated into store catchment areas, sales territories and distribution areas. The current choice of PC-based geodemographic analysis systems tends to provide an option of holding classification data at a postcode sector level, largely because it cuts down on computer storage requirements. However, it should be noted that the geodemographic classification systems which 'drive' these systems (ACORN, MOSAIC, etc.) have actually been *built* at an ED or unit-postcode level, and are merely summarised at a postcode sector level.

This is an important distinction, because the size of the unit of area concerned will affect the discriminatory power of the system. In other words, a geodemographic classification system built on units of EDs (or unit postcodes) will show much greater discrimination than one built at the level of wards or postcode sectors. The reason for this is that, in general, a large area such as a postcode sector (average 2,500 households) will be much less *homogeneous* than an area the size of an ED (average 150 households). I gave an example of this in a contribution to Stephan Buck's book, *The 55+ Market* – see References. Relate this to your own experience; think of neighbourhoods that you know, then consider the area covered by the postcode sector within which you live. Usually, there will be far more variation in terms of 'neighbourhood characteristics', the larger the area. The implication of this is that accuracy of targeting is much improved if the unit of area you are targeting is as small as the data will allow. Nevertheless, there is clearly a trade-off between volume of data and the requirement for precision, which recurs often in geodemographics. The key is to think through the *application(s)* carefully, in order to take a view on whether the additional targeting power inherent in holding data at an ED level, is worth the extra cost – as against operating in units of postcode sectors. (If one of your requirements is to use the system for *customer* profiling, then you have no choice; you will need to hold the classification on a 'postcode directory', within which each *unit* postcode is classified.) However, for *area* profiling, if you can operate satisfactorily by aggregating postcode sectors, say into catchment areas, then either option is viable.

Defining Areas for Profiling

Once you have decided on the units of area which you will use, this may well influence the way you then define your areas of interest. To take the most obvious example; if you have chosen to use postcode sectors, and you have a system which includes 'digitised' postcode sector boundaries, then the logical way to proceed will be to *aggregate* postcode sectors into larger areas, such as catchment areas or sales territories. Various ways of defining retail catchment areas are described in Chapter 9. If, however, you have decided to use ED-level data, and unless you have decided to acquire ED boundaries (an option since the 1991 Census – see Chapter 13), then you must use a different method. I mentioned earlier that OPCS produce the SAS data for census EDs together with a 'centroid' for each ED – its nominal centre point, expressed as a map grid reference. Without boundary data, this is the only way of locating EDs, and forms the basis for area analysis. All the PC-based geodemographic systems have facilities for 'drawing lines' on maps, to create new boundaries. The simplest is to specify a grid-reference for a centre-point (which could be the address of a store, say, 'converted' from its postcode to a grid-reference, automatically) and then specify a radius around that point, in miles or kilometres. The system will then draw a circle accordingly. If you want to analyse the Census characteristics of the area within the circle, the system will identify all the ED centroids within the circle, aggregate them, and produce a profile from the total of those EDs. A similar procedure is used if you wish to define a square, rectangle, or irregular polygon on the screen, perhaps because you wish to include a number of retail outlets, or put a 'box' around a town on the map. Again, the system will perform what is called a 'point in polygon' search, include all the EDs whose centroids come within the polygon, and sum their data in the form of a profile. Please note, if you have used the 'point in polygon' methodology to include Census EDs, the total of households (or other variables) included in the defined area will be necessarily approximate. If an ED centroid is *included* in the search, all its data will be included in the analysis; if its centroid is *excluded*, so will all its data. In the normal way, this will not matter (that is, if you have defined a reasonably large area) because there will be a 'swings and roundabouts' effect. If precision is important, it is best to use an ED boundary file and thus define the area of interest more precisely.

Thus you can establish the total numbers of households and individuals within the area you have defined and look at their characteristics. You will be able to specify the *base* for the profile, either as GB or as another relevant area, for comparison.

Area Potential Methodology

In essence, there are two basic methods of deriving area potential using geodemographics. One is to use standard demographics from the census (which I have usually referred to as 'raw' census variables); the other is to use a neighbourhood classification system. Both methods require a research source as the basis for the calculation of potential.

Dealing first with the method using standard demographics from the census; this was in use in the UK grocery trade long before the start of the geodemographics industry to which I referred in Chapter 2. To my knowledge, J. Sainsbury were using this methodology, using ward-level data from the census, at least 20 years ago. A similar methodology, although using ED-level data, was used by Pinpoint from 1985. It was known as 'Retail Potential Report' methodology and was developed by David Rogers of DSR Marketing Systems Inc., Deerfield Illinois. Since I am familiar with this system, I will outline the methodology by way of illustrating the principles of this approach. (I understand that URPI's Data Consultancy also use a similar methodology.) The startpoint is the FES, conducted annually by the social survey division of the ONS. The FES reports on all aspects of family expenditure, and respondents' characteristics are reported in some detail. As well as the normal hard-copy FES reports, it is possible to commission special analyses, which provide demographic detail which can be matched to census characteristics. The geodemographic systems are set up to analyse those particular census variables (in defined areas, as explained earlier) and to multiply out these variables by the £ sterling amounts derived from the FES analysis. Thus, for all the types of expenditure collected by FES and analysed by these systems, the Retail Potential Reports will produce annualised estimates of potential expenditure within the defined areas. In practise, FES is being used mainly for the demographic breakdown it provides; *absolute* values of national expenditure within the various expenditure categories are 'corrected' from national income and expenditure 'Blue Book' figures. Other features of the reports are the application of regional weighting factors, and an estimation, for each merchandise type, of the market value accruing to different retailer categories; for example, the relative share of confectionery sold by CTN's and specialist confectioners, as against the share sold through grocers. Most types of merchandise sold through retailers is covered by the Report series. So, in summary; the systems pick up the numbers of households in various demographic categories within the study area, and convert that information into a measure of sterling value for specified categories of merchandise.

The other methodological type, although similar in principle, uses neighbourhood classifications to make the link between survey research and geographical areas. I explained in Chapter 5 how geodemographic cross-tabs may be produced from the various syndicated research surveys and panels. Such a cross-tab is the start-point for the methodology covered here; it provides the *profile* of buyers or users of the product or service in question, ideally with some value or volumetric measure of demand. As Chapter 5 explained, the profile is comprised of differential penetration rates for each of the neighbourhood types concerned. The way the area potential methodology works, is to compare the *buyer* penetration with the *area* penetration, the latter being derived from an area profile. To look at it in 'disaggregated' form; we are taking each individual neighbourhood type, and measuring its buying rate for the product in question from the research source. Then we are 'trawling' the area of interest, to see how many households of that neighbourhood type are present. Finally, we are producing a potential demand estimate for all the individual neighbourhood types, and summing them to produce a measure of potential for the area. As in the methodology previously covered (using standard demographics), the results are improved by regional factoring.

An alternative data source to the market research source discussed here is a customer database, if you have one. It will need to hold transactional data in order to make this approach viable; and it will need to be coded up with a geodemographic classifier. Given these two criteria, it can be used to measure apparent potential for your product within areas. This is not quite the same as using a research source, in that market research will usually measure *all* products in the market sector, not just yours; thus giving you a much truer idea of where the overall opportunity lies. Of course, if you look at both aspects (market potential, and your current actual) within areas, you can measure your market share, and look at the residual that you have to go for, area by area. It can be powerful stuff!

The MAU Problem

In this current context, MAU is the Modifiable Areal Unit problem – which sounds very technical, and indeed it is.

There are two components to the MAU problem, and they are described very succinctly in Chapter 2 of *Spatial Analysis; Modelling in a GIS Environment*, edited by Paul Longley and Michael Batty (See References). I can do no better than quote the authors:

> '*These components are defined as follows.*
>
> *The scale effect is the tendency, within a system of modifiable areal units, for different statistical results to be obtained from the same set of data when the information is grouped at different levels of spatial resolution (e.g. census blocks, tracts, districts, counties and regions).*
>
> *The zoning effect is the variability in statistical results obtained within a set of modifiable areal units as a function of the various ways these units can be grouped at a given scale, and not as a result of the variation in size of those areas – i.e., the difference in results which follows from merely altering the boundaries or configurations of the zones at a given scale of analysis.*'

Perhaps some further interpretation is in order. Certainly, *Spatial Analysis* is written in a far more technical style, and for a different readership, than is this book. 'Modifiable areal units', in a UK marketing/retail context, are probably most likely to include census EDs, and units of 'postal geography', e.g. postcode sectors or districts. So the 'scale effect' might be observed if the same analysis were conducted on census EDs on the one hand, and postcode sectors on the other (and in this case, the problem does not relate to the fact that ED boundaries and postcode sector boundaries tend to overlap). The 'zoning effect' relates to the issue of exactly where the boundaries (of whatever geography) are drawn; in many cases the boundaries are 'accidents of history' or matters of administrative convenience. 'Imposed', rather than 'natural', geographies.

The underlying difficulty that gives rise to the MAU problem, is the tendency of households to 'group' and 'cluster' in particular ways, on the ground. Ironically, these are the very traits which make geodemographics 'work'. To take a practical example of MAU; say you are analysing a customer database, and you decide to map customer numbers by postcode sector, to get an idea of customer concentration within a geographical area. The resultant area shading will give you an *apparent* answer; but it could be very misleading. You could improve it to some extent by expressing customer numbers as a *penetration* of the underlying population (e.g. as a penetration of all adults, by postcode sector). But the basic problem is that the postcode sector shading may actually *disguise* the true pattern on the ground. Particularly in cases where you are studying catchments where a store or branch is in a town centre, and the catchment extends out into surrounding rural areas, you will generally find that the bulk of the population in a sector lies in that part nearest the town centre, and the sector is more sparsely populated as you go further out. Or there may be settlements concentrated in particular parts of the more rural sectors.

If you have ED boundaries available to you, then it would be instructive to repeat the exercise using these boundaries (in household terms, an average 2,500 households in a postcode sector plays an average 170 households in an ED). You will see the evidence for MAUP before your very eyes! If you do not have ED boundaries on your GIS (which will be the situation for the majority), you can get a good proxy for population density by plotting the ED centroids on the map ; see how the 'populated' areas cluster within the postcode sector boundaries. You may indicate those EDs where you have customers – or, as a further sophistication, *penetration* of customers within EDs – by changing the colour of the ED centroid points on the map accordingly. Or you could simply plot the *postcode* centroids of your customers. Whichever method you choose, you will be able to see how area shading may obscure the actual 'scatter' of customers on the ground.

The practice of mapping the results of an analysis is deservedly popular ; it can show the patterns in a way that no other technique can match. However, it is important to bear the MAU problem in mind, lest the results are misinterpreted. Wherever possible, look beneath the surface of an area shaded ('Chloropleth') map, to establish the *real* locations of customers and prospects. Still use the shaded map by all means; but understand what it *really* shows. Readers wishing to delve deeper into MAU (and the ecological fallacy) could read *Spatial Analysis*, as mentioned earlier in this section; but unless they are very familiar with geographical analysis, they may find it hard going! Another very interesting reference is Martin Callingham's paper entitled 'Will the MAU problem defeat turnover estimation modelling?' which he presented at the AGI 1996 conference. Martin is group market research director at Whitbread , and has done some pioneering work on catchment analysis and sales forecasting for a number of restaurants in the Whitbread estate. He presents a case history, and a hypothesis that it is possible to identify which catchments will be seriously affected by the MAU problem, to the extent that sales forecast models for those catchments will be unreliable; while those catchments that are relatively unaffected by MAU are capable of being forecast more accurately. This has the considerable benefit of being actionable in the commercial world!

CHAPTER 8

GEOGRAPHICAL INFORMATION SYSTEMS

Introduction

GIS are undoubtedly one of the phenomena of recent times, insofar as marketing and retail applications are concerned. GIS themselves had their origins in the US in the early 1970s, in environmental analysis and land-use applications; indeed, one of the pioneers (and still a world-wide market leader) is ESRI, whose full name gives us the clue – Environmental Systems Research Institute, of Redlands California.

Over time, GIS 'migrated' into other applications, such as defence (the locations of all the missile silos – theirs as well as ours!), local government, local authorities and utilities. In the case of the latter two segments, the main function was asset management; a system to locate and manage all the assets such as street furniture, cables, pipelines, switches and valves – essentially replacing all the paper maps that had previously served this purpose.

Retail and marketing applications came much more recently on the scene; since the mid-1980s, in fact. There were a number of reasons for this. In my view, one of the main ones was the growth of geodemographics, and the fact that this new way of looking at the world led naturally on to mapping, and thus to geographical analysis in general. Certainly, the geodemographic agencies 'made the running' in terms of marketing desktop analysis and mapping packages to the retail and marketing communities in the UK. SPA (Sales Performance Analysis) were the first, starting the development of their 'Marketing Machine' software in the mid-1980s. CCN then licensed SPA's software, and 'badge-engineered' it, relaunching it as MOSAIC Systems in the autumn of 1987. During the next year, two other systems joined the fray; InSite, written in-house by CACI (with Atlas Mapping as the computer mapping 'back end'), and GEOPIN from Pinpoint – geodemographic applications on PC-ARC/INFO software.

A government initiative helped to stimulate interest in GIS. A committee of enquiry was set up to investigate best practice in geographic information handling. Chaired by Lord Chorley, it became known as the Chorley Committee. It took evidence during 1986, and published its report in May 1987 (Department of the Environment 1987, *Handling Geographic Information*, HMSO.) Its recommendations led directly to the setting up of the Association of Geographic Information (AGI) in 1989. The publication of the Chorley report significantly raised the profile of GIS, particularly in the commercial sector. This, taken together with the efforts of the geodemographic agencies, caused the commercial sector marketplace to grow rapidly in the late-1980s/early 1990s.

Admittedly, the majority of the commercial sector systems had little in common with 'traditional' GIS installations. The latter could be very large and complex; for example, a utility GIS installation would contain all the detail of the underground pipeline or cabling, where all the switches, valves, etc. were located, their characteristics, maintenance history, etc. This needed to be very precise in terms of mapping scale and geographical location. A typical marketing or retail GIS deals in very different datasets, which operate at more of an 'overview' level, and need much less geographical precision. Thus (as a generalisation), they need much less 'heavyweight' GIS than do the big public sector users. PC-based GIS is, in the majority of cases, perfectly adequate for commercial sector applications. So the explosion of desktop computing over the last decade has fuelled the growth of GIS in the commercial sector. Major software producers such as MapInfo and Tactician have exploited this growth.

The Power of Mapping

Almost invariably, the results of geodemographic analysis are enhanced by *mapping* the output. Maps are a powerful way of showing the *patterns* revealed by the analysis; useful not just to the person who has commissioned or conducted the analysis, but particularly valuable in presenting these results to colleagues or management. Maps help understanding – you can show the 'hot-spots' of demand, differences across areas, how customers or prospects cluster on the ground. Gurmukh Singh used to make the point very eloquently at Pinpoint; he used to show a map of the results of an analysis, next to a huge pile of computer printout – which was the data represented by the map. Maps can be understood by (virtually) everyone. They represent an effective presentation tool for showing the results of analyses to colleagues, to the committee, to the board. Maps on paper are good; maps on computer screen can be better, particularly if you can show the 'layers' of data building, layer by layer, until the final pattern is revealed.

Hence the enthusiasm for computer mapping among early geodemographic practitioners. However, the computer mapping software used in that context was not GIS *per se*. Perhaps now would be a good time for a definition; the one I favour is slightly more user-friendly than some:

> *GIS are computer-based systems for storing and manipulating information that can be related to specific locations or areas.*

In this context, the locations could be, for example, customers' home addresses, stores or branches; the areas could be store catchment areas or sales territories. GIS are *more* than just computer mapping systems. They are 'driven' by relational databases, which will hold relevant information (for example, customer databases, store attributes, facts about store catchment areas), and via the geographical references, will *relate* these data to the maps. The data are held in 'layers' in the system, and a series of new layers of data can be superimposed on what lies beneath. For example, basic geographical features (coastline, rivers, etc.) overlaid with urban settlement boundaries, overlaid with roads and railways, overlaid with the boundaries of 'postal geography', overlaid with store locations, overlaid with geodemographic data, etc.

In 'true' GIS, you can 'interrogate the map', and analyse its features (for example, point to a store location, and call up details of its attributes from the database; update these details on the screen, and they will also change on the database). If the system is a computer mapping package, this will not be possible. Whether this matters will largely depend on what you wish to do with it; if you merely wish to visualise sales data, it may be irrelevant. However, the cost of basic PC GIS packages is now so low that you might as well have GIS functionality, which gives you flexibility to expand into more sophisticated analyses as required.

Most of the computer mapping or GIS systems that are encountered in a marketing context are *vector* systems. They can display three types of elements:

- *Points*, which might be branches, sales calls, town centre points, customers' addresses, etc.

- *Lines*, which might be roads, rivers, railway lines, etc.

- *Areas* (i.e. the areas enclosed by polygon boundaries), which might be catchment areas, sales territories, media regions; or units of area, such as postcode sectors or EDs.

The use of different symbols/colours on the points, and different colours on the lines (such as differentially-coloured lines of A and B-roads, etc.) will aid understanding. And perhaps the most powerful visual aid of all; different colours to shade areas according to relative customer penetration, potential, or whatever. (Our technical colleagues call this 'chloropleth' shading.)

The Relationship between Geodemographics and GIS

Back in the early days of UK geodemographics, the practitioners – while clear that what they were doing was a form of geographical analysis – would not have applied the term 'GIS' to the systems they were building. They viewed geodemographics as primarily a market segmentation system; although clearly, having identified the segments of interest, the next step was usually to *locate* them, which involved computer mapping. However, this was done with a view to 'showing the patterns' and/or locating the target neighbourhoods, rather than producing a full GIS solution.

As the 1980s rolled on, and particularly once geodemographic analysis and mapping gravitated to the desktop, the value of GIS as a 'delivery system' for geodemographics became clear. Previously, the geodemographic companies had tended to operate on a bureau basis. Clients would brief the project, and the agency would conduct the analysis on its mainframe or mini-computer, and deliver the report (plus maps, if appropriate) to the client. Now, clients could be provided with the wherewithal to conduct their own analyses and produce their own reports and maps.

Few of the 'traditional' GIS suppliers have made inroads into the commercial sector. There are the exceptions that prove the rule – ESRI, Smallworld, and LaserScan – but in each case, with only a few installations to date. They tend to be installed in major players, predominantly retail. In some cases they have formed alliances with geodemographic agencies, in order to source the demographic data needed for these applications; in other cases, the purchasing organisations have processed these data themselves, or have dealt separately with the geodemographic suppliers. I think it is fair to say that in every case, these GIS vendors have needed to learn for themselves what the longer-established geodemographic companies had known for some time – what clients *need*, in terms of functionality and applications, in the commercial sector. These tend to be very different from 'traditional' GIS business, and indeed, are closely akin to what the geodemographic agencies had previously supplied. The key difference is that the 'heavy-end' GIS suppliers can provide the computing power to deliver the solutions that (say) major retailers need – which is much more than can be delivered by a PC-based system.

Meanwhile, the geodemographic agencies have succeeded in selling a large number of desktop systems in to the commercial marketplace. Research conducted among the geodemographic suppliers in 1995 (on the basis that only *aggregated* figures could be produced) produced a total estimate of 575 systems sold at that date, with an expectation of a further 275 system sales in the following year (which, if achieved, would total some 850 systems by the end of 1996). The degree to which this process was accelerating is shown by the fact that the 1996 estimate amounts to 47 per cent of the previous cumulative total! As mentioned earlier, by 1995, PC-based geodemographic systems had been sold since 1987, i.e. for some eight years.

While a few of the geodemographic agencies have developed their own Analysis/GIS systems, others have taken existing desktop GIS software and written geodemographic applications to run on these. MapInfo has proved to be the favourite platform, just as it has become market leader in the wider market. The link-up with Microsoft (the first manifestation of which was a 'cut down' version of MapInfo appearing in Microsoft's Office software suite) could be a pointer to the future. A mapping package on every desktop?

So, while you can have GIS without using geodemographics – and while you can use geodemographics without using a GIS – in marketing and retail applications, the chances are that you will use both. It makes good sense!

What Data Will You Need?

Retail and/or marketing GIS will normally contain most or all of the following datasets:

Dataset	Example
Natural geography	Coastline Waterways
Man-made geography	Settlement names Roads Railways 'Urban sprawl' boundaries
Imposed boundaries	Administrative (counties, districts, etc.) Postal (areas, districts, sectors) Media (TV areas, ILR boundaries, etc.)
Retail data	Store locations Store catchment areas
Demographic data	Census data Lifestyle data Geodemographic classification Customer data
Geocoding data	Postzon or Addresspoint

Most of these data are either self-evident or are covered in other relevant chapters. However, some commentary may be helpful here. I'll come to some of the geographic issues shortly, but first I'll deal with the demographic data. *Census data* may be held at the ED level (see Chapter 3), or may be aggregated to postcode sector level. The choice will largely be determined by the level of detail at which you wish to work (and the attendant flexibility; clearly, data held at ED level will enable much more precise areas to be defined, than will data at postcode sector level). The attendant issues are cost (census data at ED level attracts a much higher ONS royalty than if the same data are held at postcode sector level) and computer storage, for obvious reasons.

Geodemographic classifications are usually held as 'postcode directories', that is, a national directory of unit postcodes (sourced from Royal Mail) with a geodemographic code attached to each postcode (in excess of 1.6 million postcodes for GB). This enables customer files to be coded (via their postcodes), and profiled, given relevant software. Alternatively, classifications can be held as profiles for postcode sectors (which saves on storage – and cost – but does not allow for customer profiling) . However, it does permit *areas* to be profiled, so long as they are expressed as aggregations of postcode sectors.

Lifestyle data is most unlikely to be held as 'raw' data (for a number of reasons, including data protection); it is most likely to be summed to a unit postcode level, and held as a postcode directory. For example, Claritas UK's 'FIND' directory gives, for each unit postcode, various measures of household income (arithmetic average, median, rank, and spread). Additionally, it gives proportions within postcode of – retired households, homeowners, households with children (and number of delivery points).

Geocoding has been covered elsewhere, but in order to make this chapter as self-contained as possible, it is repeated here. It simply means adding map references to addresses, so they may be located on a digital map. The most common way of doing this is via the unit postcode, and this is achieved via the Postzon file, which gives a national grid reference for virtually every postcode. One problem with this is that the grid reference is not the complete 12-digit version, but the eight-digit version, which actually locates the South-West corner of the 100 metre grid-square within which the centroid of the postcode is located (sorry that this is bound to seem tediously detailed – but there is no quick way of saying this!). What this means is that postcodes cannot be *precisely* located using this file. If precision is important, you will need to use Ordnance Survey's 'Addresspoint' ('son of PAC' – see Chapter 1), which is a very accurate grid reference for each individual address. Naturally, it is expensive if you have lots of locations to code; a compromise is the Ordnance Survey's postcode centroid grid reference (branded Data-Point) which was launched in spring 1997.

There are several alternative sources for the digital mapping data – Ordnance Survey (OS), Automobile Association and Bartholomews are the principal ones – which are produced at varying scales and at varying costs. Normally, if your GIS has been sourced in 'packaged' form (meaning you have not had to put it together yourself, from the various components) your supplier is likely to recommend the option which he has tailored to his system. This may or may not be negotiable! However, it is worth discussing this with your would-be supplier (or suppliers) and reviewing the options. Some of the issues that may inform your discussion will be:

- The computer hardware and operating system that you are running. Frankly, given the enormous increase in PC power (and the inroads made by Windows '95 and NT) since the first edition of this book, this is likely to be much less of an issue now than it would have been then. The relative cheapness of high-speed Pentium processors, and of hard-disk storage, means that you should not be unduly constrained. Nevertheless, different solutions do require different magnitudes of storage – see below. The other thing that has changed dramatically is the availability of Windows versions of low-to-mid-priced GIS and GAS (Geographical Analysis Systems).

- What mapping scale will you want to work to? Or, to put a similar question a different way, do you need to map accurate detail? If you do, then you will need to use mapping data that has been digitised at a large scale. Translating that into English: maps can be 'digitised' (i.e. computerised) at various scales. If you think in terms of the paper maps that are probably familiar to you, the most familiar is likely to be the OS 'Landranger' 1:50,000 scale map (1.25 inches to the mile). You may also be familiar with the OS 'Routemaster' maps (1:250,000 scale, or one inch to four miles); and possibly the OS 'Routeplanner' map (1:625,000 scale, or one inch to ten miles). When you are using these maps in digitised form, within a GIS or computer mapping system, you *can* reproduce them at any scale you want; for example, you *could* have the OS 1:625,000 map (i.e. digitised at that scale) and print off an overlay on film or acetate, to 'overlay' on a 1:50,000 paper map. But if you were unwise enough to do so, it would not fit! The detail of the features (roads, etc.) would not be there in the 1:625,000 map, so roads would seem to 'cut corners' when laying the overlay down on the paper underlay.

    The reason for making this point, which probably seems rather tedious, is that you need to think about the maps that you finally intend to produce, before deciding on the system, and the scale of digital mapping which it contains. If you intend to print transparent overlays to OS 1:50,000 maps, then it would be a mistake to acquire a system loaded with data digitised at 1:625,000 (although you might well 'get away with' 1:100,000 digital data). Apart from this practical point, there are two other 'crunch' points; cost and disk storage requirements. Generally speaking (and for good reason), the larger the scale of the digital data, the more it costs. It also takes up considerably more storage space on hard disk.

- Do you want to see 'proper' maps on screen, underlying your data? This is largely a matter of individual preference. Many people seem perfectly happy to deal with the 'vector' mapping that typifies computer maps; boundary lines, points, area shading. So long as they can 'get their bearings' by means of the road network, rivers, etc., they can manage. Others seem lost without the familiar features of (say) an OS map. For those people who come in the latter category, raster maps are the answer. Raster maps display the full detail on screen, just as paper maps; you can then call up the detail you want from a vector system to superimpose on the map image. ESRI, LaserScan and Smallworld employ both mapping systems within their product; recent versions of MapInfo can also handle the raster 'backdrop'.

Are you committed to a particular neighbourhood classification system? If so, you may have little choice of GIS if the author of the classification system has already developed (or integrated with) a specific GIS. This is not *necessarily* as cut and dried as it might seem. However, if you favour a particular GIS, but wish to use a particular classification not already linked to it, by all means ask the classification system author. It should be possible, so long as the cost of customisation software is not prohibitive.

– This does raise a related issue which is crucially important. Some of the least expensive GIS systems do *not* have any geodemographic functionality, unless third-party software has been written for this purpose. In other words, these systems cannot perform the tasks that a geodemographic application will require (such as profiling). This is not a criticism – they were written as GIS, not geodemographic systems – but clearly this should be a major consideration when evaluating the options! See the next section.

GIS Market Segmentation

I have referred several times to the types of GIS available in the UK marketplace. In this section, the intention is to review the way in which the market segments, and to give some indications of the costs involved. Concentrating specifically on the marketing and retail sector, the GIS market segments as follows:

(a) 'Big systems' (e.g. ARC/INFO, LaserScan, Smallworld).

(b) PC analysis/mapping systems (e.g. Geodemographic Systems).

(c) Low-priced GIS/mapping systems (e.g. MapInfo, Tactician).

(d) Spatial decision support systems (e.g. GMAP).

I shall comment on each segment in turn.

(a) 'Big Systems'

The three suppliers mentioned (ESRI, with ARC/INFO, LaserScan and Smallworld) have all come from the 'traditional' GIS public sector market, but have made some inroads into the retail and marketing sector. Given their pedigree, unsurprisingly they are powerful systems, capable of handling large volumes of data at some speed; for example, if reviewing 'what if?' scenarios, they can rebuild such scenarios 'on the fly'. They are suitable for the heavyweight analytical tasks typified by large retailers, and indeed this is where their greatest concentration is found. LaserScan 'broke through' with Marks & Spencer, back in 1989 (see case history in Chapter 12). ESRI built an ARC/INFO installation for J. Sainsbury, Smallworld won the contest for Tesco, LaserScan won Safeway, Smallworld won Boots. ARC/INFO installations may be found in a few other major commercial sector players – but confidentiality precludes their mention.

These installations involve large sums of money, relative to the other segments which I am about to cover. Investments of £1 million or more (so far!) are represented in some of the installations mentioned above. A large part of this investment goes into the applications software which customises the GIS to the client's requirements. Typically, a number of users may access the system simultaneously, and indeed, different departments of the client may be involved.

(b) PC Analysis/Mapping Systems

The history of these developments has already been mentioned, both in Chapter 2 and earlier in this chapter. Most of the geodemographic suppliers have either written their own systems, or have developed geodemographic functions on existing software 'platforms'. The following companies and systems come in this segment:

- CACI, with InSite, whose Windows '95 version was launched in autumn 1995;

- Experian (formerly CCN), whose MOSAIC System was relaunched as MOSAIC Micromarketer, Windows '95 based, in autumn 1996.

- CDMS, who market Prospex, originally developed by GeoMatrix and now sold and supported by Beacon Dodsworth (also Windows '95-based).

- Claritas Market Analysis, who launched their CATALYST system in June 1996, based upon MapInfo and Microsoft Access on the Windows '95 OS.

- Equifax, who have just switched from SIA's Datamap to a MapInfo platform, therefore Windows '95-based branded MicroVision PC.

- EuroDirect, whose DemoGraf system was written in-house and runs under Windows '95.

- Business Geographics, who have written CENSYS95 based on MapInfo, in Windows '95.

- The Data Consultancy, whose Illumine software uses a MapInfo platform.

The biggest changes in the last few years have been the almost universal move to Windows (making the systems easier to use), and the strong growth of MapInfo, now used as a platform by half of the above suppliers. In fact, CACI has a second system (InSiteMaps) which is based on MapInfo – which is part of the legacy of their takeover of Pinpoint (it was formerly branded GeoMap).

All these systems have as their startpoint the analysis of geodemographic information, so they 'come with the functionality' that this implies: area profiling, customer profiling, ranking and reporting – as well as mapping and other GIS functions (such as proximity analysis). Additional modules are available for some systems, such as drive-time analysis, statistical modelling, scorecard building, etc.

Costs start at around £12 – £15k (sometimes each year, rather than one-off) and for some systems, £30 – £50k each year; this can be higher, depending on the data and modules taken. Indeed, the data are often a large part of the total. Some more detail of individual systems will be found in Chapter 12.

(c) Low-Priced GIS/Mapping Systems

The market-leading system, MapInfo, is sold both by the MapInfo Corporation, and by a number of VARs (Value-Added Resellers). Some of these VARs were mentioned in (b) above, where geodemographic functionality has been added to the basic MapInfo software. Another popular system is Tactician (sourced from the US, but supplied by Tactician UK, sister company to GEOPLAN). Tactician was devised for sales and marketing applications, and is very fast. It comes in two versions; the more advanced (and much more expensive!) version comes with much enhanced functionality, including gravity modelling and profiling.

ESRI, already mentioned as a 'heavy-end' system provider, has also moved into the lower-priced market fairly recently with ArcView, which has impressive GIS capability (unsurprising, given its pedigree). Other newcomers are GeoConcept (French in origin, marketed in the UK by Kingswood), and WinGis (Austrian), marketed by Soft Toolrack. Least expensive of all is Maptitude, marketed by SSI Ltd.

The cautionary note here is that you cannot expect to buy a fully-functioning geodemographic/GIS system for just the software price of these systems. Most of them do *not* have geodemographic functionality (unless it is added, as in some of the examples in (b) above); and usually, the data (which is extra) will cost much more than the software. As a rule of thumb, you are unlikely to be able to get started with a geodemographic analysis system plus mapping, for much less than £10k (of which, £2k might be the base software).

A system which is different in concept from the others mentioned here, but is also lower in price, is Cenario from Capscan. Cenario provides a facility to analyse 'raw' census variables (supplied on CD-ROM) at either postcode sector level, or at census ED level; then to link the results of the analysis to postcodes. The base-level product starts at £3k (postcode sector level), and goes up for the more detailed level of data.

(d) Spatial Decision Support Systems

In a general sense, one could describe *all* GIS as being spatial decision support systems. However, in the context of this chapter, I am referring to the methodology employed by GMAP. GMAP was 'spawned' by the School of Geography at the University of Leeds, and built upon work conducted through the 1970s and 1980s by Professors Wilson and Clarke and their colleagues. GMAP itself was formed in 1989, and is unusual in that it is a limited company operating in intimate proximity with academia!

GMAP's methodology is centred on spatial interaction modelling (more commonly, if slightly inaccurately, known as *gravity modelling*). In crude terms, the principle behind it is to measure the 'gravitational pull' of one shopping centre against another (or, in a different part of the retail market, one superstore versus another). The objective is to model 'flows' between origins (residential areas) and destinations (stores or shopping centres). Using this technique, GMAP will build a model of the existing competitive scenario, which then enables 'what if?' analysis; for example, 'what would be the effect on my existing stores and my competitors if I were to open a new 30k sq. ft. superstore at location x?' Another shorthand name for this type of modelling is 'impact analysis'.

GMAP have built a substantial business on the application of their methodology to commercial decisions, notably the optimisation of branch networks. This subject will be picked up again in Chapter 9. For now, suffice to say that GMAP's *modus operandi* takes a consultancy approach, in which they work with the client to model his existing network. This is usually a time-intensive operation, which is likely to cost of the order of £250k to model a national operation. GMAP's solution will include the facility to visualise the data (in a GIS sense) – but is far removed from 'conventional' GIS.

Readers wishing to delve deeper into some of the issues involved in using GIS in the marketing and retail areas might read *GIS for Business & Service Planning*, edited by Paul Longley & Graham Clarke, and published by GeoInformation International. There is a fascinating mix of the academic and the commercial!

CHAPTER NINE

RETAIL APPLICATIONS

Introduction

The retail sector is now a 'heavy user' of geodemographics. This is likely to increase, in my view. Chapter 1 made the point that geodemographics, by virtue of its locational aspect, is very relevant to retail applications. Chapter 7 demonstrated how geodemographics is used to model retail potential. This chapter shows how the combination of GIS, geodemographics and lifestyle data can be used in retail applications; commencing by explaining the various ways in which users may define the catchment areas of their stores or branches.

Catchment Area Definition

The concept of the catchment area for a store or branch is a vital one to retailers. I realise that this will be a statement of the obvious to retailers, but of course this report is written for a wider audience, some of whom may not have given such issues much thought! The catchment area is the area from which a store's customers will be drawn. The reason for its importance is that it is no use having a stunning retail prospect if the target market to whom it appeals are not within reach of an outlet (to take an extreme example); the retailer can only do business with those potential buyers who are able to visit his branches. Or, in those frequent cases where a retailer operates in a competitive marketplace, where shoppers have plenty of choice as to which store to use, then the location of the outlets in contention will play a major role in their success. In this case, the trading area within which these retailers compete may well be a more important issue than their individual catchment areas, since shoppers may visit a centre containing a large number of outlets, without any one being the dominant reason for their visit. In this case, substitute trading area for catchment area in what follows.

The definition of the catchment area of the store or branch in question is a necessary pre-requisite to the analyses and activities that will be described in this chapter. Given the techniques and tools available to us in a GIS/geodemographic environment, how might we define a catchment area?

The first two methods require access to customer data. For organisations which routinely capture customer data on computer, this is relatively straightforward. For organisations which do not, this task is more forbidding; it requires them to implement some scheme for the collection of customer addresses. This might tie in with promotional activity, in part derived to capture such addresses; it might form a part of a customer care scheme, whereby customers are asked to give their name and address in return for mailings about special offers, etc. (Either activity could lead on to the opportunity to implement a customer database, of course; that issue is covered in the next chapter, whereas here I am simply concerned with customer addresses to give locational information.)

So, given a reasonable number of customer addresses per branch (say 500 if difficult to collect, but ideally 1,000) and ensuring they are fairly representative, rather than skewed to any one type of customer, we can use these addresses to indicate the overall catchment area. We need to add postcodes to the addresses; they may already be present, but if not, PC-based automatic postcoding systems are very reasonably priced these days – or use a bureau to do it. Then 'feed' the postcoded addresses into a GIS, which will then *geocode* the addresses, and you can then map them as a scattermap (geocoding simply means attaching a map grid reference to the postcode). The scattermap will indicate the extent of the catchment area, and its relationship to the store or branch (which should also be located on the map, naturally). The density of clustering of the 'dots' will also indicate where the majority of customers come from. To complete the exercise, run a proximity analysis programme (most decent GIS should have one) to produce a boundary defined by the (say) 80 per cent of customers nearest to the branch; this can then be used as a catchment boundary, and the areas within it used as the definition of the branch catchment area, for further analysis. The reason for excluding customers beyond the 80 per cent catchment is to cut out the 'outliers'; people who may have visited the store in question while visiting a relative, perhaps, or while on holiday – not regular shoppers. It is also the case that these customers on the fringe of the catchment lead to sampling error, which makes any modelling inherently unstable.

An alternative means of catchment area definition, given customer addresses on computer, is to use postcode sectors as units of area, and combine postcode sectors to create catchment areas. This method has the merit that the postcode sectors can subsequently be used as units of area for targeting marketing activity (such as door-to-door distribution). Again, the customer addresses must be postcoded. In this case, compute the penetration of customers within each postcode sector (using either PAF addresses, or census-based households, as the total within each sector). You can either set a cut-off of a minimum percentage penetration, below which you will exclude sectors and/or allocate sectors to 'competing' branches (where two or more branches have customers in the same sector) by allocating the sector to the branch with the highest penetration. It is important to map the results as you conduct this process, or some silly catchments may result! If they do, edit them on a commonsense basis. And remember MAUP! (Chapter 7.)

Another means to define catchment areas is by means of market research. This might entail exit interviews (which would be similar in principle to collecting customer addresses as mentioned above) or a survey of the trading area within which the branch or store trades. This latter method would pick up customers to competitive branches or stores, as well as your own, which raises an important point; although it is very useful to know your own catchment area, it is also helpful to know how it *competes* with other outlets. The major grocery supermarket operators tend to field trading area surveys on a regular basis, to check how they are competing, as do some other major retailers.

A specific research exercise with which I was associated was the SHOPPiN study, conducted by Pinpoint in association with Nielsen Marketing Research. When Nielsen were conducting the establishment survey for the recruitment of their 'Homescan' consumer panel, they involved Pinpoint in the design of the sample frame. They required the sample points to be well dispersed geographically, as well as requiring the sample to be fully representative. The reason for requiring dispersed sample points was in order to avoid the possible problem arising from a clustered sample, where source of purchase data may be skewed where clusters fall into the catchment areas of specific grocery multiples, but possibly under-represent other multiples. For a very similar reason, the geographical dispersion also suited the needs of research into shopping patterns. Pinpoint proposed a series of questions about shopping habits to be asked by Nielsen, and results of around 80,000 housewife interviews were processed by Pinpoint and 'packaged up' as SHOPPiN. This was, so far as we were aware, the first fully-national large-scale survey of UK shopping habits, and it showed the shopper 'flows' from residential areas to grocery stores, on the one hand, and to shopping centres on the other. (Separate questions were asked about food shopping and 'non-food' shopping, the latter typified as clothing, footwear and electrical goods shopping.) The data were processed by Pinpoint as tables and maps, the latter adding up to 'the shopping geography of the UK'.

So, whether a large-scale survey like SHOPPiN, an exit interview, or *ad-hoc* trading area survey, market research can provide very useful information about catchment or trading areas; including use of competitive outlets or centres, if the questions have been designed accordingly. Information from lifestyle databases can be used in a similar way – more about this appears later in the chapter.

The fourth method of defining catchment areas is via drive-times. Most of the PC-based analysis systems now contain software to generate drive-time 'isochrones' (these are simply the 'contour lines' on a map reached after, say, five minutes driving, ten minutes, etc.). The software works on the road network and assumed traffic speeds on the various classes of roads; some systems allow you to change these assumptions. Before these systems were developed, retail executives would drive outwards from the site in question, marking their position on a map after 5 minutes driving, etc. I understand that some still do! It goes without saying that you need to choose a common day of week and time of day for drive-time calculations; Saturday afternoon and Monday mid-morning would give wildly differing results of course.

The drive-time approach to catchment area definition has most relevance to grocery superstores, DIY 'sheds', and shopping centres or retail parks; in other words, sites which represent specific destinations for car-borne shoppers. It is much less relevant to outlets visited more casually, in the course of other activities or at lunch-time from the work-place.

Finally, if all else fails, use a radius or polygon, 'drawn' by your GIS around the site in question. In practice this works perfectly well for market towns or similar, where the conurbation is surrounded by sheep country! It works much less well in larger conurbations (such as metropolitan areas) where it is very difficult to 'guess' where shoppers come from when you are studying one of the sub-centres.

One more point about catchment area definition. If you have used your own customer data to establish where customers are currently coming from, this on its own will not tell you where they might potentially come from. This is why it is worth comparing more than one method of catchment definition; if you try a research-based method (or a drive-time, if appropriate) you may well discover that shoppers from particular residential areas are visiting the general vicinity of your outlet, but not visiting the outlet itself. If you find this sort of pattern, it may be worth experimenting with local marketing activities (such as door-to-door leafleting) to see whether the current catchment area can be expanded, and new customers thus gained.

The 'Hierarchy' of Catchment Area Analysis

Having defined the catchment area, it seems to me that there is then a 'hierarchy' of analyses that can be conducted:

(a) A simple 'headcount' of population in the area;
(b) The demographics of these people;
(c) The geodemographics (i.e. neighbourhood types);
(d) The merchandise potential inherent in the above.

At the very least, a retailer is likely to be interested in the total population available to his store; this gives some outline indication of potential. It becomes more interesting and useful if some basic demographic breakdown of that population is available – the types of variables available from census analysis, such as age profile, household composition (i.e. presence of children, etc.), household tenure, some measure of social class or social grade, etc. The retailer will be able to match this population profile to his ideal customer profile, and thus look at the catchment population in terms of apparent value to his retail offer. In reality, there are very few retailers who have a 'flat' customer profile; even the grocery retailers, where you might expect this to be the case ('everyone eats food') have different positionings, or serve different niches; or have certain types of customer who are most valuable to them.

Geodemographics (of the neighbourhood classification variety) takes this an important stage further. With their use (as you will no doubt see, having persevered this far in this report!), we can identify and locate our core target market even more precisely. The profiles of alternative areas can be compared more easily, if we are engaged in screening possible areas for new sites. Then, the final level in this hierarchy of data is the potential for the product or service in question, within the defined catchment area. The methodology for this application was reviewed in Chapter 7. Each of these methods provides useful information in its own right; they also provide input to the other applications, reviewed below.

Store Location Analysis

This is a very important application of geodemographics. The most sophisticated retailers (in this regard, and in others) spend very large sums of money on 'getting it right'. Generally, they will have developed an in-house function to evaluate existing and potential store sites, and to produce revenue forecasts from these sites. Even excepting these market leaders, many retailers have embraced a similar approach to site selection in recent years; not abandoning the judgmental approach, involving experienced executives, but supplementing their experience with geodemographic and related data. Jonathan Reynolds, research fellow at the Oxford Institute of Retail Management, reviewed this in his 1992 paper 'Managing the Local Market'. (See References.)

There can be said to be two distinct levels of analysis associated with site location analysis. The first is a 'site screening' overview, designed to produce quick top-line data on candidate sites, perhaps sites which have been put forward by agencies for the retailer's consideration; the property decision-maker wants a swift view of likely viability, rather than an in-depth study. The other level is an in-depth study, which includes a detailed review of the likely catchment area and revenue forecasts based on an analysis of its potential. As with other retail analyses, the first step is to define the catchment area in question. Note the point made earlier in this chapter; a proposed new site where the retailer will be a focal point for car-borne shoppers (such as a superstore) will require a completely new catchment to be defined (perhaps by drive-time analysis), while a comparison retailer taking a site in an existing high street needs to be concerned with the existing 'shopping geography' – the trading area of that high street.

The 'overview', site-screening approach may simply analyse the overall catchment population, perhaps with some key indicators of population type (i.e. measures like car ownership, social grade, family composition), or it may use a geodemographic profile to see if the profile of the candidate catchment matches the 'ideal' profile of the desired target market. A caveat on this latter point; while the overall profile of the catchment population is of considerable interest, the real question should be whether there are sufficient numbers of the desired neighbourhood types available to the proposed store. So, while the overall profile of a large catchment area or trading area may not look promising – the 'desirable' neighbourhood types in the profile are 'diluted' by less desirable types – so long as there are *sufficient* of the former, this may not be a problem. It will simply depend on the ability of the store, once trading, to attract enough 'desirable' types, to be viable. This is a similar issue to that discussed in the interpretation of geodemographic profiles in Chapter 6.

The site-screening methodology may also address the supply-side presence in the catchment areas under consideration; I have chosen to cover this aspect in the next section.

Market Share Analysis

This type of analysis tends to merge with the more detailed version of the store location analysis, outlined above. Here we are not merely concerned with a 'top-line' view of apparent viability for a new site, but with a much more detailed analysis of what market share (and therefore turnover) might be expected for the new store. There are two elements involved; the potential *demand* from the catchment area, and the total *supply* (in terms of other retail outlets selling similar merchandise) present within the same area. Given a GIS approach, containing both geodemographics linked to research or customer data to produce the demand estimate (see Chapter 7) and the locations of other retail outlets, own and competitors, this is not a difficult exercise. You can estimate the total level of residential demand. If you have an existing branch or branches in the catchment, you know your own sales; there simply remains the task of allocating market share to competing outlets. You may have some hard information about competitive turnover, or you may be able to estimate sales per square foot fairly reliably. You may be able to look at total selling area in the catchment (from Goad, or similar) and either apportion the market equally by square foot of selling area, or 'factor' it depending on the relative strength of competitors. However you do it, the data exist to produce a reasonably accurate estimate of actual or potential market share.

Those retailers (or quasi-retailers) who rely for much of their trade on 'non-shopping' trade – for example, fast food outlets, pubs – will also need to take account of workplace 'populations' and travel patterns. Special workplace statistics are available from the ONS, derived from the census of population, which analyse origin (home) and destination (place of work) 'flows'. In addition, some of the databases of company information (such as Dun & Bradstreet and Market Locations) can supply staff numbers at workplaces; such data can be manipulated within a GIS to 'fill the gap' left by the other data sources mentioned above. Financial services locations (such as bank and building society branches and ATMs) have a particularly complex problem to solve, because their services can be used in the course of various other activities; shopping trips, leisure outings, lunch-break from work, journeys, even special trips from home. This complex pattern is further complicated by the frequent habit of leaving the account wherever it was first opened, but after moving home, using another branch or ATM. Even such complex problems are susceptible to analysis, and again using a GIS can reveal the patterns.

Chapter 4 covered the activities of the lifestyle database companies, and mentioned the former collaboration of CMT with CCN, which led to the 'checkout' product. Although that actual collaboration ended some years ago, both companies have continued with similar products (CCN, now Experian, using its 'Chorus' database). This methodology uses a different approach to market share analysis from the geodemographic modelling approach outlined above. The 'checkout' product and its successors took responses from the lifestyle databases in question, and used them directly. For example, in the grocery market, the questions on grocery store most used, weekly expenditure on groceries, and reasons for choice of favourite store; and analysed them within postcode sectors, to give estimates of market share by all the major grocery retailers. This analysis is run (and mapped) within Experian's MOSAIC Micromarketer PC system; or within Claritas UK's Catalyst system. This is a very interesting application of lifestyle data – subject only to the caveat of the penetration of (and representativeness of) the lifestyle data within postcode sector.

Branch Performance Analysis

This section deals with the regression modelling approach to branch performance modelling. An alternative approach, gravity modelling, is dealt with in the next section.

The objective in the regression modelling approach is to build a model which explains the performance of branches in the retailer's network. The model can either be used to evaluate how well existing branches are performing (with a view to improving performance, where some branches are under-performing), or to evaluate the likely performance of new branches. The method involves collecting data for a sample of branches (at least 30, ideally 50); these branches should be representative of the network. If the network includes very different types of branches (different in size, or type of location), then separate models will be needed for each type.

The model needs different sorts of data; data about the characteristics of the catchment area, and data about the branch itself. Under the former category come the types of analysis covered in this chapter and Chapter 7, for example:

- Extent of catchment area
- Total population

- Population in core target market
  - □ Demographic
  - □ Geodemographic
- Workplace population
- Potential expenditure on merchandise in question.

Data about the branch itself will include some or all of:

- Sales area
- Product range (where this can vary)
- Size of frontage
- Decor/facia (where this can vary)
- Other store-specific features
- Branch turnover
- Car parking (proximity).

Additionally, *locational* variables should be collected:

- Competitive presence, proximity and size
- Type of location (e.g. high street, mall, edge-of-town, etc.)
- 'Pitch' of site (prime, secondary, etc.)
- Accessability to pedestrian flows, *or* vehicular traffic flows (depending on type of store)
- Proximity to 'anchor store' (if appropriate).

Finally, if some stores have benefitted from advertising support when others have not (for example, regional television campaigns have been run), these data should be collected.

Having collected all these data for each of the sample stores, the next stage is to build a multiple regression model, testing variables until an optimal solution emerges. The aim of the model is to *explain* store performance in terms of a particular combination of variables, which effectively *predict* store performance. For example (simplistically), the performance of an individual store might require a particular level of presence of the target market in the catchment, a certain minimum sales area, and absence of key competitors (although paradoxically, in 'comparison goods' markets, *presence* of competitors in the vicinity may *enhance* performance). The model should be able to identify which of the variables tested does contribute to good performance, and to what extent. Store turnover is the 'dependent' variable, that is, the one which the model is trying to predict.

Once the model has been built and tested, it will be run on all the stores in the portfolio. In each case, actual turnover will be compared with predicted turnover for each store. Not only can remedial action be taken at branches seen to be under-performing; the model may well indicate that some branches are poorly sited, and stand little chance of performing adequately *whatever* is done. This is a good method of setting sales targets for branches, and for 'weeding out' branches with poor prospects. A variation on this 'evaluative' model is to extract a sample of stores which represent the desired future direction for the retailer in question, and build a 'predictive' model; the methodology is exactly the same. Clearly, it must be possible to collect all the 'external' data for the site under consideration, when running the predictive model; although the aspects of the branch that are under the retailer's control can be specified from the model. It is prudent, having developed a model, to test it on an additional sample of stores before implementing it.

Gravity Modelling/Impact Analysis

Gravity modelling, sometimes known as impact analysis, is a technique which can be used as an alternative to some of those outlined above. The principle behind gravity modelling is the 'gravitational pull' of some stores or centres, against others. It deals with 'flows' of shoppers from residential areas into these competing stores or centres, and estimates the relative 'pull' of each centre. This technique can be used for market share analysis and branch performance analysis, as it will generate estimates of turnover for particular centres or outlets; but its main application, as its alternative name suggests, is for modelling the *impact* of proposed changes in shopping geography. A classic example of this is the planning of new grocery superstore sites. Clearly, opening a massive new superstore is likely to have a major impact on existing stores in the trading area, both competitive stores and, if present, existing stores owned by the retailer in question. So a gravity model would be constructed of the trading area under consideration; which would need to be a reasonably self-contained area, without too much 'leakage' into neighbouring areas. The study area would then be divided into residential zones (usually units of postal geography) and population characteristics and demand estimates produced for each zone (by the techniques mentioned earlier).

The next step would be to locate all the competing stores (i.e. within the grocery market) in the study area; in practice, the smaller 'corner stores' would probably be ignored. Turnover estimates for competitor's stores would be computed (clearly, you would known your own!), perhaps based on selling area, or some more concrete information. Then a model of the 'dynamics' of the trading area would be constructed, using special software developed for this purpose. Some models use the digitised road network, and compute travel distances from centres of residential zones to stores; others use 'crow-fly' distances. The model would then be calibrated with some flow data (data such as that produced by the SHOPPiN survey is ideal for this purpose), and the model run through several iterations until the calculations of residential demand and supply-point turnover were robust. (If this sounds jargonesque, I promise you I'm letting you off lightly – I haven't used the word 'spatial' once!)

Once the model of the area is performing satisfactorily, then some 'what if' questions may be asked. For example: what would be the effect of siting a new 35,000 sq. ft. superstore at grid-reference x? What 'steal' would result from competitive stores? What 'cannibalisation' would there be from existing stores owned by the retailer concerned? The model will provide estimates of these impacts, thus allowing sensible decisions to be taken with confidence. Perhaps the best-known exponent of this technique is GMAP (see end of Chapter 8).

Local Store Marketing

Retailers are heavy users of local media, particularly local press. As has been mentioned earlier in this report, most media may be targeted using geodemographics. I have written a new chapter on media applications for this second edition – Chapter 11 – so it would not be productive to repeat some of it here. However, in essence, retailers can use GIS and geodemographics to assist in their media planning and buying. To take a simple example, they can compare the geography of their catchment areas with the 'footprints' of local and regional press to establish matches and mis-matches; they can mail within catchment areas, they can target door-to-door distribution, and other media too. This subject is covered in more detail in Chapter 11.

It is obvious that store loyalty cards have the potential to revolutionise local store marketing, provided that the operators can master the 'data indigestion' problem. Detailed records of all purchases, product combinations, frequency and value, could allow for a very sophisticated programme of promotional stimulation. These data also provide raw materials for custom segmentation – which is easier to manage than 'one-to-one' dialogues.

End Note

Speaking personally, I am very pleased that the last six months (spanning late 1996/early 1997) have seen no fewer than four conference platform appearances by the Marks & Spencer site location team; and by coincidence, I have been involved with organising/chairing all four. Having been aware of the work of the department since it was 'reformed' in the late 1980s, I have watched its progress with great interest. There is no doubt that they are at the leading edge of the application of GIS and geodemographics in UK retail applications; and by extension (given their multi-national activities), *world* retail applications. It is good that they are prepared to share their experiences with a wider audience. One by-product of this is the case history that appears in Chapter 12 – for which I am grateful. Although, in essence, it is one story which is being told, I have been privileged to see it in four different dimensions; at the AGI 1996 conference, tailored to a GIS audience; at an Admap conference, pitched at a marketing audience; at an MRS census interest group seminar, 'tweaked' for a research audience; and at a DMA evening event, where the stress was on customer targeting.

One issue, which was highlighted in David Broom's presentation at the Admap conference ('Can a Retailer Find the Right Information Systems', Targeting Consumers 2000 conference, Admap 1996), is the *dynamic* nature of demand over time, and the need, when looking at (say) a 15-year planning timescale, to project demographic trends forward accordingly. I think it is a very fair criticism that, occasionally, we get so caught up in the detail of geodemographic analysis, that we forget that demographics is in a state of change over time. We tend to be reminded of this once a decade, with the new census data!

Readers wishing to know more about the techniques mentioned briefly in this chapter may be interested in the following books which cover this area in much more depth.

Davies, R.L. & Rogers, D.S. (Eds.), 1984, *Store Location and Store Assessment Research*, John Wiley, Chichester.

Wrigley, N. (Ed.), 1988, *Store Choice, Store Location and Market Analysis,* Routledge & Kegan Paul, London.

Jones, K. & Simmons, J. 1990, *The Retail Environment,* Routledge & Kegan Paul, London.

Guy, C. 1994, *The Retail Development Process – Location, Property and Planning,* Routledge & Kegan Paul, London.

CHAPTER TEN

DIRECT MARKETING APPLICATIONS

Introduction

The growing influence of direct marketing (DM) has long been a feature of the UK marketing scene. Having come from its origins in catalogue and mail-order trading, DM has spread into many other markets and has even impinged on fmcg. The reasons for its growth have been well-rehearsed; the fragmentation of markets and media on the one hand, and advances in computing technology on the other. The same revolution in computing that has assisted the development of geodemographics and lifestyle databases, has also fuelled the growth of 'relationship' marketing, driven by customer databases. The speed of change is accelerating (a phenomenon which seems to be fairly general!), and the factors which have changed since the first edition include:

- the influence of the Internet
- the growth of loyalty schemes
- the advent of the ER on CD-ROM
- the influence of Don Peppers, and his one-to-one marketing message
- the physical size of lifestyle databases
- the proportion of marketing companies having customer databases
- developments in response analysis
- links to market research.

But first, let's look back briefly at some history. The explosion of financial services DM from the mid to late-1980s both assisted the growth of geodemographics and lifestyle databases, and also 'fed' on these data. This market sector (within the geodemographics marketplace) grew to dominance virtually overnight, it seemed. To a large extent, the financial direct marketers and the geodemographic suppliers were sharing a mutual learning experience. I will touch on the way in which the marketplace has changed in this chapter.

First perhaps, I should clarify some terms. DM does not equate to direct mail; direct mail is very easy to define, simply being communication with customers or prospects by means of the mail. DM also embraces telephone marketing, direct response advertising ('off the page' advertising in the press, and the equivalent on television – DRTV – or radio). Internet marketing is in essence an electronic form of 'off-the-page' advertising, in that viewers have to seek out your web-site. Its particular power lies in the facility for a dialogue, if the viewer can be persuaded to register his interest and to respond. Direct marketing implies a *direct* relationship between marketer and customer or prospective customer; sometimes referred to as 'one-to-one marketing' or 'relationship marketing'. Enter yet another kind of 'DM' – 'database marketing', which is the means by which the dialogue with the customer can be managed. More about this later in the chapter, but before moving on, one more point which perhaps needs to be flagged. Direct marketing does *not* necessarily imply that the product or service in question is being sold by mail order. DM can be employed for products and services which are sold through retail channels, indeed it can be used to *direct* customers to those retail channels. But it can also be used to collect and organise *information*, the better to understand customers and potential customers, and to assist with targeting marketing activities.

This chapter is not about direct marketing *per se*, it is about the use of geodemographic and lifestyle data in direct marketing.

Development and Transformation of the Targeting Marketplace

The targeting marketplace has gone through several revolutions since the beginning of the 1980s. The first was the adoption of geodemographics for targeting direct mail. Even before the introduction of ACORN, census data had been used as one source of information for prospect modelling – on the huge Reader's Digest database. But it was the growth of the 'ACORN industry' which introduced census-based targeting to a much wider audience.

In essence, the new methodology was straightforward. First, profile your customers (either from your own customer addresses, or from a research source, such as TGI). Then, use this profile to select the best customer types – generally from the ER. In the early 1980s, there was only one source for this methodology: CACI, with their ACORN typology, using the ER supplied by CCN. As I mentioned in Chapter 2, in addition to CACI selling this facility, from late-1982 onwards the Direct Mail Sales Bureau (DMSB) also presented and sold ER targeting via ACORN, usually based on TGI cross-tabs. Their presentation of this 'product' was branded the Consumer Location System, and it was presented to most of the major advertising agencies (the DMSB's brief was to get direct mail accepted as a mainstream medium). As I also mentioned in Chapter 2, with hindsight it is probable that the enthusiastic selling of ER mailing, targeted by geodemographics, to clients new to the medium may have set up unrealistic expectations of likely response rates. I think it is fair to say that there was little appreciation of the importance of 'mailing responsiveness' among those mailed (that is, a predisposition to buy things through the mail).

In any event, ER mailing continued to grow through the mid-1980s, boosted particularly by the Financial Services Act, and the explosion of DM activity which this Act stimulated in the financial services marketplace. Huge volume 'cold' mailings took place (that is, prospect mailings to 'cold' lists, such as the ER). The financial services vendors were prepared to 'pump' huge resource into recruitment by direct mail. Even if they used rented lists first, the volume requirement was such that they would 'top up' with ER selections.

Those days are long gone! A number of factors have changed:

- economic factors, combined with 'junk mail' considerations, have consigned these huge volume 'cold' mailings to history;

- sophistication has grown, and there is a more general realisation of the importance of 'mailing responsiveness', which cannot be qualified by ER targeting alone;

- lifestyle databases have arrived and have reached a 'critical mass' – they offer literally millions of names for list rental, about whom specific facts are known.

This does not mean that there is not still a place for targeted ER mailings, far from it; I have recently heard case histories of its continuing, effective use – but the scenario has nevertheless changed markedly over the decade. Also, refer back to previous chapters for additional enhancements to the ER (additional, that is, to geodemographic segmentation), and to the way in which the lifestyle database operators are using the ER to 'extend' their lists. A fairly recent development has seen the ER marketed on CD-ROM; five or six vendors are now making it available in this form. The biggest single change (apart from the flexibility implied by having the ER in-house) is in the *pricing*; formerly it would cost of the order of £100,000 per annum to acquire the ER on magnetic media from one of the (relatively few) organisations which data-capture it, now it costs about £5,000 on CD-ROM. Thus we are likely to see a much larger volume market. The CD-ROM products tend to have geodemographic classifications attached, plus (in some cases) the ER-based discriminators – see Chapter 5. Some vendors sell the names of the CD-ROM by the thousand – you pay them to 'unlock' a tranche at a time! This flurry of activity is likely to increase the volume of ER-based mailings. No doubt the new users will have to go through the same learning process that their predecessors did before them.

Apart from the ER, it is *relatively* unusual to find rented lists that may be segmented by geodemographics; although there are a few very large lists which are available with this feature. Consult your list broker!

Cross-Selling and Database Enhancement

Cross-selling is an activity which has made considerable use of geodemographic segmentation. This activity requires an existing customer database. There is no doubt that there has been a huge growth in the penetration of customer databases, even in sectors which were formerly slow to adopt them; for example, fmcg companies and retailers (loyalty cards provide a potent mechanism). The objective of cross-selling is to make a selling proposition to existing customers for one product, which persuades them to buy another product. Depending on the size of the database segment, it is possible to mail *all* the prospects in that segment with the new proposition; however, this may prove to be wasteful. Geodemographic segmentation is one way to priorise prospects for mailing. Let's take an example – say a large building society. It has hundreds of thousands of customers for an existing savings product, and it plans to launch a PEP. It holds a geodemographic classification system on its customer database, so it is able to classify all its customers accordingly. It also subscribes to industry market research; it commissions a geodemographic profile of purchasers of PEPs, and uses the results to select the 'best' geodemographic types from its database to mail with the new product. I have seen it done – and it works!

This is an example of the use of a geodemographic classifier on your own customer database, for segmentation purposes. In practice, this would normally be achieved by linking a postcode directory of the classification, to the database. There are other ways of using a geodemographic classifier on the database; other than for cross-selling, that is. For example, the classifier can be used in response analysis. This could either take the form of a simple *profile* of the respondents by the classification (see Chapter 6), so you could determine the best neighbourhood types to mail next time; or the geodemographic classifier could act as one of the variables in a *response model*.

Response modelling is rather beyond the scope of this chapter, but briefly, it entails building a model which identifies the combination of variables that lead to response (variables such as personal characteristics – if held on the database – transactional information, length of time on the database, plus geodemographic type, again if available). As mentioned previously, the geodemographic type can be simply attached to the customer's postcode. Regression modelling is used most commonly in UK DM, but techniques such as CHAID and neural networks are being employed more commonly these days. (CHAID is described later in this chapter.) Response modelling is widely practised nowadays. A particularly interesting example, developed over the last two years, is the 'Prospector' system, which analyses response to DRTV campaigns on Carlton TV. Respondents are analysed by the PRIZM geodemographic system, and a model of likely conversion is constructed. For more details, see Caroline Hunt's paper from the 1996 Admap conference, Targeting Consumers 2000.

One of the applications of lifestyle databases is customer database enhancement. Chapter 4 explained the technique of *matching* respondents on a lifestyle database file, with customers on a client customer file; in that context, the purpose was to *profile* the customer file, using the extra information on a lifestyle database. If the purpose is to enhance the client customer database, then appropriate extra information is transferred from the lifestyle database to the customer database. This process is known as data tagging, and the objective is to enrich the customer file with additional data, generally for modelling purposes.

There is no doubt that database marketing will continue to grow, and particularly to grow into non-traditional markets. The ability to identify key customers, and 'converse' with them, is very powerful; and, if you can get the economics right, very profitable. Both geodemographic data and lifestyle data can play their part in this very exciting scenario. The publicity generated by Don Peppers on his visits to the UK in 1995 helped to boost the 'one-to-one marketing' concept. In 1996, Garth Hallberg came over to publicise his book about differential marketing, *All Consumers are not Created Equal*, which concentrates particularly on fmcg markets. See References for details.

Lifestyle Database Selections

The primary purpose of the lifestyle database operators is to collect names and addresses for mailing purposes – which is of course a key aspect of DM. Companies with an existing customer database will mail selections from that database. These are 'warm' mailings, because by virtue of the fact that these are existing customers, the database owner knows they are interested in his company and products. When the database owner wants to recruit new prospects, essentially he has two choices; to *advertise* (i.e. direct response advertising, in whichever medium), or to *mail* a prospect list. This latter activity is known as *cold list* mailing, and these days, the lifestyle database operators are a prime source of cold lists. This is not to suggest that they are the only source, by any means; there are numerous lists available for rental, some of them very large. But few can compare with the potential volume of the lifestyle lists, or the wealth of data about the individuals on the lifestyle databases. Another issue – mailing responsiveness – which was touched on earlier in this chapter, will be covered in more depth later.

In essence, you can make selections on any variable, or combination of variables, held on the lifestyle database in question. The selection might relate to demographics (for instance, a certain age band, or people owning their own homes), to existing product usage, to sports, hobbies or interests, to charitable giving, or to any of the other details collected from the questionnaires. These types of selection are known as *'knowledge-based'* selections. The main alternatives to this are to select on a *profile*, or to *model*. The profiling method was covered in Chapter 4; it involves matching individuals from the client's customer file and the lifestyle database, then looking for patterns in the other facts known about those customers, from their questionnaire responses. The variables which occur most frequently among the customers that are profiled, will then be used to select 'lookalikes' from the remainder of the lifestyle database; and a prospect list will be extracted, ranked in order of greatest apparent similarity to existing customers. This technique uses regression modelling as the 'driver'. An alternative technique, used by CMT, is to use the CHAID technique to select the variables which hold greatest promise of response. CHAID identifies the strongest response variable (say, homeowners) and splits the file by that variable (i.e. homeowners in one section, non-homeowners in the other). Then it carries on splitting the file (like an upside-down tree, or dendogram). Each cell is given a response index and you mail the cells with the highest indices.

I have mentioned prospect (or 'cold') mailings, but CMT conduct an activity which is rather different from 'run-of-the-mill' prospect mailings. I described CMT's operation in Chapter 4; it is particularly geared to fmcg marketing. It collects information (to order) about respondents usage of fmcg products and brands; brand used, weight/frequency of usage, competitive brands occasionally used, etc. When the questionnaire containing this information is returned, the information is keyed into the Behaviourbank database. The information is then used to 'trigger' the follow-up couponing activity. Personalised, laser-printed coupons are produced – and they can be targeted very precisely. For example, you could mail competitive brand users with high value coupons to encourage brand-switching, while mailing your own loyal users with (for example) an offer which requires a number of proofs of purchase – a lower-cost promotion. Non-category users would not be mailed; occasional users could be mailed a product sample – depending, of course, on the nature of the product! So the mechanism could be adjusted very sensitively to get maximum promotional benefit, and could continue indefinitely. Indeed, the lifestyle database companies have built and handled customer databases for many clients, on a bureau basis, in fmcg markets as well as durable, and other, markets. Thus, the contribution which the lifestyle database operators are making to the DM world is considerable.

Door-to-Door Distribution

Much of this chapter has been concerned, in one way or another, with mailing. Door-to-door distribution offers an alternative to mailing in some scenarios. To state the obvious; while a mailshot can be targeted at individual addresses (or unit postcodes, if geodemographically targeted), door-to-door cannot be this precise.

Generally, the door-to-door distributors, whether Post Office HDS or the commercial contractors, operate on units of postcode sectors, averaging 2,500 households. A recent innovation by two of the major commercial distributors (Circular Distributors, and MRM – the latter having been subsequently taken over by The Leaflet Company) has been to offer targeting at the level of free newspaper delivery rounds, which averages 200 households. This is clearly much finer targeting than that at a postcode sector level. Circular Distributors have also developed a new targeting geography (which they call Micro Sectors), where they have subdivided postcode sectors into smaller geographical units averaging some 600 – 700 households each. Because the areas in question were defined geodemographically – to make the new sectors as demographically homogenous as possible – they offer very efficient targeting units. Analysis has shown that their targeting efficiency is similar in practice to the newspaper delivery rounds – because in the latter case, these rounds were devised with no reference to geodemographics.

You may say 'if the targeting comparison is sectors, of whatever size, versus individual households, why should I want to choose the former?'. The answer lies in the relative costs of those two alternative distribution methods. Door-to-door generally costs about one-tenth the cost of mailing (more or less, depending on whether the distribution is solus to that item, or shared with others). This cost benefit can make door-to-door very attractive, particularly where the target market does not require great targeting precision (if it *did* require great targeting precision, postcode sectors would not be the ideal units of area!). So, particularly in markets such as grocery, DIY, catering (i.e. mass-market restaurant chains) – wherever the market can be fairly broadly defined – door-to-door comes into its own.

Having said that, a completely broadscale distribution, devoid of any form of targeting, is unlikely to make sense unless the deliberate intention is to cover *all* households (for example, a government communication). So targeting of various sorts has been practised in the door-to-door industry for many years, even pre-dating geodemographics. Back in those far-off days, the method was to use a rough and ready 'social class' segmentation, decided on the basis of the distribution companies' field management knowledge, i.e. ABC1 versus C2DE. The problem was the very considerable variability in the judgment of individual field managers – still, possibly better than nothing.

Targeting improved dramatically with the introduction of geodemographics. Now, the sectors could be profiled by geodemographics, and a process called 'postcode sector ranking' (PSR) could be employed. First, the desired profile will be established (usually from a customer profile, or a market research cross-tab). The key neighbourhood types of interest will thus be established. Then these key types will form the 'brief' for the PSR exercise. All the postcode sectors in the area in question will go into the analysis, and the computer program will rank the sectors by penetration of these 'desirable' types. The sectors containing the highest concentrations will come top of the ranking, and so on down to the lowest-penetration sectors. Then you select from the top of the ranking, either until you have reached the number of households to which you wish to distribute, or alternatively, to a pre-determined cut-off point of percentage penetration (say, 60 per cent penetration of desirable neighbourhood types). This technique enables you to calculate the apparent level of wastage inherent in any specified distribution, and ensures that such wastage is minimised.

These analyses used to be performed on a bureau basis by the geodemographic agencies, but nowadays the more sophisticated contractors have in-house targeting systems utilising one or more of the proprietary classification systems. Another filter which will be employed is to conduct PSR only within the catchment areas of relevant retailers, thus cutting out potential wastage by not delivering to areas where consumers could not avail themselves of the product in question. There is no doubt that the door-to-door industry has made great strides in recent years, partly by developing greater sophistication in targeting, but also by initiatives like forming the Association of Household Distributors (AHD) to maintain standards, by commissioning industry research, and by gearing themselves up to undertake very precisely targeted operations such as 'knock and drop' exercises. Hiding behind this rather unfortunate name is a very powerful technique for product sampling, whereby the fieldworker knocks on the door of each call, asks a qualifying question about brand usage, drops a product sample or coupon accordingly, and (in the most sophisticated cases) completes a questionnaire on product and brand usage for subsequent analysis. State of the art practice, which generates an extremely powerful database.

Some Observations

I mentioned 'mailing responsiveness' earlier in this chapter, initially in the context of the use of the ER for mailing. The ER tells you the name of the adults (eligible to vote) living at an address; you can then add additional targeting information via the ER 'indicators' (mentioned in Chapter 5), and of course, you can select the address using geodemographics. However, none of this tells you anything about how *mailing responsive* the occupants will be. The situation with lifestyle database respondents is somewhat similar, except for two factors – a question about purchasing by mail-order is asked in some cases, and the lifestyle database operators will say (quite reasonably) that the very fact that respondents *have* responded by mail, proves the point.

Nevertheless, aficionados will know that, however precise the targeting, whether you use targeted ER or lifestyle selections, the best of the rented lists will out-perform such selections in terms of response rates. The basic reason for this is that the customers on these rented lists have a greater propensity to buy by mail order – that is, they are more mailing-responsive. In practice of course, these very mailing-responsive lists tend to be heavily used (and potentially, over-used) in a relatively short period of time, and response rates then drop. Again, this does not mean that you should always go for rented lists, rather than geodemographic or lifestyle targeting! It simply means there are 'horses for courses'; you need to know what the options are, and to be able to evaluate the pros and cons of each in particular circumstances.

This can be a complex area. One of the crucial prerequisites for success is to understand the *data* that you are using, its *quality*, and the underlying *assumptions*. Hopefully, the nature of geodemographic and lifestyle data has been covered adequately in this report; *quality* is a rather more difficult issue to address. Perhaps the best advice is *caveat emptor* – ask the data vendors the crucial questions about data robustness, 'up-to-dateness', and integrity. As an example of the latter: you cannot necessarily assume that everyone completing a lifestyle questionnaire has done so with absolute honesty, as some respondents may be cute enough to work out that a particular answer may generate a higher value coupon than another! (For example, a Maxwell House purchaser, if ticking the Nescafé box, might get a high-value Maxwell House coupon, which is what they really want.) This may not be a widespread phenomenon, but clearly it will be present in some degree.

In referring to the 'underlying assumptions', I mean issues such as the 'neighbourhood' nature of geodemographic data, and the assumptions that will go into modelling approaches, such as area potential estimation or response analysis. These issues are deserving of a reasonable level of understanding if you intend to use these products in your business. One of the issues involved is what I tend to refer to as:

what is known, versus what is modelled

which is, I think, a useful criterion to keep in mind. What is *known* about an individual is (hopefully) certain; what is *modelled* can only be a probability. Knowing the probability is useful in itself, however! (That is, being able to put a statistical probability on whether an individual is likely to respond, for example.) Of course, you can get everything right in terms of the targeting, and *still* not make a sale, because if the respondent to a mailshot is 'in the market' in a general sense, but not at that particular moment – he won't buy. That is human nature, which is extremely difficult to model in individual cases, although possible to model in aggregate. Notwithstanding this human 'quirkiness', it still pays to do everything possible in targeting terms to maximise your chances; you'll be improving the odds in your favour.

Finally, although we do ideally want to address each customer or prospect as an individual, in practice it will generally be necessary to place customers in *categories* or *segments*, purely from the point of view of practicality. Thus we will employ some form of segmentation on an existing customer file, whether it be by means of scoring techniques, simple selections by (say) purchase history, or by geodemographics. Similarly, when prospecting for new customers, generally we will want to target towards the optimum segments in the overall market by similar means, whatever the source of the data. If using geodemographic or lifestyle data we will generally want to target profile-based 'lookalikes'.

Market Research Meets Database Marketing

The coming together of the market research industry with database marketing is finally happening, and in my view, much to be welcomed. When the lifestyle databases first appeared in the UK, they were condemned by many members of the 'traditional' market research industry. The main reason was that the MRS code of conduct states: 'No information which could be used to identify people or companies shall be revealed to anyone, except to those who need it to check the validity of the data or who are engaged in the processing of them' – the rule of respondent confidentiality. On the other hand, the whole purpose of collecting data on lifestyle questionnaires was to use those data for list rental purposes, thus diametrically opposite to the MRS ruling. Certainly, one could fill in the lifestyle questionnaire and then tick the opt-out box, but relatively few respondents did so. So, the argument ran, members of the public would associate the completion of questionnaires with the subsequent receipt of 'junk mail', thus damaging 'proper' research. There was the associated accusation that lifestyle database operators were 'sugging' – 'selling under the guise' of market research.

There is little doubt that the growth of lifestyle databases – particularly when they reached their very large volumes, from the late-1980s onwards – did have some effect on market research, and probably helped to depress response rates. However, lifestyle databases, along with database marketing, of which they were merely the most visible part, were not about to go away. There needed to be a way to accommodate those business managers who not only wanted to use both, but who ideally wanted to combine information from both sources. The professional standards committee of the MRS published guidelines for the handling of databases in February 1995; these allowed members of the MRS to link their research data to other databases, so long as the processing was conducted by their staff on their own premises, and confidentiality was thus maintained. In effect, the research data can be linked at *individual* level, but this linkage must then be used to *model* across the database in question, rather than the respondents being identified to the database owner.

Several high-profile research services have seized the opportunity opened up by this decision. Perhaps the one which has received the most publicity is the link between Taylor Nelson AGB's Superpanel and Claritas' Lifestyle Census. (At the risk of repeating earlier information – but at least it keeps things self-contained – Superpanel is a 10,000 household continuous panel which records panellists' purchases of grocery and other fmcg products. The Lifestyle Census contains the key variables from the merged CMT and NDL databases – some 16 million households.) The Lifestyle Census dataset includes grocery shopping information (e.g. which store used). AGB holds the Lifestyle Census on its premises which it matches at an individual and household level from this dataset to its own Superpanel homes. It then models characteristics of product purchase from Superpanel onto the Lifestyle Census (for instance, for targeting mailings).

Similar in concept, BMRB's TGI can also be 'fused' with the Lifestyle Census. Thus the wealth of information carried on the 25,000-respondent TGI can be modelled across the individuals on the Lifestyle Census. Andy Brown and Anne Mackay presented a paper at the 1996 Admap Targeting Consumers 2000 conference, which explained what had been done, and the results of a validation exercise. The next step was seen as linking TGI to customer databases in another ground-breaking development. The BMRB paper was entitled 'It's lifestyle – but not as we know it'. Tony Cowling of Taylor Nelson AGB also presented a paper, entitled 'New information systems', which covers the development outlined above, and others.

Finally, in yet another development in which market research meets database marketing (with a vengeance), Berry Consulting developed a segmentation system on NOP's FRS – the exotically-named FRS FRuitS. Taking a 'classical' database marketing approach, Barry Leventhal (Berry Consulting's research and statistical director) segmented the FRS respondent database on three interlaced dimensions – product portfolio (ownership and use of financial products); lifestage (based on demographics of respondents); and financial strength (interlacing household income and data on savings and investments). All 60,000 FRS respondents per annual survey can be allocated to one of the eight FRuitS types. Each financial market can be profiled by FRuitS; clients can even create their own customer workbench and attribution approach, thus segmenting their own customers by FRuitS. Powerful stuff indeed!

CHAPTER 11

MEDIA APPLICATIONS

Introduction

As I mentioned in Chapter 2, the launch of geodemographics into the commercial sector effectively took place at the MRS conference in 1979, when three colleagues from BMRB presented a paper showing the discrimination of the new classification (CRN, subsequently rebranded ACORN) on the TGI. One example was discrimination in broadsheet newspapers; using conventional social grade and age, the readership profile of the *Telegraph* seemed very similar to that of the *Guardian*. However, using CRN – with its locational element – showed clearly that *Guardian* readers tended to be 'Inner City High Status'; while *Telegraph* readers were predominantly 'Suburban High Status'. The fact that this work had been done on the TGI – and, fairly soon thereafter, ACORN analyses could be conducted on the TGI, quickly and inexpensively – led to the situation where ACORN was quickly perceived as a media planning tool. The TGI was, and still is, extensively used for media planning, because of its 'single source' nature (product and media consumption on the same survey). The media research and planning community were quick to pick up on this new tool, and ACORN was well used in a media targeting application.

But we're in a fashion business! New methods and techniques come and go – some of them reappear from time to time. I think it would be fair to say that geodemographics is not nowadays much used for targeting 'main', national media (commercial television and press), but is used quite extensively in 'local' media (regional press, door-to-door, mailing). One reason for this (apart from the obvious relevance of geodemographic to 'locational' targeting), in my view, is the fairly early positioning that took place in the UK marketplace. After the initial 'flurry' of media targeting using ACORN, in 1979 and the early 1980s, the Consumer Location System was launched (I think in late-1982) by the Direct Mail Sales Bureau (DMSB). The DMSB was charged with promoting direct mail as a medium, and conducted many presentations to advertising agencies. The Consumer Location System was based on ACORN/TGI cross-tabs, and encouraged ER mailings targeted by ACORN. While a sensible initiative for the DMSB, in my view it served to position geodemographics (to the agency community) as a means of targeting direct mail, therefore 'below' rather than 'above' the line. Add to this the fact that it has not been possible to target commercial television by geodemographics (more about this below), and the 'local media' application has been dominant.

Television

As readers will probably know, commercial television airtime has traditionally been bought on a fairly crude target market definition – largely age and sex, social grade, and perhaps family composition (for example, 'C1C2 housewives aged 25–35 with kids', or similar). While this worked well in the 'old days', when a mass-market audience was easy to buy, it is not very useful in today's fragmented media market. Consequently, Pinpoint agreed with BARB to add geodemographics to the BARB measurement in 1991; the service, called 'Viewpoint', was launched late that year. It stimulated quite a lot of interest but was not commercially successful. It was easy enough to produce an analysis to show (for example) that using FiNPiN rather than 'standard' demographics would enable much tighter targeting of certain financial products; the difficulty came in persuading the TV buying community to *use* the facility! There seemed to be a number of reasons for this:

- it was not part of the culture;

- it would have made the cost per thousand figures look worse (purely as a result of the tighter target definition) and this was seen as undesirable; and

- it would have interfered with the argument that people *outside* the defined target were also potentially 'in the market', therefore prospects.

Of course, there is some validity in the third argument (although not, if we are honest, in the first or second!). One can simply take the view that a 'broadcast' medium like TV cannot be tightly targeted; that is not my view. Indeed, one could speculate that, given the way the media market is moving, that view is an admission of future defeat. Certainly, the technology inherent in digital TV (due in less than one year's time, in its terrestrial form) means that it could be eminently targetable. No doubt market forces will eventually sort this one out!

An interesting development that I was first made aware of in autumn 1995 was the 'Prospector' system, developed for Carlton TV by Prime Prospects. This takes a database marketing response analysis approach to Direct Response TV (DRTV). Having run the DRTV campaign, respondents are datacaptured, then analysed by geodemographics (PRIZM in this case) and lifestyle profile. The resultant analysis enables market size assessment, and responses can be ranked by closest fit to the customer profile. Cost per response can be calculated, as can likely conversion to sale. So campaign effectiveness can be measured, and forecasted ahead, while the campaign is still in progress. It's a very good idea, and by all accounts, works well – having been validated over a number of campaigns. But – what a pity that the output (i.e. geodemographic targets) cannot be put into the loop, and fed in to the spot buying process! Maybe one day…

Cable Television

Of course, cable TV is in a very different position. It knows exactly where its customers live, so could easily use geodemographics, both to analyse 'best' customers for its own purposes (as well as for potential advertisers' purposes), and thus, where it should lay its cables. Perhaps surprisingly therefore, there was little apparent use of geodemographic techniques in the early days of cable TV in Britain. Reasons why this may have been so range from (a) the fact that the old rediffusion networks were predominantly in council estates, where housing density and existing wayleaves dictated the initial strategy, to (b) the American owners of British cable franchises simply adopted the US cable model; lay the cable, then send in the 'heavies' (salesmen) to sign up the punters, confident that mass sales would result. The practice often proved less profitable than the theory, apparently.

In recent years, I have heard several case histories extolling the virtues of the geodemographic approach (and its enthusiastic implementation). It has proved relatively easy to build a geodemographic model, which identifies the most valuable customers (and the most potentially valuable neighbourhood types) who spend the most with the cable companies and – rather importantly – actually pay their bills.

So 'churn' can be minimised and profitability maximised. It is a classic application for geodemographics. An excellent case history was presented by Andrew Chamberlain of Berry Consulting at the MRS Census Interest Group seminar 'Geodemographics for business decisions', March 1996 and subsequently published in *New Perspectives*, June 1997 (see References)

National Press

I mentioned that, in the early days of geodemographics, there was a fair amount of activity in media applications of this new technique. Many of these related to national press. Given cross-tabulations with TGI (and later, with NRS too), readership of any publication measured on these surveys could be expressed in geodemographic terms. This was a new and interesting way of defining readership profiles. Given that it was also easily possible to generate buyer profiles of products and services on TGI, the sales departments of publications could build selling propositions to prospective clients, too. On the other side of the buying/selling divide, agency planners and buyers could conduct similar analyses to explore the suitability of candidate publications for the product or service which they were advertising.

This practice still goes on, to a degree, but varies in intensity dependent on the extent to which the participating organisations have embraced geodemographics. If anything, there has been a resurgence since desktop analysis systems made it possible for agencies to conduct their own analyses in-house. BMRB's 'Choices' software (which contains TGI data) can be interfaced to some of the geodemographic analysis systems, making such analyses straightforward.

Regional Press

Geodemographics has been used in the regional and local press market since the early days of the technique. The former Regional Newspaper Advertising Bureau (RNAB) used a geodemographic analysis system based on postcode sectors from the mid-1980s, and that development work was then consolidated into the PressAd database, run by the Newspaper Society. The PressAd database holds mechanical ad data for regional newspapers, plus circulation data; it also holds the 'footprints' of both free newspaper distribution areas, and paid-for titles' circulation areas. This is supported by geodemographic data at postcode sector level, so it is possible to relate (say) freesheet distribution to a geodemographic profile. Thus the target profile may be compared against distribution or readership profiles. Again, in a strictly geographical sense, retailers' catchment areas may be matched against the 'footprints' of competing titles. Apart from the advertisements in the newspapers, the targeting system is clearly relevant to the coupon or leaflet inserts carried by the titles.

Many regional and local newspapers have themselves taken desktop geodemographic systems in-house, mainly as a selling tool to produce sales aids and presentation material for selling advertising; although I gather that geodemographic analysis is sometimes used by the editorial departments too.

Door-to-Door

(Door-to-door was also covered, in more detail, in Chapter 10; but I try to keep each chapter as self-contained as possible!)

Door-to-door distribution has been a heavy user of geodemographics ever since the technique was first introduced. There is a very obvious relevance, as door-to-door is organised by 'units of geography', generally postcode sectors. Clearly, the ability to target their distributions geographically is very helpful in improving the efficiency of the medium. The usual methodology is to conduct a postcode sector ranking (PSR) exercise. This starts with a definition of the desirable target market in geodemographic terms – generally the key neighbourhood types for the product in question – then the PSR program analyses all the postcode sectors in the defined area, placing them in rank order of penetration of the target market. The output is a table showing the postcode sectors in rank order, highest penetration at the top. This enables a cut-off point to be specified, either at a particular penetration point (for example, all sectors containing 60 per cent or more of the target market) or at a total number of households to be covered.

Door-to-door is a strong medium, particularly in fmcg manufacturing for launch or relaunch activity. Product sampling is a particularly lively area, reflecting the ability of this medium to get samples into the hands of consumers quickly and economically. The medium is also used extensively by fmcg retailers for new store openings or tactical marketing; the fact that the store catchments can be defined by postal geography is clearly helpful in that PSR runs can be confined to the catchments, and no material wasted in peripheral areas. Sometimes, of course, it will be appropriate to door-drop in certain parts of the catchment area where apparent potential exists but where few customers are presently visiting the store. Whatever strategy is being used to 'drive' this medium, geodemographic targeting can help with 'wastage reduction'.

Posters

Given the nature of the poster medium, it is unsurprising that geodemographic analysis of one sort or another has been applied to this medium since the early 1980s. The Mills & Allen Poster Targeting System, designed by Total Media and implemented by Pinpoint Analysis, was launched in 1983. Since then there have been several initiatives, similar in concept but differing in detail, including in the early 1990s, MAI's 'PosterPiN' and Portland's product. In practice, the tricky thing about applying geodemographic analysis to posters is that, although the sites are static, clearly the audiences are not, and account needs to be taken of both pedestrian and vehicular traffic flows. Sites can be categorised as follows:

- 'Locality' posters, sited in local areas (for example, small neighbourhood shopping parades), likely to be seen by only 'local traffic', both pedestrian and vehicular; the geodemographic profile of the *locality*, perhaps a 300-metre radius, should be indicative.
- 'Catchment' posters, sited in the catchment area of a small/medium shopping centre or a superstore (on its feeder roads, or within its centre) where the profile of the *visitors* to the centre should apply.

– 'Roadside' posters, on main through-routes (the majority of important cases, and the most difficult!). This requires knowledge of journey patterns and origin/destination matrices – but is still capable of being modelled.

In the work leading up to the implementation of POSTAR, the poster industry's successor to OSCAR, there was some experimentation with the use of geodemographics; POSTAR was launched in April 1996 and, so far as I understand, does not utilise geodemographics at present. However, in my view, the technique could usefully be applied, and should add value if this were to happen.

Media Boundaries

As I mentioned in Chapter 8 (Geographical Information Systems), 'media geography' is often a useful geography to add to marketing and retail GIS applications. For example, ITV regional boundaries, which come in two forms; non-overlap boundaries from ISBA, and overlap boundaries from BARB. Clearly, these are most useful on a national or regional view, to see which stores (for example) are covered by which ITV station; although they are relevant at a local level too. More obviously 'local' are the independent local radio (ILR) boundaries, showing the geographical coverage of the ILR stations. Of course, the notion of a precise boundary delineating radio (or indeed, TV) reception is rather artificial; but it provides a practical indication. (By the way, RAJAR, the audience research system for radio, can be analysed by geodemographics.) Boundaries of cable TV coverage are useful local media indicators. 'Footprints' of regional and local press were mentioned earlier in this chapter; as was the possibility, using GIS, to overlay such media boundaries on the catchment boundaries of stores, in order to measure 'best fit'.

CHAPTER 12

GEODEMOGRAPHICS AT WORK

Introduction

The aim of this chapter is to provide readers with information on two aspects of the geodemographics market; an overview of the census agencies and their products and services on the one hand, and some selected case histories on the other.

All the agencies currently recognised by ONS and the other census offices are profiled below – other than Chadwyk Healey, which does not deal with the commercial sector. Contact details for all these agencies can be found in Appendix 4, and their main classifications were described in Chapter 3, with details provided in Appendix 2. A profile of Claritas was included in Chapter 4 (under Lifestyle Database companies; contact details of these organisations are in Appendix 5).

Case histories have been provided by three market-leading organisations; Marks and Spencer, Standard Life, and Whitbread. I am grateful to the executives involved for their help, and to these companies for giving their permission.

Profiles of Census Agencies

Business Geographics Limited

Business Geographics Limited was set up in 1993 by former CACI and Pinpoint executives. It became a census agency in 1995. Business Geographics is a Mapinfo Value-Added Reseller (VAR), and has developed a number of marketing GIS applications on this platform. When Business Geographics became a census agency it went on to develop a census analysis package called Censys 95, which as its name implies, runs under Windows '95 on Mapinfo. Business Geographics was the first (and at the time of writing, only) UK census agency to offer on-line access to local area demographic reports on the Internet (web site http://www.geoweb.co.uk).

Business Geographics is strong in the media/media research sector, also operating in the publishing, retail, financial and market research sectors. One of the company's specialisations is sample design and sample frames for the latter sector, using geographical and geodemographic filters to provide wholly representative samples. Business Geographics also conducts statistical analysis and modelling of demographic, geodemographic, market research and business data.

Business Geographics supplies a range of census and GIS-related data, and has a close working relationship with BMRB, and its TGI service.

CACI Information Services Limited

CACI (originally California Analysis Centres Incorporated, but just known as CACI for many years) was set up in 1962 – in California, unsurprisingly. It opened a London office in 1975 and initially operated a site analysis service on a bureau basis. However, CACI's UK market analysis division really started to grow rapidly once ACORN had been 'taken aboard' at the turn of the decade. Now CACI is one of the major players in the UK marketing services arena, operating in market analysis, information systems and direct marketing. Shortly before this book went to press, Business Geographics announced that IPM, the Poster Specialist agency and subsidiary of the InterPublic advertising group, had taken a financial stake in Business Geographics. Poised for expansion?

CACI's market analysis business is strongly centred around ACORN and its variants. ACORN is now one of only two neighbourhood classifications based entirely on census data; however, CACI's formerly resolute stance against lifestyle data changed in 1995 when CACI entered an agreement with ICD to utilise the latter's data, both for list rental, and also for geodemographic applications. A number of products have come from this data source. A third strand of CACI's strategy has been to look for third-party agreements with other data providers and/or trade bodies – examples below.

ACORN benefits from being the first UK neighbourhood classification, the most widely known, and to some extent the generic term (cf. Hoover). It has now been in existence in some form for 20 years. See Chapter 3 for an outline of its methodology. It has been joined by a series of variants; Scottish*ACORN, Northern Ireland*ACORN, and Financial*ACORN. The first two are self-explanatory, having been built from the census data of Scotland and Northern Ireland respectively, and therefore containing some unique neighbourhood types. Financial*ACORN is similar in concept and construction to the old FiNPiN, utilising as it does FRS data, and describing neighbourhoods in terms of their financial characteristics. Another ACORN variant, Investor*ACORN was built using an investor file overlay, to identify areas with a propensity to spend on high-value products. Yet another ACORN variant, Change*ACORN – which examined area changes between 1981 and 1991-based census data – was effective when first launched, but is now getting rather 'long in the tooth'. CACI also markets other census-based 'market indicators' (following in the footsteps of Pinpoint's 'wealth indicator') – lifestage, housing, wealth, and ethnicity indicators.

Another 'tranche' of new products has been developed from ICD lifestyle data. Generally they operate at a postcode level (although they will be aggregated to ED-level if necessary for 'robustness') – they are:

- Paycheck – income profiles
- Auto*Plus – car ownership potential
- Fuel*Plus – cooking/central heating fuel type
- Mail Order*Plus – propensity to use mail order
- House Age*Plus – age of housing stock.

Although the lifestyle data provides the 'base' for these products, census information and market research sources have also been combined to model propensities. These 'single dimensional' indicators tend to be used as overlays, perhaps on ACORN analyses.

CACI has a number of research sources which it can use for modelling small area potential. The longest-standing of these is TGI (see Chapter 7); CACI use Verdict Research data to 'calibrate' the national volumes or values. Recently, FES data has become available to CACI as a source for area potential methodology. GfK data are used in the home improvement and electrical markets. The recent development which made DVLA motor licence data available through agencies has provided CACI with a new dataset; in CACI's case, they have formed a strategic alliance with the Society of Motor Manufacturers and Traders (SMMT), which is one of the agents for the DVLA data. The SMMT has a registration query system called 'Winscreen'; CACI has integrated this with its InSite analysis/mapping system to produce Winscreen Auto*InSite. This particular product is exclusive to SMMT members; it is planned to develop a separate product which will be available to all clients. The detailed data of vehicle registrations by postcode sector can be combined with CACI's demographics to provide a very powerful market analysis tool.

Another example of using 'whole market' data for analysis, is CACI's Mortgage Market Database. CACI has persuaded the institutions responsible for 96 per cent of the UK market for mortgages to 'pool' their data; CACI acts as 'honest broker', taking monthly data from each, and publishing market totals by postcode sector. A similar service is being set up for the savings market. Yet another market analysis service has been devised for the pub trade – called Inn*Focus. This involves analysis of pub catchment areas, analysing both supply, and potential demand. Supply is covered by Quantum/CGA pubs database; potential demand is indicated by demographic profiles from the census of both domestic (i.e. residential) neighbourhoods, 'workplace' demographics (derived from ONS Special Workplace Statistics); and modelled demand for both 'drinking out', and 'eating out', derived from the TGI. This includes frequency of eating out in pubs. Finally, modelled household income is also included.

CACI operates a bureau for 'phone-in' area analysis (it has since its initial set-up in the UK). The service is now branded 'AreaData', and offers very comprehensive types of analysis on 24-hour turnaround. CACI also offers consultancy, on site if required; and specialised training, through its CACI*Skills. For large users, the InSite GIS option is recommended – an analysis and mapping system containing a variety of modules, and loaded with databases to suit the applications required. InSite was originally launched in 1988. The system was completely relaunched in 1995 to run under Windows '95 and NT (this involved writing a proprietary database). InSite modules and applications-specific variants include:

- InSite*Direct (for DM applications)
- ACORN*Profiler (profiling module)
- InSite media module (can link to the PressAd database)
- Insite*Retail (contains Retail Locations database)
- Orphan handling (for insurance company 'orphans')
- Impact modeller (for impact analysis)
- Drivetimes premier (drivetime module).

CACI has had a retail division for many years; unsurprisingly, this being a key market sector. CACI's retail offer includes consultancy, InSite of course, and some specific retail products:

- Retail*Direction (shopping centre catchment definitions)
- Centre classifications (types of shopping centres, classified)
- Shoppers*Choice (retailer share within catchment – uses ICD lifestyle data)
- Provision (supermarket gravity catchment model, and clustering of stores by catchment characteristics)
- Market*Scan (scanning GB for suitable catchments).

Another key division of CACI marketing division is direct marketing. Naturally, this division utilises a number of the ACORN classifications in making name and address selections – as appropriate to the market sector in question. Classifications such as Investor*ACORN are particularly useful in this application. CACI have also devised the 'MONICA' methodology, which uses ER data and predicts age from 'given' name (e.g. Sharon and Gary 'play' Ethel and Percy – see Chapter 5); putting MONICA together with other ER-derived variables, + ACORN, gives Household*ACORN (formerly called ACORN Lifestyles). CACI can also market ICD lifestyle data, for list rental, as well as geodemographic applications. The 'Lifestyle Plus' overlay products, referred to earlier in this section, are also valuable for mailing purposes. The Directors Residence database is also marketed by CACI for list rental. Modelling and scoring systems can be constructed for clients, and indeed, marketing database building also comes within CACI's area of competence.

CACI were the first census agency to exploit the Special Workplace Statistics (SWS) from the census – initially in the 1981 Census decade. These data utilise the 'place of work' question on the census, and produce origin/destination matrices from ED of residence to postcode sector of workplace. Thus, workers in industrial/commercial areas can be profiled; this is particularly useful in analysing the 'workplace' potential for retail or catering outlets in town centres. The SWS data took a long time for ONS to process this census decade; but CACI have fairly recently sorted out the trip matrix, and have launched Workforce*ACORN.

Briefly, other products and initiatives worthy of mention include:

- Market Analysis for Business-to-Business (a link between CACI and Market Location);

- Private Medical Insurance (PMI) modelling – based on TGI, FRS; also, now on lifestyle data;

- 'share of wallet' modelling in the financial services market;

- an arrangement with Brann Software to use Brann Viper software, both for bureau applications, and for supply to clients.

In a more significant move, CACI recently acquired SPA Fieldforce Planning (former sister company of SPA Marketing Systems Ltd; the latter continues as an independent census agency). SPA Fieldforce Planning, as its name implies, had specialised in the optimisation of sales and service territories. CACI has now acquired the specialised software and services developed by SPA, and has merged it with CACI's own Fieldforce Planning business. The SPA name will be used for the newly-formed operation, whose key product offer is Totem97, now 'bundled' with JourneyPlan as a module within InSite.

Capscan Limited

Capscan is well known in the mailing industry as the author of postcoding and address management software. Capscan became a census agency in 1994, and developed a census analysis product called Cenario (in association with Royal Mail, who also sell the product). Cenario is different from other census analysis products, in that it makes 'raw' census statistics available to users on a CD-ROM, with user-friendly software for manipulation.

Cenario is available at different 'levels' -

- Level 1: 50 most commonly-used census variables
- Level 2: an additional 200 variables
- Level 3: access to all the 9,500 variables in the Small Area Statistics.

Different geographical levels (i.e. units of area) are also available –

- Postcode areas, districts, sectors, and TV regions
- As above, plus local authority wards and districts
- As above, plus EDs (with access by unit postcode).

Thus one could run a profile using this most detailed version, and convert it directly to a mailing target using PAF.

Capscan is also agent for two other census-based products:

- SCAMP-2, a census analysis and mapping package for schools;
- CD91, which contains the complete set of 1991 Census Local Base and Small Area Statistics on CD-ROM.

CCN/Experian

CCN was set up in 1981 by Great Universal Stores (GUS), the retail and mail-order group. CCN operated as a credit bureau, and initially its clients were mainly within the GUS group, but it gradually expanded into a third party client base – finance houses, banks, building societies and retailers. CCN specialises in on-line credit information; its credit referencing business is the largest part of the company's business, although it is the targeting part (CCN Marketing) which is of the greatest interest in the context of this book.

At the end of 1996, the CCN Group merged with Experian, one of the largest suppliers of marketing information in the US. GUS acquired Experian for $1.7 billion; Experian had turned over $540 million in the previous year, as against CCN's £120 million. However, there was no doubt that CCN would effectively run the newly merged company, and that CCN's targeting expertise would be made available to Experian's client base. It was decided (effective 2 June 1997) to change CCN's name to Experian, worldwide.

Leaving aside Experian's credit businesses, and Experian Business Information, the remainder of this section concentrates on Experian Marketing. This division splits into two; Experian Marketing Services, and Experian Marketing Analysis. Marketing Services includes the following services:

- address management;
- credit screening (i.e. mailing pre-screening);
- print and mail;
- telemarketing (inbound/outbound)
- list rental (e.g. ER);
- lifestyle ('Chorus' – see Chapter 4);
- marketing database building, on a bureau basis.

A notable product launch in early 1997 was 'Prospect Locator', which provides the ER on CD-ROM, together with a variety of discriminators – the 'standard' ER-based selection criteria, plus MOSAIC – and the names and addresses, once selected, can be paid for on a 'per thousand' basis. This was not the first CD-ROM of this type on the market – see Chapter 10 – but the option of paying for names as you need them for mailing is a nice feature. Experian was the first company to capture and market the ER, back in the early-1980s, and remains at the leading edge of its use.

While still making use of the ER, Experian is 'backing both horses' since it started to collect lifestyle data with Chorus; so it can offer its clients the option of either route for cold list mailings. On the marketing database front, Experian has found that the big, bureau-service databases, built and held on behalf of clients, have shown a resurgence. After former moves by clients to take customer databases in-house, there has been a reversal of this trend, and clients often find it more cost-effective to outsource this activity.

Experian Marketing Analysis is responsible for developing and marketing segmentation systems and the associated software. The main 'product', of course, is MOSAIC, first launched when CCN entered the geodemographic market at the turn of 1986/7, and relaunched in 1993 refreshed with 1991 Census data. As well as the 'general purpose' product, there are now variants; Financial MOSAIC, Scottish MOSAIC and Northern Ireland MOSAIC. MOSAIC segmentation systems now operate in many other markets across the world; I believe it is 15, at the latest count. In recent years Experian has ventured into 'industry specific' discriminators in the UK. Apart from Financial MOSAIC, it has developed 'Clientele' for the alcoholic drinks market. Clientele classifies neighbourhoods into 14 different types, in terms of usage of pubs and catering; it also profiles the number of 'drinking occasions' that each type is likely to take. The behavioural data is sourced from the PAS beer market survey.

In addition to its segmentation systems, Experian has also developed products for estimating small area potential. Products based on TGI have been around since the late 1980s; recently FES has joined Experian's portfolio of data sources. It is now possible to attach MOSAIC codes to FES respondent data, thus producing a variation on Retail Potential Report methodology (see Chapter 7). Experian has also developed a methodology for modelling small area potential for financial products, using market research data (formerly FRS, about to switch to MFS). Predicted scores are modelled at a suitable level; this could be unit postcode, pseudo ED, or postcode sector. Given suitable penetration, market shares can be modelled at a product level. In another market, motor registration data from DVLA became available to Experian in spring 1997; once processed, that data source will give CCN the facility to model motor potential in some detail. Although individual records are very detailed, they are only provided to agencies at postcode sector level.

CCN launched 'Psyche' in February 1995. Psyche was a psychographic segmentation system, based on Synergy's Social Value Groups (see Appendix 3), where CCN 'scored' all the unit postcodes in the country to predict which Social Value Group predominated in each postcode (geodemographics meets psychographics!). The agreement with Synergy will expire in autumn 1997, and Experian will replace it with an agreement with RISC, which has a ten-cell segmentation system. See Appendix 3 for more details.

Experian's delivery system has fairly recently (autumn 1996) been rewritten, this time to operate under Windows. The previous DOS version had been rewritten a number of times since the original, which was SPA's 'Marketing Machine', rebadged MOSAIC Systems when CCN signed a marketing agreement with SPA in autumn 1987 (CCN went on to purchase the software outright in autumn 1990) . The latest (1996) version was branded MOSAIC Micromarketer; it links to SPSS for modelling. Although completely rewritten, it is similar in functionality to the previous version, with internal connectivity between modules. Experian places great store on customer support and training, and sells this as part of the package. Experian has sold literally hundreds of systems over its years of operation.

Experian Marketing Analysis also operates a bureau, at three levels of service:

- 'Data on Call' – basic data, either faxed or posted, with a 24-hour turnaround;

- MOSAIC Solutions – 'traditional' bureau analysis, more sophisticated analyses, modelled potential, etc;

- Retail Consultancy – various forms of modelling, including regression and gravity modelling, catchment analysis, and sales forecasting; and 'qualitative' site analysis, involving production of site reports.

Experian's acquisition of Chas. E. Goad in 1996 fits very well with its retail consultancy. Goad are responsible for producing Goad Plans of shopping centres, which are heavily used by the participants in the retail property market. Goad put all their plans on an ARC/INFO GIS in recent years; this enables not only very flexible mapping output, but also a very flexible database of retail property. CCN's intention is to integrate these data with its demographic data (and vice versa), and to 'export' Goad's expertise into some of the overseas markets where CCN already operates with MOSAIC. As mentioned earlier, Experian has MOSAIC up and running in around 15 countries.

Holland was the first outside the UK, back in 1987; now (at the time of writing), MOSAIC is in ten European countries, four 'old Commonwealth', and the US – where it launched in 1996. More are in the pipeline. EuroMOSAIC has been in existence for a few years; now Experian have developed Global MOSAIC, which takes 14 'groups', common to most countries within which MOSAIC operates. There is obviously more scope for expansion here, and this is clearly a major plank in Experian's strategy. The Experian takeover will give CCN far more firepower in the huge US market than it enjoyed formerly – and will allow it to compete in that biggest, and most competitive, geodemographic market. It has also given CCN a new name!

CDMS Limited

CDMS is owned by the Littlewoods organisation and is one of the longer-established players in the geodemographic marketplace. Its main product is the SuperProfiles neighbourhood classification, which was first launched in 1986 (originally by another company, Demographic Profiles, but subsequently acquired by CDMS in 1987). SuperProfiles was updated, with various improvements, in early 1994. Detail of the design and construction of the new version will be found in Peter Batey and Peter Brown's contribution to *GIS for Business and Service Planning*.

CDMS has developed a suite of Windows-based software products which allow users to manipulate SuperProfiles and associated data. GEOPROFILES allows users to view key census variables for any catchment area made up of postcode sectors (for example, retail site analysis). ROLLCOUNT software provides fast and accurate household counts by SuperProfiles and household type (from the ER) and can be used to target mailings and household distribution. SOLUTIONS establishes the geodemographic and geographical distribution of a customer file by using the full postcode (i.e. a profile plus geographical analysis). CDMS also offer the PROSPEX desktop GIS system, under licence from Beacon Dodsworth.

CDMS provides a range of services – including database management, list rental and credit referencing – on a bureau basis. It operates across most market sectors, and is particularly strong in the automotive, leisure, and financial sectors.

Equifax Europe (UK) Limited

Although Equifax has been operating in the UK credit referencing marketplace since 1988, until recently it has not been a major player in the UK geodemographics industry. Equifax (Europe) UK Limited is part of the huge US-based Equifax Inc., which turns over approximately $2 billion worldwide. Equifax initially took a 50 per cent stake (with the Next Group) in Precision Marketing International in the UK. This included the former Wescot credit referencing business, indeed, the credit 'arm' of Equifax has been the larger part of its activity in the UK. It built market share gradually, until in late 1994, it took over Infolink, which not only gave Equifax a much larger critical mass in the UK credit referencing market, but also brought with it two existing geodemographic classification systems – DEFINE (which was essentially census-based), and PORTRAIT (based mainly on NDL lifestyle data). Infolink's PORTRAIT, launched in October 1994, was ironically, taken over about a month later by Equifax. Subsequently, NDL renegotiated their data supply contract, and PORTRAIT was taken back into the Calyx group (and subsequently replaced by PRIZM).

This background helps to explain why Equifax Decision Solutions, the consultancy 'arm' of Equifax UK, spans *both* geodemographic and credit applications, and incorporates products like risk models alongside more 'traditional' geodemographic products; while Experian, which also operates in both the credit referencing/scoring and geodemographics markets, keeps these two areas of expertise in separate divisions. In essence, Equifax Decision Solutions adds value to the Equifax data resources, and builds client solutions from these resources. Data resources include:

- ER, including derived attributes such as years of residency at that address, household composition, 'attainers' (i.e. of age 18);
- a generic risk score (derived from credit referencing activities);
- age and income estimates (derived from ICD data);
- 'credit activity' indicator (derived from credit referencing activities);
- credit worthiness indicator (based on penetration of CCJs);
- DM response indicator (derived from ICD data);
- geodemographic classifications (see below);
- ICD data (lifestyle data covering 6 million individuals);

- census data (Equifax is an approved ONS census agency);
- directors database (sourced from Companies House – Infocheck).

Perhaps unsurprisingly, Equifax will be utilising many of these data sources to produce a new geodemographic classification – MicroVision. This will effectively replace DEFINE (it is an ever-changing scene, as readers will have noticed!). MicroVision will be unusual in several respects:

- it will utilise *both* census *and* lifestyle data;
- it will exist in three distinct forms:
    - a generic 'all purpose' classification;
    - market specific versions for example, insurance, other financial services, leisure, motor;
    - custom – a bespoke solution built around customer data.

To be specific MicroVision will be built from the following data sources – census, ICD lifestyle data, ER, credit, unemployment, directors, shareholders.

At its most detailed level, MicroVision will consist of no fewer than 200 clusters, which will then be aggregated into one of the three versions (generic, market specific, or custom) – which are the levels at which the solution may be used. The 200-cluster solution forms the 'building blocks' from which the other versions will be constructed. Equifax' strategy is to provide *multiple* classifications to its clients, rather than a single classification directory.

Equifax markets its basic data resources under the 'Dimensions' brand. Dimensions provides a highly-segmented consumer list, for list rental. A recent development has seen this resource released on CD-ROM, following EuroDirect's similar initiative. Equifax has an agreement with ICD to use the latter's Lifestyle list for list rental purposes (as well as within other derived products, including MicroVision).

Recently, Equifax signed an agreement with Berry Consulting to market the latter's 'FRuitS' segmentation system, built on NOP's FRS. 'FRuitS' takes a database marketing approach to market segmentation, looking at FRS respondents on dimensions of both product holdings, and Lifestage (see Chapter 10). The agreement allows Equifax to append the FRuitS classification to the ER, and/or to client databases.

Another collaboration, this time with Synergy Consulting, has led to the second 'marriage' between psychographics and geodemographics, the first having been CCN's Psyche (launched in February 1995). Like the CCN product, Equifax has modelled the predominant Social Value Group (SVG) at a unit postcode level, and markets it as the 'Social Values Directory'. There is an intention to build customised psychographic directories; experience suggests that, although this will be a more expensive option, it is likely to work better than a general purpose solution.

In autumn 1996, Equifax launched a MapInfo-based delivery system, branded MicroVision PC. Its PC Profile software links in to MicroVision; other modules include 'Builder', which enables users to build scorecards for response modelling, and 'Monitor', which monitors mailing selections for response, and builds that information into the next selection. (The MicroVision brand now refers both to the neighbourhood classification system, and the delivery system – MicroVision PC.)

To better address retail applications, Equifax has formed a relationship with The Data Consultancy (see separate entry), whose 'Illumine' software handles area analysis and profiling. The Data Consultancy has developed expertise in the retail sector over many years; which will no doubt help Equifax up the learning curve. Equifax' previous expertise has been concentrated mainly in the financial services sector, and in DM applications.

As the name Equifax Europe (UK) suggests, Equifax has much wider European ambitions than 'just' in the UK. So far, this has led to operations in Spain, Portugal and Eire. The Iberian venture involves credit referencing, DM, and geodemographics (a MicroVision classification has just been developed in Spain). In Eire, Equifax formed a joint venture with the Irish Post Office, the result being PMI (shades of Equifax' UK heritage!) which has – so far – developed DM capabilities. Developments are pending in other European countries.

A recent restructure within Equifax Europe (UK) created vertical market teams to service four business sectors (financial services, motor and manufacturer, retail, and communications/utilities). All information sources, analytical tools and consultancy services are supplied by the Decision Solutions Group into each vertical market team.

EuroDirect Database Marketing Limited

EuroDirect was set up in the early 1990s with the strategy of providing data and software at relatively low cost, to enable marketing people to conduct their own analyses. Its software product, DemoGraf*, was first launched in 1992, running under Windows; the first market analysis software to run on this operating system. EuroDirect's 'Neighbours & PROSPECTS' neighbourhood classification system was launched at the same time. EuroDirect also offered ER selections; so a user could profile a customer file and convert 'best' Neighbours & PROSPECTS types into postcodes for ER mailing.

EuroDirect has developed a number of new products in recent years. Neighbours & PROSPECTS was rebuilt with 1991 Census data (relaunched in 1994), and more recently, a series of data overlays have been added. These overlays operate at unit postcode level: they are -

- – the *financial* overlay (for assessing credit risk);
- – the *investor* overlay (for assessing implied affluence);
- – the *income* overlay (for assessing income band).

An additional overlay – the media overlay – comprises a set of media boundaries for use with EuroDirect's GIS – DemoGraf*, and for mailing selections from their ER products.

EuroDirect has recently developed and launched a census-based classification for Northern Ireland – Neighbours & PROSPECTS Northern Ireland.

EuroDirect also provides ER-based products for database building and cleaning, supplied on CD-ROM. It was the first UK company to provide the ER on this medium; its products are -

- – the UK Residents Database (a prospect database enhanced with household overlays and neighbourhood classifications);
- – RollCall (for verifying and cleaning databases);

– RollCall Trace (for locating individuals at any level of postal geography).

EuroDirect offers a range of DM services, either on a bureau basis, or provided to customers for in-house use. The latter are usually supplied on the DemoGraf* GIS platform, which has been extensively rewritten since its initial launch. DemoGraf*'s functionality includes market analysis, profiling, catchment area definition and evaluation, and mapping.

GMAP Limited

GMAP (Geographical Modelling and Planning) was founded in the University of Leeds School of Geography in 1989. GMAP is unusual in its blend of the commercial with the academic; its management team continue to lecture within the School of Geography, while also running a very successful business. This business is centred on the spatial interaction modelling originally developed in the School of Geography during the 1970s and 1980s (see Chapter 8 for more detail).

GMAP has refined this modelling technique, and used it across a variety of clients in retail, retail financial services, automotive, petroleum and pharmaceutical markets. The process involves the creation of market models, which then enable GMAP's clients to understand their competitive position, and to formulate strategies accordingly. The main applications are to:

– improve strategic network planning;

– measure outlet performance;

– predict the impact of market changes;

– identify areas for further growth;

– measure consumer behaviour;

– gain competitive advantage.

GMAP is a census agency, and offers standard 'packs' of census variables, which may be ordered by country (i.e. England, Scotland, Wales, GB and Northern Ireland); and also a Residents and Workers product (derived from the SWS) of flows of workers.

SPA Marketing Systems Limited

SPA was set up in Leamington Spa in the mid-1980s. Over the intervening period the original company developed into a number of areas, one of which was retail consultancy. This is SPA Marketing Systems' business (the sister company, SPA Fieldforce Planning, had recently been sold to CACI when this was written). SPA's forte is retail segmentation and local market analysis.

SPA Marketing Systems is a small consultancy which works with a relatively small number of large clients on strategic projects. Apart from consultancy, SPA also supplies and supports databases and software to run on clients' own PCs. The company is licensed by CCN (now Experian) to supply MOSAIC Micromarketer, and the MOSAIC classification; SPA can also supply the Tactician desktop GIS. SPA has written the 'Blueprinter' system, which analyses store and catchment data in order to facilitate store segmentation and branding.

In addition to census data and the MOSAIC products, SPA also supplies a series of locational databases:

- Tourist Attractions;
  Cinemas and Theatres;
- Shopping Centres;
- BR and Underground Stations;
- Universities, Colleges, Institutes and Halls of Residents;
- Airports;
- Banks and Building Societies.

SPA's customer base includes a number of large high street retailers, the drinks industry, and service industries, especially travel, leisure and finance.

The Data Consultancy

The Data Consultancy is a part of the URPI group, which was set up in 1975. Its main business is the supply of spatially-referenced digital datasets for use in geographical analysis. It has a catalogue of over 1,000 datasets; all of which have been rigorously checked, translated (if required), and enhanced. The key strategy is to provide data 'off-the-shelf', so users may work productively with the data straight away. A key dataset is the 1991 Census (the 1981 Census is also held); a large range of 'packs' of census data can be supplied, including the Northern Ireland data. Digital map datasets are also important; a full range of products derived from Ordnance Survey and AA mapping data. Boundary data for GIS (including census, postcode and administrative boundaries) are supplied. The Data Consultancy is a member of the ED-LINE Consortium which created the 1991 Census ED boundary file. Neighbourhood classifications are provided under licence from their authors, and retail outlet files are also supplied.

The Data Consultancy is a MapInfoVAR (and was MapInfo European Partner of the Year in 1996), holding regular training courses on MapInfo and MapBasic. The Data Consultancy's own Illumine for Windows software provides census analysis, mapping, market and spatial analysis on a PC, on the MapInfo platform. The Data Consultancy has also written the award-winning Drivetime system for generating drive time isochrones. By working at street level, with a road network of 2.4 million links, Drivetime can generate isochrones and routes of great accuracy.

Area analyses are also provided on a bureau basis for any area, however defined. These include census demographics, population updates, area component reports, neighbourhood profiles, population projections, consumer analyses, retail business turnover potential reports, drive time isochrones, retail outlet reports, market penetration reports, and census mapping. The Data Consultancy has a very wide client base across many sectors, both commercial and public sector ; from large multi-nationals to small estate agents.

(*The Data Consultancy have asked us to highlight the fact that Illumine is a registered mark and Drivetime is a registered trademark of The Data Consultancy.*)

Yellow Marketing Information Limited

Yellow Marketing Information is the holding company for three subsidiaries; Geoplan, Tactician UK, and Market Profiles.

Geoplan has built a solid business on the base of postal geography boundaries, produced in association with Royal Mail. More recently, on becoming a census agency, Geoplan has enhanced the boundaries by producing 'packs' of census data at postcode sector, district and area levels. A special feature is quarterly updates to reflect any changes to postal geography made by Royal Mail. All these data – boundaries and census data – are available in digital form and in a wide range of formats. Geoplan also publishes the *Postcode Marketing Directory*, a hardback book containing detailed information (including census data) about every postcode area in the UK.

Tactician UK is the UK distributor for Tactician, the desktop GIS (see Chapter 8). A recently developed application, Tactician Situate, is a GIS designed specifically for the analysis and mapping of retail catchment areas and producing area population profiles; it incorporates 200 census counts at postcode sector level, plus postcode information from Geoplan, and maps derived from OS data. Tactician UK creates customised systems with applications such as sales territory management, distribution planning, retail location analysis, DM analysis, and media selection.

Market Profiles is a strategic marketing consultancy, which utilises the resources of Geoplan and Tactician UK as required in the formulation of solutions.

Marks and Spencer Case History

Introduction

Marks and Spencer (M&S) needs little introduction – it is the UK's most admired retailer, and arguably its most successful over the long term. This case history reviews the rationale for setting up the Footage Assessment Unit (FAU) within M&S; the data they use, and the methodology which they employ.

A small team was assembled which reviewed the GIS market, chose a short-list, bench-marked candidate systems, and chose to go with Laser-Scan. Then the FAU team worked very closely with Laser-Scan in implementing the system, including the embedding of M&S' gravity model into the GIS. The success of the FAU may be judged from the fact that now, no retail developments, UK or worldwide, are undertaken without the involvement and input of the FAU.

Rationale

In 1990 the company identified a need for a more rigorous approach to setting the strategy for the store development programme. The reason for this was that a substantial budget was being spent in driving forward the acquisition of real estate, and there was a real desire to maximise the business benefits. As a consequence, the business created the FAU in 1990.

Although the brief was simple, the implications were far-ranging. The newly created unit undertook an analytical understanding of current markets and the way the business traded into them. With the knowledge gained, it could identify areas where sales could be further increased, either by improving merchandise on offer, or by store development. This process would lead to identification of specific areas or sites that could be targeted for acquisition by the property arm of the company.

In addition to driving the strategic overview for development, the process could provide sales forecasts for individual store developments, and indeed predict how those stores would perform over the full evaluation period of 15 years.

The company's aim was that the unit became a centre of excellence for utilising technical solutions in support of every day business decisions.

In setting up the approach to this agenda, certain analytical principles had to be established which would see the unit through its developing years. These were:

- all techniques must be applicable worldwide;
- these techniques must be flexible to local data availability, and indeed local trading knowledge where it existed;
- the results of all analysis, however detailed, must be clearly and simply understood by members of the board who needed to take the investment decisions.

For the results of the analysis to be truly universal in application, it was important at an early stage to identify the relevant sources of information, whether they existed within the company or not. The data came eventually from four main sources: the census, the customer, the market and data modelled from all three. For maximum flexibility the use of the analysis and data had to be available at a suitable building block level for the UK and indeed in most areas of the world. This now tends to be the existing local postal geography.

The UK building block is the postal sector, of which there are 9,000 within the UK, each containing some 2,000 – 3,000 households.

Key Data

1. Census

The census provides the fundamental data essential to the understanding of trading catchments and the prioritisation of store opportunities. Population and household data are of obvious significance in any modelling process. Similarly, the study of population densities allows us to understand rurality/urbanity which in turn affects different types of stores in different ways. Ethnic origin variables are of great importance. Interestingly this is the case worldwide where, for example, in some of our stores in European cities, the significance of the ethnic minority 'English' is important for M&S' sales performance. Lifestyle profile information is being used by many organisations, usually via off-the-shelf proprietary systems supplied by a handful of market analysis consultancies. This information is used extensively within M&S as it has enabled it to identify groups who are more likely to respond to the company's offer. Real commercial advantage will be gained by those organisations who can bespoke customer segmentation processes by introducing their own commercial data to the process. Household characteristics are important because they allow quality checks to be made on measures regarding affluence, for example owner occupation, car ownership, etc.

2. The Customer

The company has undertaken an extensive quantitative research programme over the last six years. During that time over 700,000 people have been interviewed, covering nearly two-thirds of the M&S chain. This information has proved invaluable in allowing the company to understand the expenditure patterns of its customers, and to identify the lifestyle profile of its customers. The data has been of paramount importance in enabling M&S to identify trading catchments for the chain of just under 300 stores. Over time, the method of defining catchments has improved substantially in terms of accuracy.

M&S has found little benefit in defining catchments of stores in terms of a crow-fly distance or a uniform drive time from the centre. People do not behave in this way when they plan their shopping trips.

It became obvious from the initial survey data that there was far greater significance being attached to 'mental maps' as opposed to purely physical proximity or drive time. The significance of the motorway system in facilitating retail trips was also apparent. Catchment areas could become extensively elongated if a motorway passed through in one direction, and considerably narrowed if there were only local roads passing through in a different direction. Similarly, people's reluctance to travel 'out of their patch' was clearly shown in certain areas of the country. For example, there is a marked reluctance among people in Lancashire to travel to shop in Yorkshire, and vice versa, and this cannot be explained away by distance, because in some cases the distances involved are very small indeed.

M&S now uses a combination of sales penetration and spatial proximity of postcodes to define and smooth the trading catchments of their stores. Increasingly the value of the M&S chargecard database is becoming obvious. Over five and a half million customers regularly use their card. The amount of information being provided enables shopping patterns and basket profiles to be understood more clearly along with distances travelled by people to shop within M&S stores. Fascinating insights are also gained into how a customer interacts with a small hierarchy of stores, for example, edge-of-town, regional centre, high street or food neighbourhood.

3. Market Data

The key data item under this heading is obviously the market sizes available to M&S by key product area. The creation of this dataset is usually the first one that is undertaken whenever analysis is carried out in a new country. In addition, information on the physical characteristics of retail destinations is of great importance, for example, sizes, location of competitors, turnover, etc.

4. Modelled Data

By pulling together the data from the key sources already identified, the modelling process is undertaken to produce new datasets which drive the strategic and site-specific analysis which is required by the company. The results of this analysis manifest themselves in three key areas.

i) Sales Forecasts

Sales forecasts are undertaken using various methods depending on the type of estimate required, i.e. a new, stand-alone, edge-of-town location requires a different approach to an estimate for an extension to an existing high street store. The core analytical tool however, is a form of the traditional retail gravity model. The key components of the model being a recognition of:

- catchment definition;
- distance decay;
- market size;
- customer profile;
- store attractiveness; and
- competition.

Under the confines of the form of the traditional model, there are a series of sub models which are used to predict the individual model parameters. For example, the expenditure component of the model has multiple regression models of its own which take account of existing market share, customer profile, and footage provision, provided both by the company and other retailers. The output from the model is simply a parameter value which is fed into the main gravity model.

The parameter for the attractiveness function has been modelled over the entire store chain where survey data exists, i.e. in some two hundred stores covering some 700,000 customer records. The parameter for the distance decay component of the model has been modelled in a similar way. Both parameters are derived iteratively in SAS using the PROC NLIN function.

Traditionally distance decay has been considered as a form of the negative exponential function. M&S' own studies indicate that in fact a gamma function is a more robust way of modelling, especially when using drive time from postcode centroids to a store location. This is due to the fact that not much trade is generated to the store from the first one to five minutes, where traditionally this would be non-residential town or city centre locations, the majority of spend starts to peak at around five or six minutes, and then tails away in a traditional negative exponential pattern.

ii) Market Share

A form of the basic gravity model is used to 'scan' the entire country and disaggregate store sales back down to postal sector level. This disaggregation when compared against the databases of consumer expenditure, allows the company's performance to be checked by way of market share. This is undertaken once a year at the end of the financial year and offers a snapshot in time which progressively monitors how the company is performing and identifies where stronger or weaker areas exist geographically.

iii) Uplift Potential

Market share on its own does not allow a strategic view to be taken as to where sales could be increased. A modelling process has been put into place which, by taking the evidence of newly-developed stores and their effects upon the local market place, seeks to identify areas where the potential to drive the additional sales can be maximised in the most cost-effective manner. The process is meant to address several key issues, mainly:

- Are areas of existing low market share ever likely to change regardless of M&S activities? For example, does the profile of the customer base in the area make it unlikely market share could ever be increased?

- Does the existing market share look low simply because people living in the area do not have a full M&S representation available to them, and therefore could they be turned on to higher levels of spending activity with an expanded or new offer?

- In areas of high market share, has saturation point been reached, and would further investment in those areas be uneconomic? Is a new store's sales only driven by cannibalised trade?

- There are certain parts of the country where although the existing market share is very high, it can be driven still higher by offering a wider and broader range of M&S products, known within the business as the 'Camberley effect'. It is essentially a high elasticity of demand for M&S products.

By looking at the uplift potential map both nationally and locally, areas of priority can be identified which drive the strategy for store development. This approach is used in all countries where M&S is either trading or is looking to trade in the future.

The initial aim of the unit was to become a centre of excellence within M&S, offering an independent and consistent input to the process. This has been achieved, and now there are no developments anywhere in the world, authorised by the board without a FAU analysis and recommendation. Accountability is high because tills do not lie! The analytical principles have been adhered to as the techniques discussed in this case history now are applied in the UK, France, Spain, Holland, Belgium, Germany, Switzerland, Italy and Japan.

This case history is based on the paper presented by Steven Bond, senior manager research & development in the FAU, to the MRS Census Interest Group's seminar 'Geodemographics for Business Decisions', March 1997. I am grateful to Steve for his permission to use it; also to his colleague Mike Fishwick for his additional insights into the work of the FAU.

Standard Life Case History

Introduction

Standard Life is the largest mutual life assurance company in Europe with over £40 billion of assets under management. The company sells life assurance, pensions, unit trusts, PEPs and health insurance products through two main distribution channels in the UK:

- the Independent Financial Advisor Division services approximately 6,000 independent agents (IFAs) who offer financial advice and planning to the public and can sell the products of any life company;
- the Direct Customer Division (DCD) sells only Standard Life products through the company's own sales force of 300 financial planning consultants (FPCs) and 100 appointed representatives (companies that can only advise on Standard Life's products).

This case history focuses on the use of GIS, geodemographics and statistics to define the strategy and develop the operations of the FPCs specifically, and Standard Life's retail operations in general. It reviews the period 1989–96, and explains the development of GIS and geodemographics within Standard Life over that period.

The table below illustrates the events that occurred over the eight-year period in question, and the GIS/geodemographic systems and solutions that were adopted. CACI's 'InSite' desktop analysis system was chosen, together with CACI's geodemographic classifications (ACORN, Financial*ACORN, and PayCheck).

Year	Systems	Solutions
1989	Introduction of direct field force	InSite and ACORN	Profiling and basic reporting
1990			
1991			
1992			
1993	Separate branch structure identified	Financial*ACORN	Branch locations
1994	DCD strategy outlined New sales process developed		Territory allocation
1995	Central Lead Generation launched Marketing Database built		Customer and market segmentation
1996	Implementation	InSite Financial*ACORN Pay Check	Statistical modelling Territory potential Market segmentation

The first significant event in this period was the establishment of the direct sales force; this was initially seen as a very poor relation to the traditional broker-orientated sales channel. There was only gradual acceptance over time within the company that direct selling was a viable alternative to the 'traditional' channel of distribution. The main source of business for the FPCs was prospecting for new clients, rather than identifying cross-selling opportunities within the existing customer base. The problem was that, despite a customer base of four million people, the limited opportunities for contacting existing customers made the FPC force inefficient. The only part of that customer base open to the FPCs was the 'orphan' customers (customers introduced by an agent who is no longer authorised to give advice on Standard Life products).

The original decision to purchase a GIS and geodemographic classification was driven by the business need to bring some science to the art of setting targets for the field force. Existing target setting methodology was largely based on management judgment; there was no existing mechanism to measure apparent area potential. The target-setting methodology that had been envisaged was to:

-   develop a measure of underlying demand from market research data;
-   extrapolate those measures using GIS and geodemographics across the whole population;
-   measure the relative potential of Standard Life against market potential;
-   adjust and equalise the sales force targets against the measures of potential.

However, in the event the task proved to be more complex and difficult than had been originally envisaged. Although there were spin-off benefits, even at this stage (in terms of profiling, customer segmentation, branch catchment definition), some key lessons were learned:

-   GIS and geodemographics requires a long-term commitment to build a team of people with the knowledge to use the system and interpret results.

The presentation of results in a digestible format to non-experts is a skill that must be learned to ensure buy-in.

- Problems with data were encountered; for example, finding a market research source which could be used in a suitably disaggregated form, and obtaining suitable customer data from internal sources and systems, proved more problematic than originally envisaged.

(In the author's experience, these lessons apply fairly generally; this case history is particularly valuable in highlighting them for a broader audience.)

Branch Territory Redesign

By 1994, the DCD had increased its profile within the company to the extent that the decision was taken to separate the two distribution channels within Standard Life, both organisationally with a new management structure, and physically by locating the FPC teams in new branch premises. This project required the identification of the optimum number of new offices to efficiently service the country, and the actual location of those offices.

Working with CACI, a sample of the DCD's potential customer base (orphans) was taken and profiled using Financial*ACORN. A profile of most likely potential customers was agreed and the analysis applied across the country to define (in broad terms) sales potential. Broad criteria were applied to define and map optimum territories. A consensus figure of 20 locations was agreed and boundaries drawn to equalise potential.

The results of the work were presented and used to assist the creation of the new territories, although branch location decisions were also influenced by existing location of staff and availability of premises through the property investment portfolio.

New Strategy for DCD

During 1994, a new and more focused strategy for the DCD was developed. The primary objective was to broaden Standard Life's distribution base away from the company's traditional reliance on the IFA channel. The company also acknowledged that to make a direct field force operate in an efficient and profitable manner, the consultants' efforts must be focused entirely on selling.

The new strategy called for a number of specific projects to be run in parallel with a view to creating an integrated technological environment for the FPCs to operate within. The key elements of the new strategy were:

- a marketing database to manage customer contacts and generate selling opportunities through DM techniques;

- a call centre to centrally manage customer contacts on behalf of consultants;

- new laptop-based financial planning software to enable FPCs to quickly and accurately assess customers' financial needs, and also remain compliant with the increasingly stringent regulations controlling the sale of financial products.

Another event which occurred in late 1994 had a major effect on Standard Life's DCD strategy. The Halifax Building Society announced its intention to create its own life assurance office within the Halifax group. Thus the Halifax could no longer be an appointed representative of Standard Life. This loss of a new business stream was balanced by the immediate creation of almost 600,000 new 'orphan' policy holders who could be approached by Standard Life's FPCs. This change provided a major business impetus to start testing the new strategy. A series of DM activities and systems projects were carried out that provided substantial business benefit in terms of retaining customers and increasing customer awareness. In addition, variations on the basic strategy ideas were tested and the lessons learned incorporated into the main development project.

Implementation of the New Strategy

The implementation of the various elements of the strategy took two years to complete. During that time a number of opportunities for the use of statistical analysis and modelling, in combination with GIS and geodemographics were identified.

In the event, the new systems and the various sub-projects around them have not only created much of the infrastructure for the integration of GIS and geodemographics much more thoroughly into Standard Life, but also provided the business drivers to do so.

The major benefit has been to give direct access to customer and policy information held on the marketing database, along with the facilities of the system to enable the selection and output of specific subsets of data for further analysis using InSite. Also, the customer data is further enhanced by being linked directly to the contact and response data resulting from the DM activity. The creation of the marketing database has ensured that Standard Life has as complete a picture as possible of its customers using data that has been processed specifically for the purpose rather than culled from elsewhere.

In parallel with the new systems, two segmentation projects have been carried out to improve Standard Life's understanding of its current position.

Customer Segmentation

This project looked inward at Standard Life's existing customers as these one million 'orphans' would form the basis of the FPC's market for the foreseeable future. The methodology involved taking a random sample of customers, identifying key variables from the associated customer and policy information, and carrying out cluster analysis on these variables. Demographics and market research data were attached to the resulting clusters. Key variables proved to be age (both customer's current age, and customer's age when they first bought a Standard Life policy), and type of product held. Thirteen clusters (segments) were found. In the event, demographic differences were slight; it was hypothesised that this resulted from the fact that the majority had been introduced by IFAs, whose customers were fairly homogenous.

Market Segmentation

This project is far more ambitious and complex than the customer segmentation exercise, and only initial conclusions have been reached to date. One of the problems has proved to be the difficulty of obtaining data of sufficient quality to support meaningful conclusions. The project has taken a wider view than customer segmentation; besides gathering data on demographics and existing product purchasers, future behaviour and attitudes have also been researched. Results to date have suggested eight segments; further work is being carried out to quantify these groups and provide an accurate descriptive mechanism. CACI's products (ACORN, Financial*ACORN and PayCheck) will be used to define the attributes of each segment, and the models applied through InSite to identify and quantify present and future market potential.

The Future

The new systems which were implemented to support the development of the DCD have already been described. There is also a new collaborative project between life offices aiming to deliver high quality data about customers' current buying patterns and the value of sales. This will greatly improve current market estimates, as market share by product could be assessed geographically. The main data areas created by the new systems will be:

- customer and policy data;
- contact records;
- customer responses to DM activity;
- appointments made;
- business sold;
- future opportunities identified;
- product information requested;
- not interested.

From this data and the work that has already been completed, a number of opportunities present themselves:

- building response models for specific marketing campaigns;
- generating predictive response models to improve response rates;
- identifying cross-selling opportunities from the customer segmentation;
- cross-matching the market segmentation with the customer segmentation;
- sales territory potential measure;
- territory design and efficiency modelling;
- customer lifetime value.

The major GIS and geodemographics project will be *territory potential*. The intention is to combine data from Standard Life's own database (number of orphans, number of current clients, number of leads generated), with geodemographics and the new market size and value data to build a detailed model of business potential. The model of potential will be calculated for each postcode sector across Great Britain and then amalgamated into the FPCs territories using InSite.

It will be possible to test the predictive strength of this model using campaign results, and the follow-up data that is captured after each appointment fulfilled by an FPC. By testing a number of versions of the potential model, a reliable model should be created quickly.

Conclusion

The implementation of GIS and geodemographic applications and their integration into company strategy is a long-term process. GIS involves a significant 'learning curve' which must be progressed stage by stage to ensure that maximum return on GIS investment is achieved. At the outset, the use of these systems and techniques must be driven by a genuine business need to ensure acceptance. The requirements for systems should be incorporated into related projects at an early stage to ensure that adequate resources can be assigned to create an environment for the development of new ideas and proposals.

It must be a key objective that skills and knowledge are concentrated in a small core team, whose task should include the dissemination of the capabilities of GIS and geodemographics as well as the communication and application of analysis results. The team must become effective advocates of the benefits of GIS and geodemographics, while delivering relevant and practical project solutions to the business.

Progression along the GIS learning curve must happen in parallel with continuous improvement of other information systems which provide inputs for analysis. Hence the development of a marketing database and subsequent customer and market segmentation projects were key stages in implementing a GIS solution for Standard Life.

The publishers are grateful to Standard Life, and specifically to Graham Wilson, its database and statistics manager, for permission to use this case history. It was first presented at the AGI '96 conference in September 1996.

Whitbread Case History

Introduction

Although Whitbread is generally thought of as a brewer, in fact brewing now accounts for only about ten per cent of Whitbread's profits. The company is actually a major retailing organisation; apart from almost 4,000 pubs (managed plus leasehold), it operates over 1,600 Thresher off-licences, plus Beefeater pub-restaurants, Brewers Fayre theme pubs, Pizza Hut, David Lloyd Health Clubs, Café Rouge, Costa Coffee, TGI Friday's; and also has substantial hotel interests in Marriott Hotels UK and Travel Inn.

Whitbread was an early adopter of geodemographics, starting to experiment with ACORN back in 1980 and maintaining a keen interest in geographical analysis ever since. In 1993, Whitbread started to build a centre of expertise within the Group market research department relating to the geographical manipulation of data. This reflected the importance of this activity to the rapidly-growing portfolio of property locations. The intention was to provide a cost-effective service to Whitbread Group clients of the market research department, and also to design and develop techniques to better support Group property acquisitions and marketing promotions across the different sectors within which Whitbread operates.

Background

The case study in question was carried out for the Thresher off-licence chain for one of its newer retail concepts known as Huttons. This new brand name has actually already been widely rolled out to relaunch the existing food and drink convenience stores, however it had also been used on three much larger sites in an effort to create a broader and more comprehensive range of goods in a much less off-licence-based concept.

These three larger Huttons stores were proving to work well but the application of existing convenience store thinking was not helping them to understand the concept sufficiently to take it forward. Some store-based interviewing was carried out and while its results helped understanding of the consumers' requirements, it was their postcodes that helped Whitbread to understand the site requirements.

Method

The interviewee postcodes were geodemographically profiled, frequency weighted and the average spend applied so that we could further understand what was driving the catchment areas. Whitbread also created what it calls the 70 per cent nearest catchment area by calculating the distance of each respondent to the outlet, which helps the company to represent its core catchment area.

Let us not underestimate the value in just displaying the respondents on a map against geographical features. It was by doing this that Whitbread were able to see why one of the stores was under performing because it was on the council estate side of a dual carriageway and was quite inaccessible to the affluent, higher-spending yuppies on the other side of the road.

Using the information collected above Whitbread were able to identify the elements of the store catchment that it would then use in order to target new sites, including a realistic estimation of the catchment area, the important geodemographic types, a minimum population figure and the importance of certain physical features to the outlet.

Nationwide Search

At this stage of the project a collection of all the EDs of the correct geodemographic types was undertaken and were then used to site intersect themselves so that the isolated instances could be disposed of. Then cluster analysis (K-Means) was carried out on the X and Y co-ordinates of the remaining EDs of the correct geodemographic types in order to try and create concentration of the best types of customers.

This is probably the area in which the methodology could do with the most improvement as invariably the clusters were created by eye, using the estimated catchment as a measure of how well each cluster was forming. However, as an understanding was developed through using this iterative technique the clusters began to fall out much more easily, although this did not stop it being a time consuming process.

This process created over 700 potential sites which were then further site analysed based on the estimated catchment around the centre of each cluster, and as a result some sites were lost due to low levels of favoured geodemographic type people and total people overall. Many were also lost due to close proximity to existing sites, or to a lack of quality retail sites within the areas defined.

Implementation

The next major step was providing the Thresher site development staff with enough information in order to define these small catchment areas so as to enable their experts in the field to find the great sites to make the concept work. This was done by using maps with high quality OS road information to define the catchment areas and also address list dumps from the Post Office address file to even further define the exact area in question.

As a result of this exercise the Thresher site development team have been able to continue the rapid growth of the Huttons brand throughout the UK with this piece of work contributing to the development of around ten new large store sites. No apologies are made for the simplicity in many of these stages of analysis as this has helped in explaining the true value of the work to the development team's clients and has enabled understanding of both its limitations and its strengths.

This case history is adapted from a presentation given by Steve Binns, Research Executive within Whitbread's Group Market Research Department, at the MRS Census Interest Group Seminar 'Geodemographics for Business Decisions' in March 1997.

CHAPTER 13

PRESENT AND FUTURE

Introduction

The census of population remains as the backbone of geodemographics. However, as I have related in this book, there has been a progressive introduction of other data sources into geodemographics – even to the extent that two neighbourhood classifications have been based on lifestyle data, with no census data present. I would speculate that, when we come to the release of 2001 Census data, there will still be census agencies committed to developing new classifications based mainly on census data; but there will also be competitors choosing to use lifestyle data, and it is difficult to predict what the relative importance of the competing data sources will be. To some extent, market forces may well dictate which way this 'contest' goes. The ONS and the other census offices are currently engaged in planning the collection and dissemination of the 2001 Census, but details of terms and conditions for prospective census agencies are only likely to be firmed up over the next two or three years. The effective cost of using census data in the geodemographic marketplace post the release of 2001 Census data, may well determine the degree to which census data are used, or are substituted by lifestyle data.

Notwithstanding this observation, it is appropriate to the intentions of this book to review some aspects of census data. I have retained some of the material from the first edition, for example, a review of the differences between the 1991 Census and its predecessor held in 1981. The purpose of this is to give readers an overview of 'what is in the census', and what can be used for marketing purposes. I have also reviewed briefly the plans for the 2001 Census, and the stage that has been reached in the planning cycle of the census offices.

The chapter continues with a commentary on the main non-census data, notably lifestyle data of course; then I review the 'state of the market'. Finally, trends and influences on the market are discussed.

Differences between 1981 and 1991 Censuses

In overview, the 1991 Census was very similar to that conducted in 1981; most of the questions were common and the basic methodology of data collection and dissemination was similar. However, there were some changes which are outlined below. It is not appropriate to the scope and purpose of this report to go into too much detail; I have tried to keep in mind a 'need to know' consideration for the typical reader. Hence, the main changes are summarised here, and references given to further sources for those who may be interested in more detail.

In the 1991 Census, there were *new questions* on:

- term-time address of students;
- ethnic group (as well as country of birth, which was asked in 1981);
- limiting long-term illness;
- central heating in home;
- weekly hours worked (asked in 1971, dropped in 1981);
- information to give a count of dwellings and building types.

In addition, there were new answer categories on household tenure and economic position.

At the suggestion of the Market Research Society, a 'lifestages' classification was added to census output for the first time in 1991. It is a summary household composition/economic activity classification, designed to attempt to identify households at different stages in their development. The breakdown is (for persons, and heads of household):

- Aged 16–24
    1. With no children aged 0–15 in household
    2. With children aged 0–15 in household

- Aged 25–34
    3. With no children aged 0–15 in household
    4. With children aged 0–4 in household
    5. With youngest child in household aged 5–10
    6. With youngest child in household aged 11–15

- Aged 35–54
    7. With no children aged 0–15 in household
    8. With children aged 0–4 in household
    9. With youngest child in household aged 5–10
    10. With youngest child in household aged 11–15

- Aged 55 up to pensionable age
    11. Working or retired
    12. Unemployed
    13. Pensionable age – 74
    14. Aged 75 and over

– all analysed by whether or not living in a 'couple' household.

I have no doubt that these variables will be much-used, and valued, by the marketing community.

Other changes included some *changes in definitions*.

- Changes in some questions
    □ Couples living together, not married ('consensual union'!).
    □ Economic activity; 'current', rather than 'usual', economic activity.
    □ Those unemployed in the week before the census were only asked 'previous job' if they had worked in the previous ten years.

- Changes in coding
    □ The 1981 classification of occupations was replaced with the new Standard Occupational Classification (SOC).

There were also some *methodological changes*.

- In 1991, those households absent at census time were asked to complete a form on their return home, and post it to the census office.

- The census form required the addition of the *postcode* in 1991, and this was data-captured by the census offices. (More about this later.)

– Households absent on census night, but whom the enumerator felt were occupied (rather than vacant) were 'imputed'; that is, they were given characteristics similar to neighbouring households. This change, plus the counting of households absent on census night but who returned forms subsequently, represent a considerable change from previous practice. The totals should be more complete, but are not strictly comparable with the previous census.

Finally, changes in *output* from the previous census. The statistical results of the census are available in two forms; printed reports, and statistical abstracts. It is the latter, available in computer-readable form, that forms the 'raw materials' of geodemographics. The Small Area Statistics, or SAS, are the data available at ED level. The 1991 output contains no fewer than 9,000 statistical counts for each ED in England and Wales, and for each 'Output Area' (OA) in Scotland (more about the Scottish difference in a moment). These 9,000 counts are approximately twice as many as were produced from the 1981 Census; as explained in Chapter 3, this huge number of counts is the result of cross-tabulation of variables.

Another innovation for the 1991 Census was the production of Local Base Statistics, or LBS, which are 20,000 counts for local authority districts and wards (but not for EDs). These are used mainly for planning purposes by the public sector. More relevant to the private or commercial sector is the production by the census offices of SAS output reorganised by *postcode sector*, which is of course, a geography now much-used for marketing and operational purposes. This was facilitated by the capture of individual postcodes on each census form – an innovation for 1991, as mentioned earlier.

The General Register Office (Scotland), or GRO(S), made even more use of postcodes than did OPCS in England and Wales. GRO(S) has mapped and 'digitised' unit postcodes, specifically for census use; it has aggregated these postcodes into OAs, which average less than half the size of English/Welsh EDs, and which 'nest' into 1981 EDs, thus facilitating analysis of change over the decade. By this means, postcode boundaries coincide exactly with OAs in Scotland, whereas in England and Wales, unit postcodes may 'straddle' ED boundaries. Nevertheless, a useful innovation for 1991 was the production by OPCS of a computer-readable directory linking whole and part postcodes to EDs, with a count of households in each whole or part postcode. So, for the first time, there is an 'official' link from EDs to postcodes, rather than the situation which existed for the 1981 Census which was described earlier.

There are a few other types of output worthy of mention here. The census offices provide Special Migration Statistics (SMS), which are based on a comparison of address on census night, with address one year before the census. They also produce Special Workplace Statistics (SWS), which are based on analysis of Ward or ED of residence and postcode sector of workplace, thus providing origin and destination data. The latter source is particularly useful, giving the pattern of flows from residential areas to workplace areas. For example. it can be used to model lunchtime 'populations' in centres, relevant to catering, shopping, and so on, and the geodemographic characteristics of these populations.

Finally, another very significant innovation for the 1991 Census, is the Samples of Anonymised Records (SARs). For the first time, the census offices have released sample files (in computer-readable form) taken from individual census returns. If that makes you feel nervous, don't be; enormous trouble has been taken to ensure that privacy is fully protected, and that the files are truly 'anonymised'. There are two files; one a two per cent sample of individuals, the other a one per cent sample of households. The main benefit of these files is that it is now possible to 'get beneath' the aggregated data intrinsic with ED-based output, and see the true patterns in the individual data. The ESRC have commissioned these tables from the census offices, and they are held at the Census Microdata Unit (CMU) of the University of Manchester. Apart from the sociological research that will no doubt form the backbone of SARs usage, the CMU is authorised to make these data commercially available (under certain conditions), and I would expect SARs to find a good market among, for example, market research companies devising sampling frames, and census agencies conducting detailed research into geodemographics.

Readers wanting to know more about these topics should consult the publications which cover them in more detail; for instance: *An Introductory Guide to the 1991 Census* (edited by Barry Leventhal, Corrine Moy and James Griffin, NTC Publications); *User's Guide to the Census* (edited by Angela Dale and Cathie Marsh, HMSO); the *1991 Census Definitions* volume, referred to earlier; and the various user guides published by the census offices.

I would also refer you to Appendix 10 to this book titled *1991 Census Output Areas*, which shows very clearly the 'census geography', and the numbers of units of area of each type. You will see, for example, that there are 113,196 EDs in England and Wales, plus 38,255 OAs in Scotland. I am very grateful to Chris Denham of ONS for providing this table, and for other help with this book.

Plans for the 2001 Census

Some time after the publication of the results of the 1991 Census, there was some controversy in the media about the 'missing million'. This was founded on a discrepancy between the population that was found to be present by the 1991 Census, and the Registrar-General's mid-year estimate for 1991. (The mid-year estimates in question had been based on the 1981 Census, 'rolled forward' and adjusted for births, deaths and migration.) After some investigation, it was concluded that there *had* been some undercoverage in the 1991 Census, particularly in some inner-city areas, and particularly among young males. 'Boost factors' were published by ONS, to enable adjustments to be made to 'raw' census variables to compensate for under-coverage.

After this problem had been recognised and resolved for the 1991 Census, the census offices were naturally very conscious of the issue when laying plans for the 2001 Census. Accordingly, one of the main planks in their strategy for 2001 is a commitment to 'getting the coverage right'. Recognising that it is very difficult to physically enumerate some areas of the country – and that even the census validation study fieldwork had hit similar problems to the Census itself – the ONS is considering a 'one-number census' (ONC) as an option. This would involve conducting the census as before, but then cross-checking the results against independent sources, and producing a single version of the number of people in the country in 2001. The application of 'correction factors' to remove inherent biases from any under-coverage that occurs would improve the output from a marketing point of view. Of course, in an ideal world, a census would be just that; a count of 100 per cent of the population and households. The fact that the world is *not* ideal will have occurred to most business people; looked at another way, the 98 per cent population coverage apparently achieved by the 1991 Census provides much greater accuracy than we are normally used to. So an ONC makes good sense, and the idea has been broadly supported by groups such as the MRS Census Interest Group, and the Association of Census Agencies.

Other strategic ideas being discussed by and with ONS include:

- 'free-flow' processing, where census forms from different geographical areas are processed in whatever order they arrive (as against the former, sequential processing, when batches of forms and data from them were processed in a predetermined order);

- concurrent release, where national totals are released at the same time as local statistics (formerly, output has been in 'tranches', following sequential processing);

- 100 per cent processing of *all* variables (so the 'hard-to-code' variables, for which only ten per cent samples had been coded within EDs, would be 100 per cent coded for the 2001 data).

A number of new topics (i.e. new questions) are being considered for the 2001 Census. Chief among these, in terms of commercial sector interest anyway, is to ask an income question. In the past, the census offices have argued against asking an income question, fearing that it would reduce response. A census test has just been fielded (mid-June 1997) in eight different local authority areas covering about 97,000 households in Great Britain. (The Northern Ireland census office also conducted a census test covering some 9,400 households in Northern Ireland.) The purpose of the census test is to enable the census offices to evaluate new collection and processing methods, an alternative style for the census form, and to test public reaction to new questions; crucially, to the income question. Response rates will be compared for forms carrying the income question, and those not, so the impact of the income question may be assessed. Among collection procedures, postal methods of collection of census forms are being tested. The use of GIS software for planning ED boundaries is being tested; as is the use of automatic data capture and coding technology.

In terms of output, the MRS Census Interest Group has made a case for coding census output by the 'standard' marketing classification, social grade (ABC1C2DE) – which would be a first, if implemented. This issue is being discussed within the census offices currently. (See Appendix 8 for details of social grade.) Currently, although it is possible to approximate to social grade for 1991 Census output, it can only be done by aggregating socio-economic groups, as shown in Appendix 8. Direct coding would be much more accurate, and I have no doubt, would be widely used by the marketing and market research community (alongside neighbourhood classifications, of course!).

'Output geography' from the 2001 Census is likely to change, from that currently in use. ONS is considering having *different* units of area for 'input' and 'output' geography. 'Input' geography will be EDs as before; but it is probable that the data will be published for OAs. The details of this are still under discussion, but it is considered likely that OAs will be made up of unit postcodes (which would be defined with the use of Ordnance Survey AddressPoint data, i.e. the digitised locations of individual households). The thinking is that OAs will be bigger than the current Scottish OAs (the latter averaging only some 50 households), perhaps 150 households on average for England and Wales; that is, not much different in size from current EDs. OAs could be defined by the data, so there would be an opportunity to make OAs as demographically homogenous as possible – which would be of benefit to geodemographics. OAs would either 'nest' into postcode sectors (in which case, they would fit precisely), or into wards (where there would still be many cases of unit postcodes straddling ward boundaries, so OAs would not fit exactly into wards). Given the paramount requirement not to disclose census data about identifiable individuals, the options for different output geographies are constrained, lest it is possible to break confidentiality by 'differencing' between slightly different populations in overlapping areas. This is a complex subject, and some observers including myself view it as much more of a theoretical than a practical problem; but of course we must be mindful of the politics of this issue. The census must be *seen* to be totally confidential!

The precise *nature* of census output is far from settled at present. While it is probable that the familiar type of SAS tables will be produced once more, this is not certain. ONS are expecting much more demand for 'customised' output in the next census decade; and indeed, given the likelihood of electronic dissemination, this will be much more feasible than in the past. Bound up in this issue, of course, is the nature of the relationship between the census agencies and the census offices; to date the census agencies have effectively acted as VARs and 'sold' into the commercial sector (mainly), while ONS, GRO(S) and (now) NISRA have dealt with the other, public sectors. No doubt there will be lively discussions between the census agencies and ONS over the next few years! It is clear that in any event, there are 'tensions' between the ONS' intention to make data 'cheap and accessible', and the requirements for ONS to recover costs.

Currently, the business cases for census topics are being evaluated, as are the results of the census test. However, the forms of output will continue to be debated well into 1999. A white paper is due to be published in the second half of 1998, by which time, many issues will be clear. The census offices have had a system of user consultation in place for many years, through a series of advisory groups. For the first time, a business advisory group has been set up this census decade. There is no doubt that this has assisted considerably in making the commercial sector's voice heard. Before that, the only real forum for discussion between the census offices and the private sector was the MRS Census Interest Group, which did (and still does) an excellent job of lobbying ONS et al. The more dialogue there can be, the better the mutual understanding, to state the obvious. Readers of this book wanting to better understand the matters dealt with in this section should either contact the MRS Census Interest Group, or census customer services at the addresses given in Appendix 1.

Non-Census Data

The point has been made in various parts of this book, including earlier in this chapter, that lifestyle data now represent a viable alternative to census data in geodemographic applications. There is no doubt that the big operators who own the lifestyle databases will either market it themselves in this application, or source it to other companies to do so. As I speculated in the previous section, the 'balance of power' between census and lifestyle data will probably be driven by market forces. If an income question is asked on the 2001 Census, one of the big advantages of lifestyle data will disappear – at least while census data are 'fresh'. But to repeat a theme which I have espoused for some years – the ideal scenario for geodemographics is to use census and lifestyle data in combination, thus exploiting the strengths – and negating the weaknesses – of both.

Credit data (in the context of credit searches at a unit postcode level – a 'credit activity indicator') has become an important part of some of the neighbourhood classifications over recent years. However, it is rumoured that a change of heart among the credit granting organisations who operate the closed user groups which form the basis for credit referencing, may lead to credit search information being disallowed over the next 12 months or so – which will leave a considerable gap. Certainly, the situation is under review as this chapter goes to press.

The use of the ER, too, appears at first sight to be under some sort of threat, given recent statements by the Registrar of Data Protection (DPR). Strictly speaking, the ER – as a statutory requirement – does not fall within the remit of DPR, but nevertheless, such statements should be taken seriously, as it is always possible to change the law if sufficient pressure should build up. However, the indications are that use of ER data in DM applications will *not* be covered in the imminent white paper, which will incorporate the EU directive on data protection. More about the ER appears later in this chapter.

The Current Marketplace

The UK market for geodemographics and lifestyles has changed markedly over this decade. It shows signs of increasing maturity; a number of well-established players are competing, some head-to-head, others occupying particular niches. New market entrants are very few. The decennial nature of the census imposes a particular life cycle on the geodemographic market; it is possible that there will be a flurry of activity early in the next century, centred on the release of new census data; but in the meanwhile, it is developments in the application of lifestyle data to market analysis that are making the running.

In the geodemographics market, CACI and Experian (formerly CCN) jostle for the lead, currently comfortably ahead of their nearest rivals in terms both of turnover and breadth of products, services and sector coverage. Equifax is best placed to challenge their lead, with a new line-up of products and plenty of resource. Claritas Micromarketing comes at the market from its very different strategic viewpoint, armed with the huge lifestyle census database and the objective of 'picking off the big players'. Meanwhile, CMT's Storescan service beavers away in the fmcg arena, a far bigger player than its public profile reflects (its clients have ticked the 'no publicity' box). Most of the other geodemographic companies/census agencies are going for their own well-defined strategies, some competing with the 'majors' on price, some (like GMAP) adopting a very different approach. Others have found their own particular niches.

The lifestyle database market continues to be very competitive. It might have been expected that the coming together under common ownership of CMT and NDL would have decreased competition – not so. The two companies continue to compete for list rental business, and ICD's new ownership has certainly led to that company strongly increasing its data-gathering activity. Consumer Surveys has also made a significant impact on the market; and Experian's Chorus, although not huge in volume, has generated fresh, good quality data. Overall, there is no shortage of data for rental, or for geodemographic applications. The news that ICD is considering an entry into the geodemographics marketplace in 1998 is fascinating indeed! The impending launch of Claritas' modestly-named 'Lifestyle Universe' – where the 25 per cent of households missing from the Lifestyle Census, are 'filled in' from ER and other data sources, using data fusion – promises to be another significant development.

Looking at the international scene, there is a distinct trend towards globalisation. Experian now operates a classification system in at least 15 countries worldwide (and GlobalMOSAIC has followed on from EuroMOSAIC!). Claritas, now quite dominant in the US geodemographics market since acquiring NDS from Equifax, has continued its march into Europe. Apart from its UK operation, it trades in Germany (where it bought IFMS), France, Holland, Austria and Switzerland. And Equifax Europe has operations in Spain, Portugal, France and Ireland – as well as its UK setup, of course. It launched MicroVision Spain in mid-1997. All these international expansions have a rationale beyond the obvious desire of the companies in question to grow their businesses; they cater for multi-national clients, for whom the ability to deal with the same supplier across different markets is often important (as is the case with, for example, advertising agencies or market research companies).

In the last chapter, mention was made of the 'blending' of geodemographics with psychographics. CCN (now Experian) launched Psyche in February 1995; this involved modelling the characteristics of unit postcodes in order to attribute each one to one of seven social value groups (SVGs) with Synergy's psychographic segmentation. A current development in this fascinating area is a realignment, in which Equifax will take over the relationship with Synergy in the UK. Equifax has conducted a modelling exercise, similar in principle to that formerly done by CCN, which has resulted in a 'social values directory' of unit postcodes. Equifax intends to offer the facility to clients to build customised psychographic directories. Meanwhile, Experian is about to launch a joint venture with Research Institute on Social Change (RISC), which operates socio-cultural monitoring systems across 40 countries (including both Western and Eastern Europe and the Americas). The new development – Neighbourhood RISC – involves building statistical models for each country where the joint venture operates, to predict for each local area, the likely percentage of residents in each of the ten RISC segments. The final outcome is the assignment of a RISC segment code to every postcode, enabling targeting by psychographics. More details of both Synergy SVGs, and the RISC segments, will be found in Appendix 3.

Another development in the targeting marketplace that is happening currently is a move to make ER-based list rental accessible to smaller business users. The first initiative involved GB Information Management and ICD, and was sold through Kall Kwik printshops. GB's compiled CD-ROM (of which, more below) is used by Kall Kwik staff to generate targeted names and addresses, and the key to its success in this application is that there is no minimum order, unlike normal list rental practice. The trial conducted in early 1997 through six Kall Kwik branches was successful, and is now being rolled out. Presto Print, a competitor of Kall Kwik, is now also trialling a similar offer. There is no doubt that this distribution method is key to the viability of this idea, as the small numbers involved would not be of interest (or commercially viable) to the normal list rental operators. However, to Kall Kwik – in the business of selling low volume print runs to small businesses – this list offer adds value and makes it possible for small businessmen to generate local, targeted mailings.

Looking around at other significant developments on the scene, the move by a number of suppliers to 'package up' the ER on CD-ROM has been mentioned earlier (Chapter 10) – and the GB Information Management product was briefly mentioned above, in the context of the Kall Kwik venture. GB's product (branded The National Register) is based on ER names matched to PAF, plus ICD lifestyle data where available, and also including the PRIZM and FIND classifiers from Claritas. It is a very complete product, offering 13 applications, including mortality screening and 'gone-away' data. As mentioned previously, other organisations produce similar products, although not necessarily with as many data sources attached (for example, Equifax, EuroDirect, Capscan, Data Discoveries and Experian). When the development is taken as far as GB's product, I think its significance is the preparedness of the other data owners involved to contribute their data to this 'pool'. Perhaps we will see other examples of 'data sharing' in future.

Reviewing some of the subjects which were 'hot' in the first edition, I noted:

- the signs of lifestyle data starting to complement geodemographic data;

- the production of digital ED boundaries by two organisations – 'ED91' by Graphical Data Capture, and 'ED-LINE' by a consortium involving Taywood Data Graphics, LRC, MVA and Ordnance Survey;

- the spectacular proliferation of GIS, particularly desktop systems.

I also speculated on some things I expected to happen.

- I was right about strong growth in the geodemographics market following the mid 1993 release of 1991 Census data; but I was wrong about the number of classification systems increasing 'substantially'. They didn't.

- I expected far more 'customised' classifications, customised to markets, to client companies, to products. There has been development at the market-specific level, and I have heard of a few 'client-specific' developments, but less than I had expected.

- I predicted the 'merger' of data sources (for example, census-based geodemographics, lifestyle data, credit-based data, market research data) to form a larger market information resource. That is happening, but only just. More to come?

- I believed that the fmcg sector would embrace geodemographics more wholeheartedly, in areas such as trade marketing. There has been little sign of this, other than in areas such as Storescan.

- I expected lifestyle databases to continue to grow and flourish, and to 'swap' data and techniques with geodemographics. OK on this one.

- I saw PCs on end-users' desks as the norm, in terms of delivery systems, with GIS providing the mechanism to manipulate and map the data. It has happened to a large degree, but there is far more room for growth yet.

- I predicted the *integration* of the data sources and techniques mentioned here, into management information systems (MIS), feeding clients' information needs. Only in its infancy still, I would judge – but that should be the end game, rather than the analysis systems sitting out on a limb somewhere.

About seven out of ten, on a four-year timescale. Perhaps we should give it until the end of the decade!

Market Influences and Future Speculation

Of course, the geodemographics and lifestyles market must be seen in the context of the broader marketing and media scene. That scene has changed dramatically, and continues to change at an ever-increasing pace. The old marketing and advertising models and methods, that developed in the late 1950s onwards after the launch of commercial TV in Britain, are looking as old and tired as they are. They were still operating perfectly well in the mid 1970s, even into the early 1980s; but the combination of media fragmentation and technological advance has ensured that their days are numbered. I take no satisfaction from that observation. I was a practitioner, back in the days when those models and methods worked well, when grocery products could be successfully mass-marketed on the back of heavy ITV spend (and indeed, the very fact of a heavy ITV spend was the way to get the grocers to stock them!). The world was much simpler then – for consumers, for marketers, for ad agencies. Direct marketing was something done by relatively few, small agencies, with 'traditional' mail order clients.

It would be impossible – indeed, pointless – to try to disentangle the chicken-and-egg pattern of which change caused which outcome – society? consumers? media? advertisers? retailers? – but there can be little doubt that the main agent for change was information technology. The growth in 'computing power per pound' has been exponential. It was reducing computing cost that made geodemographics possible, first developed on mainframes and minis and delivered on a bureau basis; then in the last decade, both developed and delivered on PCs or workstations. Reducing computing costs made lifestyle databases viable, and helped them to grow to their current size. More fundamentally, reducing computing costs enabled the database marketing revolution to take place. Most consumer-facing companies are at least experimenting with customer databases; the more successful of these companies are likely to have a reasonably sophisticated database.

It was speculation on how interactive media might impact on 'traditional' mass advertising that led Don Peppers to his conclusions, subsequently published in his book (jointly authored with Martha Rogers) *The One to One Future*. In other words, the *ability* of consumers to interact with suppliers, carried to its ultimate conclusion, would demand that suppliers compete for 'share of customer' – and effectively, compete for business one customer at a time. The precise opposite of the mass production/mass media model that formerly held sway. There are a number of examples of one-to-one marketing in action – but relatively few, in the scheme of things. As technology advances, surely there will be more. But whether we accept Don Peppers' argument that one day all marketing will be like this, or not, the desire for customer dialogue is already there. Database marketing allows that possibility; relationship marketing requires it.

In my view, we are likely to exist in a transitional state between mass marketing and one-to-one marketing for a very long time. In some markets, we may never get beyond 'mass customisation'. However, it is customer connectivity that will set the agenda, and the mass media model will gradually decrease in relevance. Apart from the fact that technology will make interactive communication more widely possible, there is the parallel requirement from marketers for more *accountability* of advertising, for more *measurability*. They can get this information from their databases. While you *can* evaluate advertising effectiveness – and you should – it is much easier to evaluate the effectiveness of direct communications. Please note – direct *communications*, not necessarily direct mail! The all-powerful medium of television will be available for direct communications, once digital television has arrived.

Digital television will hasten the demise of 'mass' advertising, for two reasons. Firstly, it will contribute to fragmentation, by making many more channels available. But secondly, digital TV sets will be *individually addressable*. You will be able to target them, individually. And if set-owners take the interactive option (i.e. connecting the set to a telephone line) this will open up a much more potent interactive market than that currently offered by the Internet – which is accessible to a much more limited audience.

This new world of one-to-one communication, and/or dealing with customer segments, as the case may be – where precision, measurability and accountability will be the watchwords – will be a natural home for the data and techniques developed in geodemographics and lifestyle marketing. While the lifestyle 'crusaders' say there will be no substitute for *individual* data, I cannot agree; it will be 'horses for courses' as it is now. Individual, one-to-one dialogue may be the 'end game', but sheer practicality will still require clustering and segmenting, particularly when looking to recruit more customers. Take, as an example, the 'Prospector' response analysis system, mentioned in the media section (Chapter 11). This analyses responses to DRTV, and is presented as being based on lifestyle data. It actually uses the PRIZM neighbourhood classification, supported by the FIND income profiling systems. Both lifestyle data based, it is true; but 'raw' lifestyle data could not produce response profiles, it requires geodemographics for that. Similarly, in broader targeting applications, there are some instances where individual selections make sense, there are many more when some sort of segmentation model needs to be applied. Sometimes this will be geodemographic segmentation. So I see a continuing role for both geodemographics and lifestyles, whether in DM applications (both 'cold' recruitment, by whatever medium, and when enhancing customer databases for campaign planning); or in retail applications, where geodemographic techniques are likely to hold sway. Knowing *where* your best prospects and customers live will continue to be crucial, and modelling local area potential is the bedrock of store location strategy. GIS, whether 'heavy end' systems or inexpensive desktop systems, will continue to proliferate as the means for best understanding the geographical patterns that underlie retail or quasi-retail applications.

So, in conclusion, although the marketing scene has changed markedly in the four years since the first edition of this book, the geodemographics and lifestyles market has grown strongly; and the signs look good for that situation to continue.

Happy Analysis!

It should be noted that while not individually marked in this book, many of the brand and service names mentioned are registered to the companies involved.

APPENDICES

THE ONS CLASSIFICATION OF LOCAL AND HEALTH AUTHORITIES OF GREAT BRITAIN

Chapter 3 outlined how a census-based neighbourhood classification is produced. This appendix gives a practical illustration of two aspects of such a classification.

Table A specifies the variables that were used in the classification, both by description of each variable (e.g. 'percent of residents aged 0-4') and by the census cells utilised (e.g. L020012/ L020001*100). These cells are taken from the Local Base Statistics (LBS), rather than from the Small Area Statistics (SAS) normally used by the census agencies. LBS relate to wards and districts, SAS relate to Enumeration Districts (EDs). Thus the ONS classification, because it is built from relatively 'course' geographical units, cannot be linked to unit postcodes in the way that the commercial classifications can.

Table B illustrates the 'Families, Groups and Clusters' that were derived in the ONS classification. To give examples; 'Family 1' is Rural Areas, 'Family 2' is Prospering Areas, etc.; within these Families are Groups, for example, within Family 1 are Rural Areas in Scotland, Coast & Country, Mixed Urban & Rural. At the most detailed level, the Clusters are numbered 1–32. For example, Clusters 1 and 2 occur within the Scottish Group. The average penetration percentages are given for each input variable, for each Family, Group and Cluster (it is worth studying the tables in question to get the hang of this); so with a little work, you may understand the profile of each.

Readers requiring more details should contact:

> Census Marketing and Customer Services
> Office for National Statistics
> Segensworth Road
> Titchfield
> Fareham
> Hants
> PO15 5RR
> Telephone 01329 813800

Table A: Specification of Variables Used

Cell numbers are taken from Census Local Base Statistics. Scottish equivalents were used where necessary.

	DIMENSION: DEMOGRAPHIC STRUCTURE	
included	percentage of residents aged 0 to 4	L020012/L020001*100
	percentage of residents aged 5 to 14	(L020023+L020034)/L020001*100
	percentage of residents aged 25 to 44	(L020089+L020100+L020111+L020122)/L020001*100
	percentage of residents aged 45 to 64	(L020133+L020144+L020155+L020166)/L020001*100
	percentage of residents aged over 65	(L020177+L020188+L020199+L020210+L020221+L020232)/L020001*100
	percentage of residents identifying as black	(L060003+L060004+L060005)/L060001*100
	percentage of residents identifying as Asian	(L060006+L060007+L060008)/L060001*100
excluded	percentage of residents aged 15 to 24	(L020045+L020056+L020067+L020078)/L020001*100
	percentage of residents aged over 75	(L020199+L020210+L020221+L020232)/L020001*100
	percentage of residents identifying as white	L060002/L060001*100
	percentage of residents identifying as African	L060004/L060001*100
	percentage of residents identifying as Pakistani or Bangladeshi	(L060007+L060008)/L060001*100
	percentage of residents born in the New Commonwealth	L070055/L070001*100
	percentage of residents born in the Third World	(L070001-L070004-L070043-L070259-L070289-L070325)/L070001*100
	percentage of residents imputed	L180005/L020001*100
	DIMENSION: HOUSEHOLD COMPOSITION	
included	average number of household residents per household	L200411/L200001
	households with 4+ children as percentage of all households with children	L460241/L460001*100
	percentage of all households which are single working age person households	L430025/L430001*100
excluded	percentage of all households which are single pensioner households	L430013/L430001*100
	households with 4+ children as percentage of all households	L460241/L430001*100
	households with children as percentage of all households	(L310002-L310001)/L310002*100
	one adult households as a percentage of all households	(L310026+L310014)/L310002*100
	one adult with children households as a percentage of all households	(L310026+L310014-L310013-L310025)/L310002*100

DIMENSION: HOUSING		
included	percentage of residents in owner occupied accommodation	(L200412+L200413)/L200411*100
	percentage of residents in public sector rented accommodation	L200418/L200411*100
	percentage of residents in private rented accommodation	(L200414+L200415)/L200411*100
	percentage of residents with no central heating	L490222/L490170*100
	terraced as percentage of all dwellings	L610005/L610001*100
	purpose-built flats as percentage of all dwellings	(L610006+L610007)/L610001*100
	percentage of households in dwellings with 7+ rooms	L220008/L220001*100
	average number of rooms per person	L220009/L220073
excluded	percentage of residents in private rented accommodation (unfurnished)	L200415/L200411*100
	percentage of residents in private rented accommodation (furnished)	L200414/L200411*100
	percentage of people in households with 7+ rooms	L220080/L220073*100
	percentage of people in households living at more than 1.5 persons per room	L230055/L230051*100
DIMENSION: SOCIO-ECONOMIC CHARACTER		
included	percentage of residents aged over 1 living at a different address 12 months before	L170013/L170001*100
	percentage of residents aged 18 and over with an HE qualification	L840004/L840001*100
	percentage of residents in households where the head is in class L1 or 2	(L900012+L900007)/L900002*100
	residents in households headed by someone in class IIIn (non-manual)	L900017/L900002*100
	percentage of residents in households where the head is in class L4 or 5	(L900027+L900032)/L900002*100
	percentage of households with 2 working adults and no children	L360056/L360061*100
	percentage of households with 2 or more cars	(L210005+L210006)/L210002*100
	percentage of all dependants in lone carer households	(L300030+L300070)/L300010*100
	percentage of all children in single adult households (100% counts)	(L310022+L310034)/L310010*100
	percentage of household residents in households without a car	L210045/L210044*100
	persons in employment travelling to work by public transport	(L820002+L820003+L820004)/ L820001*100
	directly standardised rate for limiting long-term illness	age/sex specific rates calculated from tables 2, 12 and 13 applied to the European Standard population
excluded	*percentage of residents in employment, working in another district*	L820013//L820001*100
	percentage of children in unwaged households	(L360006+L360012+L360018+L360030+ L360036+L360048)/L360066*100

	lone parents with children as a percentage of families (10% count)	L860014/L860013*100
	inactive lone parents with children as a percentage of families (10% count)	L860280/L860013*100
	percentage of families which are concealed	L880113/L880105*100
	percentage of residents living in a different district 12 months before	(L150001-L150004-L150005-L150006-L150007)/L020001*100
	percentage of residents living outside UK 12 months before	(L150014+L150015)/L020001*100
	percentage of residents in households where the head is a manual worker	(L900027+L900032+L900022)/L900002*100
	crude rate for limiting long term illness	(L120001+L130003+L130004+L130007+L130008)/L020001

	DIMENSION: EMPLOYMENT	
included	unemployment rate for men and women of working age	(L080134-L080149-L080150-L080151-L080680)/(L080020-L080035-L080036-L080037-L080566)*100
	percentage of working age women who are employed	((L080571-L080585-L080586-L080587-L080588)+(L080590-L080604-L080605-L080606-L080607))/L080533-L080547-L080548-L080549-L080550)*100
	percentage of residents who are economically inactive students	L080191/L080001*10
	persons in employment in agriculture	L730002/L730001*100
	persons in employment in primary production	L730004/L730001*100
	persons in employment in manufacturing	(L730005+L730006)/L730001*100
	persons in employment in service employment	(L730011+L730010)/L730001*100
excluded	percentage of working age men are inactive (not students)	(L080438-L080457-L080453-L080454-L080455+L080472+L080473+L080474)/(L080267-L080282-L080283-L080284)*100
	employment rate for men of working age	(L080400-L080415-L080416-L080417)/(L080286-L080301-L080302-L080303)*100
	percentage of working age residents who are on a government scheme	L080115/L080001*100
	employment rate for men and women aged 16 to 24	(L090121+L090313)/(L090037+L090229)*100
	percentage of working age women who work full-time	(L080571-L080585-L080586-L080587-L080588)/(L080533-L080547-L080548-L080549-L080550)*100
	percentage of working age women who work part-time	(L080590-L080604-L080605-L080606-L080607)/(L080533-L080547-L080548-L080549-L080550)*100
	percentage of resident employees who are working part-time	L080058/(L080039+L080058)*100
	percentage of 17 year olds who are inactive students	L080193/L080003*100
	persons in employment in primary production or manufacturing	(L730004+L730005+L730006)/L730001*100
	percentage of unemployed who were formerly in primary production or manufacturing	(L940004+L940005+L940006)/L940001*100
	term-time address students as percentage of all residents	(L100040+L100079+L100118+L100170+L100209)/L020001*100
	home address students as a percentage of all residents	(L100027+L100066+L100157)/L020001*100

Note: Text in *italics* indicates variable derived from the 10% Census counts.

Table B: Families, Groups and Clusters – Family 1

Family	RURAL AREAS		
Group		SCOTLAND	
Cluster number			1
Typical district			Moray
Percentage of residents who:			
are aged 0 to 4	6.01	6.09	6.22
are aged 5 to 14	12.08	12.82	13.14
are aged 25 to 44	27.39	27.59	28.11
are aged 45 to 64	23.44	23.14	22.59
are aged over 65	18.06	17.13	16.24
identified as black	0.18	0.10	0.12
identified as Asian	0.22	0.09	0.11
moved in last year (%)	9.70	10.77	11.41
are in Social Class 1 or 2*	37.58	32.56	33.16
are in Social Class IIIn*	9.92	9.34	9.63
are in Social Class 4 or 5*	19.23	23.95	23.20
have an HE qualification	13.31	13.13	13.61
are students	3.63	3.32	3.48
Limiting long-term illness standardised rate	10.13	9.45	9.40
Children with a single adult (%)	9.61	10.20	10.49
Dependants with a lone carer (%)	18.12	17.78	18.56
Percentage of households which:			
have 4+ children	3.58	3.43	3.46
are young single persons	9.37	11.05	11.29
have 2 earners and no children	20.77	19.70	19.96
No. of people per household	2.49	2.48	2.50
Unemployment rate (%)	7.36	7.88	7.82
Working women (%)	56.09	55.93	56.65
Proportion of people in employment who:			
are in agriculture*	6.95	10.47	8.29
are in primary production*	2.81	1.17	1.26
are in manufacturing*	16.16	13.99	13.37
are in finance & services*	35.72	34.00	37.26
go to work on public transport*	5.14	5.85	7.38
People in households without a car (%)	17.36	22.45	23.51
Households which have 2 + cars (%)	27.10	20.06	19.89
Percentage of people in households which			
are owner occupiers	72.26	58.91	58.53
are renting from the local authority	16.27	26.82	27.57
are renting privately	6.24	6.84	6.58
Percentage of people in households which have no central heating	18.10	20.01	19.17
Dwellings with 7+ rooms (%)	18.84	14.20	13.68
No. rooms per person	2.16	2.02	1.99
Percentage of dwellings which			
are terraced	22.77	22.30	21.86
are purpose-built flats	8.05	11.56	13.09

Note: Variable derived from 10% Census counts.

	COAST AND COUNTRY					MIXED URBAN AND RURAL	
2		3	5	7		4	9
Berwickshire		South Shropshire	Carrick	Purbeck		Mendip	Alyn and Deeside
5.89	5.74	5.76	5.86	5.67	6.39	6.30	6.46
12.35	11.62	11.72	11.68	11.53	12.36	12.23	12.45
26.81	26.45	26.46	25.51	26.89	28.74	28.40	28.97
23.96	23.86	24.21	23.74	23.67	22.95	22.69	23.13
18.45	19.80	19.25	20.66	19.77	15.90	17.04	15.11
0.07	0.15	0.13	0.15	0.18	0.25	0.24	0.26
0.07	0.14	0.09	0.12	0.17	0.44	0.20	0.60
9.80	9.92	9.57	9.68	10.28	8.76	10.14	7.81
31.66	41.15	40.21	35.54	44.53	34.93	36.10	34.12
8.91	10.22	9.07	10.39	10.95	9.79	9.66	9.88
25.07	17.44	18.04	19.93	15.82	19.30	19.26	19.33
12.40	14.60	12.82	12.30	16.98	11.41	11.93	11.05
3.07	3.91	3.84	3.98	3.92	3.39	3.32	3.43
9.52	10.11	10.51	11.29	9.27	10.54	9.45	11.29
9.78	9.44	9.07	11.15	8.88	9.53	9.00	9.90
18.78	20.96	17.24	17.64	16.64	18.33		
3.39	3.67	3.86	4.12	3.31	3.52	3.51	3.53
10.69	9.21	8.88	9.67	9.21	8.67	8.61	8.71
19.31	20.11	20.49	17.20	21.24	22.40	22.60	22.25
2.44	2.45	2.48	2.43	2.43	2.55	2.51	2.57
7.96	7.06	6.91	9.93	5.77	7.52	6.75	8.05
54.86	54.55	52.42	49.46	58.54	58.54	58.58	58.51
13.74	7.79	11.71	6.93	5.42	3.66	5.63	2.31
1.04	2.34	2.47	2.26	2.28	4.47	2.78	5.64
14.93	13.22	14.88	9.37	13.90	21.94	20.17	23.16
29.13	38.34	33.87	37.97	41.69	32.66	34.07	31.69
3.55	4.26	2.86	4.34	5.22	6.08	4.50	7.18
20.86	15.42	14.42	18.33	14.73	17.45	14.75	19.33
20.32	28.70	29.29	24.46	30.33	28.62	30.33	27.44
59.48	74.59	74.22	73.84	75.22	76.23	75.25	76.90
25.69	12.80	12.48	14.38	12.26	15.64	14.84	16.19
7.22	7.17	7.71	7.70	6.52	4.47	5.66	3.64,
21.26	19.39	19.88	28.38	14.70	15.03	15.11	
14.99	21.65	23.12	20.27	21.28	17.13	19.67	15.37
2.08	2.24	2.25	2.23	2.23	2.11	2.16	2.07
22.96	22.76	20.87	27.08	22.01	23.04	22.53	
9.26	7.52	5.28	7.47	9.13	6.88	6.40	7.22

Table B: Families, Groups and Clusters – Family 2

Family	PROSPERING AREAS		
Group		GROWTH AREAS	
Cluster number			8
Typical district			Rugby
Percentage of residents who:			
are aged 0 to 4	6.38	6.50	6.53
are aged 5 to 14	12.33	12.41	12.32
are aged 25 to 44	29.82	30.05	29.67
are aged 45 to 64	22.90	22.61	22.48
are aged over 65	14.84	14.59	15.21
identified as black	0.50	0.55	0.68
identified as Asian	1.08	1.07	1.92
moved in last year (%)	9.92	9.90	8.79
are in Social Class 1 or 2*	46.16	43.16	40.83
are in Social Class IIIn*	11.97	11.88	12.41
are in Social Class 4 or 5*	13.64	14.72	15.96
have an HE qualification	16.68	15.15	14.65
are students	3.96	3.75	3.79
Limiting long-term illness standardised rate	8.80	9.03	9.87
Children with a single adult (%)	8.43	8.69	10.32
Dependants with a lone carer (%)	14.88	15.20	17.12
Percentage of households which:			
have 4+ children	3.29	3.35	3.51
are young single persons	9.50	9.47	10.12
have 2 earners and no children	24.74	24.86	23.56
No. of people per household	2.56	2.56	2.52
Unemployment rate (%)	5.76	5.91	6.79
Working women (%)	61.79	62.13	62.99
Proportion of people in employment who:			
are in agriculture*	2.24	2.44	1.15
are in primary production*	2.40	2.42	2.97
are in manufacturing*	17.45	18.81	22.39
are in finance & services*	42.25	40.43	38.04
go to work on public transport*	10.15	9.39	10.23
People in households without a car (%)	13.26	13.88	17.74
Households which have 2 + cars (%)	35.26	34.24	29.09
Percentage of people in households which			
are owner occupiers	78.32	77.65	79.27
are renting from the local authority	12.32	12.99	13.24
are renting privately	4.66	4.63	3.95
Percentage of people in households which have no central heating	10.22	10.76	11.66
Dwellings with 7+ rooms (%)	21.30	19.85	16.98
No. rooms per person	2.13	2.11	2.10
Percentage of dwellings which			
are terraced	22.46	23.70	24.78
are purpose-built flats	10.81	9.97	10.80

Note: Variable derived from 10% Census counts.

			MOST PROSPEROUS			
21	22	29	32		23	24
Aylesbury Vale	Cherwell	Broxbourne	Wansdyke		Surrey Heath	Tandridge
6.72	7.29	6.42	5.98	6.00	6.29	5.91
12.63	13.03	11.85	12.28	12.08	13.31	11.72
31.25	31.58	29.74	28.63	29.08	30.13	28.78
22.04	19.92	23.31	24.02	23.84	23.84	23.84
13.43	13.36	14.85	15.62	15.65	15.65	16.54
0.53	0.95	0.69	0.21	0.36	0.36	0.38
0.81	0.35	1.85	0.27	1.12	1.12	1.02
11.10	14.91	7.98	8.93	10.01	10.38	9.90
46.89	37.14	37.63	45.85	55.92	60.27	54.68
11.45	9.95	15.60	10.67	12.28	11.81	12.42
13.57	16.17	13.88	14.62	10.15	7.57	10.89
17.06	14.68	10.27	15.83	21.66	25.70	20.51
3.84	3.39	3.03	4.04	4.66	5.45	4.43
8.41	8.64	9.06	8.95	8.03	7.26	8.25
8.08	7.92	9.07	7.68	7.59	6.20	7.98
13.80	13.74	16.01	14.84	13.85	11.73	14.46
3.45	3.38	3.14	3.13	3.11	2.90	3.16
9.71	9.45	9.43	8.45	9.61	8.28	9.99
26.39	24.53	25.09	24.43	24.37	25.44	24.07
2.59	2.60	2.55	2.57	2.54	2.69	2.50
5.39	4.70	6.94	5.44	5.29	4.66	5.47
62.93	60.80	62.31	60.51	60.68	61.04	60.58
2.17	5.15	0.77	4.13	1.60	0.96	1.78
2.13	1.42	1.87	2.74	2.35	1.95	2.46
17.32	12.58	15.22	20.36	13.03	14.08	12.74
42.79	42.36	42.35	38.04	48.18	49.65	47.76
8.39	5.36	21.17	5.42	12.61	11.34	12.98
11.67	13.53	14.24	12.15	11.21	8.55	11.98
38.23	31.70	32.90	36.69	40.10	45.20	38.65
76.82	65.08	82.13	78.90	80.48	86.08	78.88
13.09	16.04	11.67	12.19	10.11	6.56	11.13
4.86	7.78	3.71	4.50	4.78	3.37	5.18
9.08	12.06	10.00	11.73	8.47	6.14	9.13
22.31	18.67	13.67	23.40	26.05	30.25	24.85
2.12	2.03	2.00	2.18	2.20	2.14	2.22
24.82	23.56	26.99	19.56	18.42	16.32	19.02
10.10	9.36	15.24	6.53	13.56	11.62	14.12

COMMERCIAL GEODEMOGRAPHIC CLASSIFICATION SYSTEMS

CACI'S ACORN PROFILE OF GREAT BRITAIN

CACI's ACORN classification profiles customers in a trading area or on a database into 6 Categories, 17 Groups and 54 Types (plus 1 unclassified). The table below shows the ACORN profile of CACI's 1997 population projections for GB.

ACORN Groups	ACORN Types	'000s	%
1 Wealthy Achievers, Suburban Areas	Wealthy suburbs, large detached houses	1,467	2.6
	Villages with wealthy commuters	1,824	3.2
	Mature affluent home owning areas	1,548	2.7
	Affluent suburbs, older families	2,123	3.7
	Mature, well-off suburbs	1,718	3.0
2 Affluent Greys, Rural Communities	Agricultural villages, home based workers	924	1.6
	Holiday retreats, older people, home based workers	399	0.7
3 Prosperous Pensioners, Retirement Areas	Home owning areas, well-off older residents	807	1.4
	Private flats, elderly people	542	0.9
4 Affluent Executives, Family Areas	Affluent working families with mortgages	1,224	2.1
	Affluent working couples with mortgages, new homes	728	1.3
	Transient workforces, living at their place of work	201	0.3
5 Well-Off Workers, Family Areas	Home owning family areas	1,486	2.6
	Home owning family areas, older children	1,721	3.0
	Families with mortgages, younger children	1,276	2.2
6 Affluent Urbanites, Town & City Areas	Well-off town & city areas	631	1.1
	Flats & mortgages, singles & young working couples	425	0.7
	Furnished flats & bedsits, younger single people	253	0.4
7 Prosperous Professionals, Metropolitan Areas	Apartments, young professional singles & couples	653	1.1
	Gentrified multi-ethnic areas	557	1.0
8 Better-Off Executives, Inner City Areas	Prosperous enclaves, highly qualified executives	428	0.7
	Academic centres, students & young professionals	371	0.6
	Affluent city centre areas, tenements & flats	254	0.4
	Partially gentrified multi-ethnic areas	407	0.7
	Converted flats & bedsits, single people	497	0.9
9 Comfortable Middle Agers, Mature Home Owning Areas	Mature established home owning areas	1,890	3.3
	Rural areas, mixed occupations	1,985	3.5
	Established home owning areas	2,299	4.0
	Home owning areas, council tenants, retired people	1,520	2.7
10 Skilled Workers, Home Owning Areas	Established home owning areas, skilled workers	2,580	4.5
	Home owners in older properties, younger workers	1,743	3.0
	Home owning areas with skilled workers	1,765	3.1
11 New Home Owners, Mature Communities	Council areas, some new home owners	2,176	3.8
	Mature home owning areas, skilled workers	1,762	3.1
	Low rise estates, older workers, new home owners	1,608	2.8
12 White Collar Workers, Better-Off Multi-Ethnic Areas	Home owning multi-ethnic areas, young families	642	1.1
	Multi-occupied town centres, mixed occupations	1,038	1.8
	Multi-ethnic areas, white collar workers	614	1.1
13 Older People, Less Prosperous Areas	Home owners, small council flats, single pensioners	1,088	1.9
	Council areas, older people, health problems	971	1.7
14 Council Estate Residents, Better-Off Homes	Better-off council areas, new home owners	1,375	2.4
	Council areas, young families, some new home owners	1,711	3.0
	Council areas, young families, many lone parents	898	1.6
	Multi-occupied terraces, multi-ethnic areas	487	0.8
	Low rise council housing, less well-off families	1,015	1.8
	Council areas, residents with health problems	1,099	1.9
15 Council Estate Residents, High Unemployment	Estates with high unemployment	645	1.1
	Council flats, elderly people, health problems	383	0.7
	Council flats, very high unemployment, singles	495	0.9
16 Council Estate Residents, Greatest Hardship	Council areas, high unemployment, lone parents	1,056	1.8
	Council flats, greatest hardship, many lone parents	518	0.9
17 People In Multi-Ethnic, Low-Income Areas	Multi-ethnic, large families, overcrowding	366	0.6
	Multi-ethnic, severe unemployment, lone parents	570	1.0
	Multi-ethnic, high unemployment, overcrowding	301	0.5
Unclassified		291	0.5
TOTAL		**57,353**	**99.8**

FINANCIAL*ACORN PROFILE OF GREAT BRITAIN

The table below shows the Financial*ACORN profile of CACI's 1997 population projections for Great Britain. The table shows the 12 Financial*ACORN Groups and 52 Financial*ACORN Types (plus 1 'unclassified') in the Financial*ACORN classification which is derived from the Government's 1991 Census of GB and data from NOP's Financial Research Survey.

Groups	Types	'000s	%
1 Wealthy Equityholders	Mature couples/families, extensive financial portfolio	349	0.6
	Professional families, life assurance, loans & mortgages	297	0.5
	Older families, esp. active in loans & deposit accounts	340	0.6
	Older couples, low pension plans, high on stocks & shares	416	0.7
	Mortgaged couples, making sensible investments, few loans	468	0.8
	Older families, with above av. loans & ample investments	518	0.9
	Mature couples, insurance, life assurance & deposit accounts	580	1.0
	Older couples, equities, pension plans & other savings	366	0.6
	Senior citizens with carefully planned savings & investments	285	0.5
	Middle aged, preferring investments in tax exempt savings	453	0.8
	Younger single executives, investing, saving & using credit	356	0.6
	Professional singles/couples, using credit & debit cards	259	0.5
2 Affluent Mortgage-holders	Younger families, extremely active across the financial range	299	0.5
	Families with kids, credit & debit cards, investing heavily	293	0.5
	Older families, deposit & savings accs. & above av. shares	480	0.8
	Young/middle aged couples investing in tax exempt savings	376	0.7
	Young singles/couples, with personal pensions	259	0.5
	Families, personal pensions, life ass. & tax exempt savings	356	0.6
	Young families, above av. mortgage & life assurance	554	1.0
	Young adults in couples, with mortgages & loans	362	0.6
	Families/younger couples, mortgages, wary of investments	410	0.7
3 Comfortable Investors	Couples, wide range of investments, especially in shares	1,079	1.9
	Middle aged couples, few loans, ample personal pensions	214	0.4
	Older couples, av. on credit, keen on tax exempt savings	2,257	3.9
	Couples with children, tax exempt saving/personal pensions	1,002	1.7
4 Better-Off Borrowers	Young families with children, using loans & mortgages	442	0.8
	Younger families/couples, high spending using credit cards	1,355	2.4
	Young singles/couples, keen on loans & personal pensions	1,102	1.9
	Families, av. financial activity apart from above av. mortgages	1,365	2.4
	Younger people, setting up home with loans & mortgages	2,137	3.7
	Family groups, especially younger families, borrowing heavily	174	0.3
5 Prosperous Savers	Older families/couples with careful savings & investments	1,531	2.7
	Mature singles/couples enjoying share ownership	859	1.5
	Older couples, deposit accounts, tax exempt savings & shares	1,589	2.8
	Young, low life assurance but high denationalised stocks	1,696	3.0
	Retired, active in shares, credit cards & deposit accounts	1,106	1.9
	Pensioners, very high share ownership, few loans & mortgages	887	1.5
6 Younger Spenders	Young adults, very active in credit cards & some investments	1,097	1.9
	Younger single people using cash & debit cards, few loans	263	0.5
7 Settled Pensioners	Older people, av. activity across the financial range	3,816	6.7
	Elderly singles/couples, some savings, generally average	2,715	4.7
8 Working Families	Younger couples, few children, mortgages & av. savings	2,907	5.1
	Families of all ages with children, above av. loans	775	1.4
9 Thrifty Singles	Young adults only av. spending, few savings or mortgages	630	1.1
	Young singles/couples, low spending & negligible savings	1,506	2.6
10 Middle Aged Assured	Middle aged/older singles, above av. life assurance	1,868	3.3
	Middle aged, well above av. life assurance, few investments	351	0.6
11 Older Cash Users	Older singles, retired or unemployed, negligible credit	5,752	10.0
	Families & single people, below av. financial products	3,102	5.4
12 Low Income Unemployed	Young families, particularly low in mortgages & credit cards	3,583	6.2
	Families with children, very little saving or spending	1,824	3.2
	Unclassified	293	0.5
	TOTAL	57,353	100

MOSAIC CLASSIFICATION

Group		%	Description	%	Typical Location
L1	High Income Families	10.8	Clever Capitalists	1.4	Whetstone
			Rising Materialists	2.4	Wokingham
			Corporate Careerists	2.5	Fleet
			Ageing Professionals	1.7	Farnham
			Small Time Business	2.8	Ruislip
L2	Suburban Semis	10.8	Green Belt Expansion	3.6	Canvey Island
			Suburban Mock Tudor	3.0	Redhill
			Pebble Dash Subtopia	4.2	Bexleyheath
L3	Blue Collar Owners	12.9	Affluent Blue Collar	3.0	Kingswood
			30s Industrial Spec	3.8	Wigston
			Lo-Rise Right To Buy	3.0	Long Eaton
			Smokestack Shiftwork	3.1	Ebbw Vale
L4	Low Rise Council	13.7	Coop Club & Colliery	3.3	Jarrow
			Better Off Council	2.0	Dalkeith
			Low Rise Pensioners	3.1	Barking
			Low Rise Subsistence	3.3	Wythenshawe
			Problem Families	2.0	Corby
L5	Council Flats	6.8	Families In The Sky	1.2	Peckham
			Graffitied Ghettos	0.3	Motherwell
			Small Town Industry	1.3	Hawick
			Mid Rise Overspill	0.7	Rutherglen
			Flats For The Aged	1.4	Clydebank
			Inner City Towers	1.8	Southwark
L6	Victorian Low Status	9.4	Bohemian Melting Pot	2.3	Tottenham
			Victorian Tenements	0.1	Partick
			Rootless Renters	1.5	Gateshead
			Sweatshop Sharers	1.1	East Ham
			Depopulated Terraces	0.8	Pontypridd
			Rejuvenated Terraces	3.5	Southsea
L7	Town Houses & Flats	9.6	Bijou Homemakers	3.5	Greenford
			Market Town Mixture	3.7	Deal
			Town Centre Singles	2.3	Tewkesbury
L8	Stylish Singles	5.3	Bedsits & Shop Flats	1.0	Boscombe
			Studio Singles	1.9	Surbiton
			College & Communal	0.5	St Andrews
			Chattering Classes	1.9	Chiswick
L9	Independent Elders	7.2	Solo Pensioners	1.9	Billingham
			High Spending Greys	1.2	Clacton-on-Sea
			Aged Owner-Occupiers	2.7	Morecambe
			Elderly In Own Flats	1.4	St John's Wood
L10	Mortgaged Families	6.4	Brand New Area	1.0	Fleet
			Pre Nuptial Owners	1.2	St Ives (Cambs)
			Nestmaking Families	1.7	Bicester
			Maturing Mortgagees	2.5	Yate
L11	Country Dwellers	6.9	Gentrified Villages	1.4	Uckfield
			Rural Retirement Mix	0.6	Stranraer
			Lowland Agribusiness	1.8	Diss
			Rural Disadvantage	1.1	Evesham
			Tied/Tenant Farmers	0.6	Stranraer
			Upland & Small Farms	1.4	Carmarthen
L12	Institutional Areas	0.3	Military Bases	0.3	Aldershot
			Non Private Housing	0.0	Beeston

FINANCIAL MOSAIC CLASSIFICATION

	Group	% GB Households	Description	% GB Households
A	Adventurous Spenders	14.1	Student Innocence	0.8
			Recession Hit Solos	3.3
			Thinking of Owning	1.1
			Poor Risk Homeowners	4.4
			Mid Market Borrowers	4.5
B	Burdened Borrowers	6.3	Brand New Areas	1.0
			Negative Home Equity	1.6
			Confident Mortgagees	3.7
C	Capital Accumulators	6.4	Young Entrepreneurs	2.6
			Wealthy Businessmen	2.6
			Captains of Industry	1.1
D	Discerning Investors	5.1	Blue Chip Portfolios	2.9
			Playing the Market	2.2
E	Equityholding Elders	4.2	Blue Blood Estates	2.6
			Wealthy Pensioners	1.6
F	Farmowners & Traders	6.5	Equity In The Land	0.8
			Farmers & Hoteliers	1.8
			Local Small Business	3.8
G	Good Paying Realists	19.6	Emerging Home Equity	4.5
			Home Nearly Paid Off	4.0
			Privatisation Buffs	6.8
			Outright Homeowners	4.3
H	Hardened Cash Payers	19.0	Low Value Homeowners	6.0
			Thrifty Estates	6.1
			Prize Draw & Gifts	2.3
			Low Expectations	3.5
			Impoverished Elderly	1.1
I	Indebted Strugglers	4.8	Overcommitted Owners	1.8
			Overborrowed Renters	2.1
			Repay When Pursued	0.8
			Rootless Singles	0.1
J	Just About Surviving	14.1	Welfare Dependency	1.7
			Victims of Recession	2.8
			Inner City Enterprise	1.2
			Resigned Tenants	4.3
			Repayment Difficulty	4.0

SUPER PROFILES LIFESTYLE CLASSIFICATION, GB

	Main Regions	Age/ Family	Property Type	Car Owner-ship	Occu-pation	Special Interests	Other Features	Distinctive Features	GB %
A: AFFLUENT ACHIEVERS									
A1 Very high income professionals in exclusive areas	SE, GL	A	SD	H	M/P	1, 2, 4	B, £	1, 2	2.06
A4 Mature families in 'stockbroker belts'	SE, NW, S	A	SD	H	M/P	1, 2, 4	B, £	1	4.34
A6 Mature families in select suburban properties	SE	A	SD	H	M/P	1, 2, 4	B, £	1	2.64
B: THRIVING GREYS									
B5 Highly qualified professionals in mixed housing	GL, SE	A	Mixed	A	M/P, WC	4	B	3	1.10
B7 Affluent ageing couples, many in purchased properties	SE	OC	SD, SS	H	WC	2, 4	B, £	1	3.09
B12 Older professionals in retirement areas	SE, SW, S	OC, VoS	SD	A	M/P, WC	2, 4	B, £	1, 4	3.00
B17 Comfortably well-off older owner-occupiers	SE, SW	OC	SD, SS	A	M, WC	4	£	5	1.56
B18 Affluent ageing couples in rural areas	SE, SW, EA	OC	RD	A	A, WC	–	B, £	6	2.43
C: SETTLED SUBURBANS									
C11 White collar families in own-occ. suburban semis	GL, SE, NW	A	SS	A	WC	2, 4	B, £	7, 8	7.02
C14 Mature white collar couples in suburban semis	SE, NW	OC	SS	A	WC	2, 3, 4	–	5, 7	1.56
C16 White collar couples in mixed suburban housing	SE, SW, S	OC	Mixed	A	WC	3, 4	£	1	2.71
D: NEST BUILDERS									
D2 Mortgaged commuting professionals, with children	SE	A	SD	H	M/P	1, 2, 3, 4	B, £	1, 9, 10	1.53
D8 Double income young families in select properties	SE	A	SD, SS	A	M/P, WC	1, 3	B, £	8, 9, 10	1.78
D9 Military families	SE, SW, EA, S	A	SD, SS	A	F	1	B, £	8, 11, 12	0.30
D13 Young families in small semis & terraces	SE	A	SS, T	A	WC	3, 6	–	8, 9	1.48
D15 Young white collar families in semis	SE, NW, S	A	SS	A	WC	1, 3, 6	T	8, 9	2.73
D27 Young blue/white collar families in semis/terraces	SE, NW, SW, Y	A	SS, T	A	WC, BC	1, 5, 6	T	8	5.08
D28 Young families in terraces – mainly council	SE	A	T	A	WC, BC	6	T	8	1.83
E: URBAN VENTURERS									
E3 High income, young professionals, many renting	GL	YC, YS	T, F	A	M/P	1, 2, 4	B, £	3, 13	1.05
E10 Young professionals in multi-racial areas	GL	YC, YS	T, F	L	M/P, WC	1, 2, 4, 5	B, £	2, 14	2.60
E20 Young white collar couples buying properties	SE, SW, GL	YC	T, F	A	M/P, WC	1, 2, 4, 5, 6	B, £	8, 9, 10	1.38
E21 Young families buying terraces in multi-racial areas	GL, WM, NW	A	T	A	WC	2	B	2, 14	1.74
E29 Young families renting accom. in multi-racial areas	GL, S, M, Y, NW	A	T, F	L	WC, BC, F	–	–	14, 15	2.74
E30 Young white collar singles, sharing city centre accom.	SE, S	YC	F	L	WC	1, 3, 4, 5	B	12, 16, 17	0.83
F: COUNTRY LIFE									
F19 Prosperous farming communities	SE, SW, S	A	RD	H	A	2	B, £	18	2.09
F25 Smallholders & rural workers	S	–	RD	H	A	–	£	11, 18, 19	0.71
G: SENIOR CITIZENS									
G22 Retired white collar workers in owner occupied flats	SE, SW	OC, VoS	F	L	M/P, WC	2	B, £	1, 4	2.50
G23 Older residents & young transient singles	SE, SW	OC, YS	T, F	L	WC	1	£	12, 13, 20	1.41
G26 Old & young buying terraces & flats	SE	OC, YS	T, F	L	WC	5	–	–	2.44
G32 Retired blue collar workers in council flats	S	OC, VoS	F	L	BC	3, 6	T	1, 4, 12, 16, 21	1.63
H: PRODUCERS									
H24 Older white collar owner occupied in semis	–	OC	SS	A	WC	–	T	4, 22	6.26
H33 Older workers established in semis & terraces	SE, S	OC	SS, T	L	BC	5	T	7, 22, 23	4.80
H36 Older & retired b. coll. workers, small council properties	–	OC, VoS	T, F	L	BC	5	T	4, 7, 16	4.28
I: HARD PRESSED FAMILIES									
I34 Blue collar families in council properties	–	A	T	L	BC	5, 6	T	15	3.66
I35 Young blue collar families in council terraces	SE, WM, S	A, SP	T	L	BC	6	T	8	0.90
I37 Manufacturing workers in terraced housing	NW, W, WM	A	T	L	BC	5	T	8, 12, 15	2.59
J: HAVE NOTS									
J31 Council tenants in multi-racial areas – high unemp.	GL, S	–	F	L	BC	6	T	2, 14, 15	2.71
J38 Blue collar families in council properties – high unemp.	–	A, SP	T, F	L	BC	5, 6	T	15	4.24
J39 Young families, many single parents – high unemp.	–	A, SP	F	L	BC	5, 6	T	16, 24	1.57
J40 Young singles & pensioners in council flats – high unemp.	–	YS, SP, VoS	F	L	BC	5, 6	T	12, 16, 17, 24	1.64

NEIGHBOURS & PROSPECTS

	Housing Type	Tenure	Family Composition	No. of Cars	Social Group	% of Pop'n
1: YOUNG & AFFLUENT NEIGHBOURHOODS						
1A Professional single home owners	Flat	Owner/O	Single	1	AB	1.1
1B Affluent singles in quality rented flats	Flat	Priv/Rent	Single	1	AB	0.8
1C Younger couples & families in single neighbourhoods	Flat	Mixed	Mixed	1	ABC1	1.4
2: WEALTHY RETIRED NEIGHBOURHOODS						
2A Affluent couples in large detached houses	Detach.	Owner/O	Couple	2	AB	3.5
2B Retired home owners in pleasant suburbs	Detach.	Owner/O	Couple	2	ABC1	3.2
2C Older flat dwellers in areas of mixed tenure	Flat	Mixed	Couple	1	ABC1	1.3
2D Couples in smaller houses	Semi-Det.	Owner/O	Couple	1	BC1C2	3.4
3: AFFLUENT HOME OWNERS						
3A Younger families in larger dwellings	Mixed	Owner/O	Family	2	AB	1.0
3B Wealthy older families, spacious homes in exclusive areas	Detach.	Owner/O	Family	3	AB	2.9
3C Affluent commuters in large family homes	Detach.	Owner/O	Family	2	ABC1	3.3
3D Wealthy older families in suburban areas	Detach.	Owner/O	Family	2	AB	3.5
3E Professional couples with school age children	Semi-Det.	Owner/O	Family	2	AB	2.9
3F Well off families in spacious semi-detached houses	Semi-Det.	Owner/O	Family	2	BC1C2	2.1
3G Affluent households in urban areas	Mixed	Owner/O	Family	2	BC1C2	1.8
4: SMALLER PRIVATE FAMILY HOMES						
4A Younger families & singles in terraced housing	Terraced	Owner/O	Family	1	BC1C2	1.8
4B Well off older families in detached properties	Detach.	Owner/O	Family	2	BC1C2	2.7
4C White collar workers in areas of mixed tenure	Mixed	Owner/O	Family	1	BC1C2	1.0
4D Suburban families with school age children	Terraced	Mixed	Family	1	C2DE	2.0
4E Younger & more affluent families in urban developments	Semi-Det.	Owner/O	Family	2	BC1C2	3.1
4F Well off families in pleasant suburban semi-det. homes	Semi-Det.	Owner/O	Family	2	BC1C2	3.3
4G Affluent households in urban areas	Semi-Det.	Owner/O	Family	1	BC1C2	3.2
4H Urban families with young children	Terraced	Owner/O	Family	1	BC1C2	1.9
5: POORER HOME OWNERS						
5A Younger families in poorer terraced housing	Terraced	Owner/O	Family	1	C2DE	3.1
5B Older families in larger dwellings	Semi-Det.	Owner/O	Family	1	C2DE	2.7
5C Suburban families with school age children	Semi-Det.	Owner/O	Family	1	C2DE	3.2
5D Young couples & families in urban areas	Terraced	Owner/O	Family	1	C2DE	3.1
5E Young families in surburban semi-det. homes & flats	Semi-Det.	Owner/O	Family	1	C2DE	2.4
5F Skilled manual workers with older families	Mixed	Owner/O	Family	1	C2DE	2.8
5G Older families in smaller terraced housing	Terraced	Owner/O	Family	1	C2DE	2.3
6: LESS AFFLUENT & RETIRED URBAN DWELLERS						
6A Active home owners in larger dwellings	Semi-Det.	Owner/O	Couple	1	C2DE	2.9
6B Mixed areas of home owners and tenants	Mixed	Mixed	Mixed	1	C2DE	3.2
6C Privately rented flats in retirement towns	Flat	Priv/Rent	Couple	1	BC2DE	0.7
6D Smaller privately owned dwellings	Mixed	Owner/O	Couple	1	C2DE	2.9
7: COUNCIL TENANTS ON FAMILY ESTATES						
7A Young families & singles – many dwelling in flats	Flat	Council	Mixed		BC1C2	0.8
7B Retired couples in larger family homes	Mixed	Council	Couple	1	C2DE	1.5
7C Poorer retired couples & singles	Flat	Council	Mixed		C2DE	1.4
8: POORER COUNCIL TENANTS, MANY SINGLE PARENTS						
8A Younger families and singles in lower quality housing	Mixed	Council	Mixed	1	C2DE	2.9
8B Poorer singles and older retired couples in flats	Flat	Council	Mixed		C2DE	2.6
8C Young families in terraced housing	Terraced	Council	Family	1	C2DE	3.0
8D Single parents in high rise flats	Flat	Council	Single		C2DE	2.0
9: POORER SINGLES						
9A Young single parents & students in small flats & bedsits	Flat	Priv/Rent	Single	1	C1C2DE	1.1
9B Young families & singles in cosmopolitan urban areas	Flat	Mixed	Mixed	1	BC1C2	0.5
9C Single parents & retired in low quality terraced properties	Terraced	Mixed	Mixed	1	C2DE	2.1
9D Young families & retired singles in low quality flats	Flat	Mixed	Mixed	1	C2DE	16

DEFINE

Codes			Market Share %
Group	**0**	**Affluent Professional Families in Owner Occupation**	**8.8**
Types	01	Mature families	3.6
	02	Families with teenage children	3.1
	03	Younger families	0.9
	04	Very young families	1.3
Group	**1**	**Less Affluent Families in Owner Occupation**	**19.5**
Types	11	Professional white collar, skilled workers in suburban semis	3.4
	12	Older white collar and skilled workers with mature families	2.2
	13	Skilled manual workers with mature families	1.8
	14	Mature families in older property	2.2
	15	Mixed white and blue collar workers with teenage families	0.5
	16	Mixed white and blue collar workers with younger families	0.6
	17	Skilled manual workers with younger families	2.9
	18	Young first time buyers	3.3
	19	Younger professional white collar workers living in terraced accommodation	2.6
Group	**2**	**Poorer Families in Owner Occupation**	**12.5**
Types	21	Families with skilled manual workers	1.9
	22	Older blue collar workers	1.4
	23	Younger blue collar workers	1.9
	24	Families with skilled, semi-skilled and unskilled workers	4.0
	25	Mature families and skilled, semi-skilled and unskilled workers	0.7
	26	Young skilled, semi-skilled and unskilled workers in manufacturing	1.1
	27	Young families with skilled manual and semi-skilled workers	1.5
Group	**3**	**Retired Home Owners**	**12.1**
Types	31	Affluent retirement	2.2
	32	Comfortable retirement	3.5
	33	Town and country singles	1.2
	34	Single person households	1.2
	35	Aged stayers	4.0
Group	**4**	**Younger Council Tenants**	**5.3**
Types	41	Blue collar workers with growing families children living in terraced accommodation	1.7
	42	Older semi-detached and terraced accommodation in manufacturing towns	0.6
	43	Inner city deprivation	1.0
	44	Mixed low-rise flats and terraced council accommodation	0.7
	45	High rise flats	1.0
	46	Scottish tenements	0.3
Group	**5**	**Older Council Tenants**	**18.2**
Types	51	Pre-War older properties	2.6
	52	Semi-detached properties in manufacturing towns	2.8
	53	Semi-rural properties	2.9
	54	Post War development	3.8
	55	Low rise council	1.2
	56	Older skilled non-manual and semi-skilled flat dwellers	0.7
	57	Older multi-ethnic flat dwellers	2.0
	58	Aged council flat dwellers	2.0
Group	**6**	**Young Adults in Mixed Tenures**	**8.8**
Types	61	Inner city cosmopolitans	0.9
	62	Young singles in rented accommodation	1.2
	63	Pre-family groups in owner occupied and privately rented accommodation	1.0
	64	Single white collar workers in mixed areas of council & privately rented accomm.	2.1
	65	Young blue collar workers in mixed areas of council & privately rented accomm.	3.7
Group	**7**	**Older Adults in Mixed Tenures**	**8.7**
Types	71	Older white collar workers in mixed tenures	3.3
	72	Extended families	0.5
	73	Mixed owner occupied and privately rented accommodation	1.6
	74	Mixed council and privately rented accommodation	1.5
	75	Elderly flat dwellers	1.8
Group	**8**	**Rural Dwellers**	**5.1**
Types	81	Older rural	3.1
	82	Intensive lowland farming	0.3
	83	Pastoral farming	0.9
	84	Hill farming	0.3
	85	Rural and semi-rural deprivation	0.6
Group	**9**	**Institutional Groups**	**1.1**
Types	91	Young military families	1.0
	92	Other institutions	0.1

DEFINE

Financial Codes				Market Share %
Type	1	**Low searches & CCJs**		30.7
Change indicators	1	Unchanged debt		26.2
	2	Decreased debt		4.5
Type	2	**Low searches, above average CCJs**		25.2
Change indicators	0	Increased debt		12.4
	1	Unchanged debt		12.3
	2	Decreased debt		0.5
Type	3	**Low searches, very high CCJs**		2.0
Change indicators	0	Increased debt		1.7
	1	Unchanged debt		0.3
Type	4	**Above average searches, low CCJs**		10.5
Change indicators	1	Unchanged debt		8.9
	2	Decreased debt		1.6
Type	5	**Above average searches, very high CCJs**		19.1
Change indicators	0	Increased debt		9.9
	1	Unchanged debt		8.9
	2	Decreased debt		0.3
Type	6	**Above average searches, very high CCJs**		2.0
Change indicators	0	Increased debt		1.8
	1	Unchanged debt		0.2
Type	7	**Very high searches, low CCJs**		3.2
Change indicators	1	Unchanged debt		2.6
	2	Decreased debt		0.6
Type	8	**Very high searches, above average CCJs**		6.0
Change indicators	0	Increased debt		3.0
	1	Unchanged debt		2.9
	3	Decreased debt		0.1
Type	9	**Very high searches & CCJs**		1.1
Change indicators	0	Increased debt		1.0
	1	Unchanged debt		0.1

CLARITAS PRIZM

The 72 PRIZM clusters can be grouped into 19 income and lifestage groupings. The 19 groups can then be grouped into a further 4 lifestages or alternatively 5 income groups.

The lifestages are:
A = Starting Out, singles and childless couples
B = Nursery Families
C = Established Families with school age children
D = Older Singles and Empty Nests

The income groups are:
1 = Most affluent 20% of population
2 = Second most affluent 20%
3 = Third most affluent 20%
4 = Fourth most affluent 20%
5 = Least affluent 20%

The 19 lifestage income groups are:
Lifestage and Income
Starting Out, Income Group 1   A1
Starting Out, Income Group 2   A2
Starting Out, Income Group 3   A3
Starting Out, Income Group 4   A4
Nursery Families, Income Group 1   B1
Nursery Families, Income Group 2   B2
Nursery Families, Income Group 3   B3
Nursery Families, Income Group 4   B4
Nursery Families, Income Group 5   B5
Established Families, Income Group 1   C1
Established Families, Income Group 2   C2
Established Families, Income Group 3   C3
Established Families, Income Group 4   C4
Established Families, Income Group 5   C5
Empty Nests, Income Group 1   D1
Empty Nests, Income Group 2   D2
Empty Nests, Income Group 3   D3
Empty Nests, Income Group 4   D4
Empty Nests, Income Group 5   D5

The 72 PRIZM Clusters Lifestage and income			% of Households
Starting Out, singles and childless couples	Urban Achievers	A101	0.34
	Upward Bound	A102	0.15
	Urban Trendsetters	A103	0.92
	Mobility Blues	A104	0.65
	Clubs & Labels	A105	1.21
	First Flats	A206	1.57
	Metropolitan Mix	A207	0.40
	Terraced Start Ups	A208	1.13
	Young Literati	A209	0.48
	Cosy Couples	A210	0.78
	New Beginnings	A311	1.45
	Right-On Renters	A312	1.89
	The Dog & Duck	A413	0.90
	Bedsits & Barstools	A414	2.08
	University Challenged	A415	0.48
Nursery Families	Silver Spoons	B116	1.17
	Kids & Cul de Sacs	B117	1.71
	Fresh Air Futures	B218	1.09
	Military Quarters	B219	0.22
	Small Town & Tots	B220	2.67
	Back Yard Gossip	B321	1.24
	Soaps and Satellites	B322	1.43
	Kids & Car Spares	B423	1.73
	Bingo & Buses	B424	2.75
	Crowded Houses	B425	0.91
	Concrete Mix	B526	0.79
	Family Scramble	B527	2.41
	Prams & Lifts	B528	2.90
	Benefit Blues	B529	1.07
	Battling Families	B530	1.77
Established Families with school age childern	Blue Blood Estates	C131	0.14
	Money & Brains	C132	1.92
	New Empty Nests	C133	1.24
	Green Wellies	C134	1.57
	Diligent Duos	C135	0.83
	Suburban Elite	C136	3.13
	Safe & Sound	C137	1.74
	Big Fish, Small Pond	C238	2.39
	Rural Idealists	C239	0.91
	Gentlemen Farmers	C240	0.18
	Rural Professionals	C241	1.10
	Farming Families	C242	0.33
	Pint & Pastie	C243	0.36
	Settled Surburbia	C244	1.33
	Canny Crofters	C245	0.15
	Forces Families	C246	0.16
	Home from Homers	C347	0.83
	Council House Converts	C348	2.07
	Mines & Mills	C349	1.27
	Down Beat Uplands	C350	0.97
	Rainy Days	C351	1.37
	Boot Fairs & Fetes	C352	1.78
	Social Club Regulars	C453	1.88
Older Singles and Empty Nests	Rural Industria	C554	2.25
	Grey Power	D155	2.88
	Rooted Blue Chips	D156	0.41
	Kick-starts & Seniors	D257	1.21
	Bungalows & Bunkers	D258	0.64
	English Riviera	D259	0.75
	Jam & Geraniums	D260	1.82
	Pipes & Slippers	D361	3.38
	Darby & Joan	D362	2.51
	Rivers & Ramblers	D463	0.33
	Gone Fishing	D464	2.38
	Doting Grandparents	D465	1.00
	Old Ecotopia	D466	2.82
	Day Trippers	D467	2.08
	Twilight Years	D568	2.09
	Woollies & Welfare	D569	1.43
	Ever Hopefuls	D570	2.79
	Launderettes & Latchkeys	D571	1.57
	Pensions & Coupons	D572	1.71

PSYCHOGRAPHICS MEET GEODEMOGRAPHICS

In 1995, CCN (now Experian) Marketing launched a product named Psyche, which linked Synergy Consulting's seven Social Value Groups (SVGs) to unit postcodes by modelling the likelihood of inhabitants of each postcode being in a specific SVG.

Details of the seven SVGs are found below. In autumn 1997, this arrangement will change, and Equifax Europe (UK) will link to Synergy. Equifax has now modelled the postcodes in a similar way, and has produced a SVG directory of postcodes.

Meanwhile, Experian have now linked with the international research organisation RISC (Research Institute on Social Change), which operates a worldwide 'socio-cultural' (as opposed to 'psychographic') segmentation system. See opposite for details of the RISC segmentation. Statisticians from Experian and RISC are building statistical models for the countries within which both parties operate, to predict the distribution of consumers by their socio-cultural types within small geographical areas, such as postcodes. The resulting product is called Neighbourhood RISC.

The Seven Social Value Groups

Social Value Group	Characteristics	1996 % GB population
Self-Explorers	Ethical, tolerant, open, understanding, introspective, non-materialistic and individualistic	17%
Experimentalists	Unconventional, technological, creative, self-confident, physically fit, risk-orientated	8%
Conspicuous Consumers	Acquisitive, competitive, assertive, conscious of appearances, self indulgent and materialistic	20%
Belongers	Conservative, pragmatic, traditionalist, conventional, self-sacrificing, tribal and pedantic	19%
Social Resisters	Altruistic, concerned with social views and supporters of standards but also doctrinaire, intolerant and moralistic	7%
Survivors	Sustenance-driven, class-conscious, community-minded, traditionalist, cheerful, awkward if treated badly but quietly hardworking if treated well	22%
Aimless	Either old, lonely, purposeless and disinterested; or young, hostile, anti-authoritarian and frequently violent	7%

© Synergy Consulting. Tel: 0181 566 2869.

Neighbourhood RISC Segments

Cell	Title	Characteristics
1	Explorers	Personal growth and social change, leading edge
2G	Moral guides	Social responsibility and strong personal convictions
2L	Care givers	Sharing and caring as the roots of social ties
3G	Mobile networkers	Assertive, success minded, pathfinders
3L	High energy pleasure seekers	Street culture and fashion forerunners
4G	Guardians	Firm rationality and strict sense of duty
4L	Rooted traditionals	Longing for the past and seeking reassurance
5G	Survivors	Overwhelmed by routine, in need of security
5L	Social climbers	Materialistic drives and pragmatic attitudes
6	Avid consumers	Down-to-earth, local interests, and search for fun

Note: Percentage in each cell varies by country and over time.
Source: Neighbourhood RISC, contact Experian, Tel: 0115 934 4805.

CENSUS AGENCIES OPERATING IN THE UK

The following organisations are 'official' census agencies, thus licensed by ONS/GRO(S) to supply census data and value-added products.

Business Geographics Limited
8–10 Dryden Street
London WC2E 9NA
Tel. 0171 520 5800

CACI Information Services Limited
CACI House
Kensington Village
Avonmore Road
London W14 8TS
Tel. 0171 602 6000

Capscan Limited
Tranley House
Tranley Mews
London NW3 2QW
Tel. 0171 267 7055

CDMS Limited
Business Administration Centre
Kershaw Avenue
Crosby
Liverpool L23 0XA
Tel. 0151 949 1900

Chadwyck-Healey Limited
The Quorum
Barnwell Road
Cambridge CB5 8SW
Tel. 01223 215512

The Data Consultancy
7 Southern Court
South Street
Reading RG1 4QS
Tel. 0118 958 8181

Equifax Europe (UK) Limited
Capital House
25 Chapel Street
London NW1 5DS
Tel. 0171 298 3000

EuroDirect Database Marketing Limited
Onward House
2 Baptist Place
Bradford BD1 2PS
Tel. 01274 737144

Experian (formerly CCN Group)
Talbot House
Talbot Street
Nottingham NG1 5HF
Tel. 0115 941 0888

GMAP Limited
GMAP House
Cromer Terrace
Leeds LS2 9JU
Tel. 0113 244 6164

SPA Marketing Systems Limited
1 Warwick Street
Leamington Spa
Warwickshire CV32 5LW
Tel. 01926 451199

Yellow Marketing Information Limited
14–15 Regent Parade
Harrogate
North Yorkshire HG1 5AW
Telephone numbers of subsidiaries
(GEOPLAN – 01423 569538)
(Tactician UK – 01423 560064)
(Market Profiles – 01423 566755)

LIFESTYLE DATABASE COMPANIES OPERATING IN THE UK

*Claritas Group Limited
Causeway House
The Causeway
Teddington
Middlesex
TW11 OJR
Tel. 0181 213 5500

*Claritas Micromarketing
Causeway House
The Causeway
Teddington
Middlesex TW11 OJR
Tel. 0181 213 5500

*CMT
Causeway House
The Causeway
Teddington
Middlesex TW11 OJR
Tel. 0181 213 555

Consumerdata Limited
Bailey House
215 Barnett Wood Lane
Ashtead
Surrey KT21 2DF
Tel. 01372 278999

Consumer Surveys Limited
Unit 1A, Southwark Bridge Office
Village
60 Thrale Street
London SE1 9HW
Tel. 0171 403 6885

ICD Marketing Services Limited
Garden Floor
Bain House
16 Connaught Place
London W2 2EP
Tel. 0171 664 1000

*NDL International
Park House
Station Road
Teddington
Middlesex TW11 9AD
Tel. 0181 407 7000

(* companies in the Claritas Group)

ORGANISATIONS OPERATING IN THE GEODEMOGRAPHICS/LIFESTYLES TARGETING MARKETPLACE

This (fairly selective) list is comprised of organisations addressing the commercial sector, within the same general market as the geodemographic and lifestyles companies. It does not include direct marketing agencies, computer bureaux, etc. – or the list would be very long!

Ken Baker Associates
73 The Greenway
Ickenham
Middlesex UB10 8LT
Tel. 01895 637413

Beacon Dodsworth Limited
90 The Mount
York YO2 2AR
Tel. 01904 638997

Berry Consulting
2 Charterhouse Mews
London EC1M 6BB
Tel. 0171 490 5840

Data Discoveries Limited
1 St. Bernards Row
Edinburgh EH4 1HW
Tel. 0131 332 8800

Demographic Decisions
8 Hugh Street
Pimlico
London SW1V 1RP
Tel. 0171 834 0966

Dolphin Consulting Group
10 Collingwood House
Dolphin Square
London SW1V 3ND
Tel. 0171 789 8465

Experian Goad Limited
8–12 Salisbury Square
Old Hatfield
Hertfordshire AL9 5BJ
Tel. 01707 271171

GB Information Management
Winster House
Herons Way
Chester Business Park
Chester CH4 9GB
Tel. 01244 683222

Kingswood Limited
Canal Court
155 High Street
Brentford
Middlesex TW8 8JA
Tel. 0181 568 7000

MVA Systematica
MVA House
Victoria Way
Woking
Surrey GU21 1DD
Tel. 01483 728051

PMpL Limited
Old Bank House
39 High Street
High Wycombe
Buckinghamshire HP11 2AG
Tel. 01494 463235

QAS Systems Limited
7 Old Town
Clapham Common
London SW4 OJT
Tel. 0171 498 7777

Retail Locations
30–31 The Broadway
Woodford Green
Essex IG8 OHQ
Tel. 0181 559 1944

Synergy Consulting
5th Floor
Bilton House
54–58 Uxbridge Road
London W5 2TL
Tel. 0181 566 2869

TRAC Consultancy
Silverdale House
64 Pepys Road
New Cross
London SE14 5SD
Tel: 0171 639 9825

AWARENESS AND USAGE OF MARKET ANALYSIS, GEODEMOGRAPHIC AND LIFESTYLE DATA

1. Background

The geodemographic industry has now been in existence in the UK for more than 15 years. However, there has never been (so far as the writer is aware) a comprehensive survey of awareness and usage of the companies and the products available in this marketplace. This survey, conducted in early 1995, aims to fill this gap.

In addition to the population census, which has formed the 'backbone' of geodemographics in the UK, other data sources have gained in importance in recent years. Notable among these is lifestyle data (from the lifestyle database companies); this data source is also covered by the survey. Finally, PC-based market analysis systems are an important delivery system these days, and geographic information systems (GIS) are impacting this marketplace too; awareness and usage of these systems was also covered.

2. Method

A postal survey was conducted by T.M.C. in January 1995. The sample was drawn from the readership of *Marketing* magazine; the following business sectors were surveyed. Only companies employing 100+ employees were surveyed. Job titles selected were:

- marketing manager;
- sales/marketing manager;
- account director;
- account manager.

On this combination of criteria, the numbers available for mailing by business sector were:

Fmcg manufacturer	1,078	28.6%
Consumer durables manufacturer	435	11.6%
Retail/wholesale	438	11.6%
Consumer services	426	11.3%
Media owner	308	8.2%
Finance/financial services	656	17.4%
Charity/society	38	1.0%
Advertising agency*	384	10.2%
TOTAL	**3,763**	

Note: * Includes direct marketing agencies.

It should be noted that, given the consumer-based nature of geodemographics and lifestyle data, no business-to-business sectors were selected; in the event, eight business-to-business responses were received – presumably due to database coding errors – these responses appear as 'other' in the analysis.

3. Management Summary – Key Findings

Of the 151 organisations responding to this survey, key findings were as follows.

3.1 Seventy-five per cent of respondents currently use geodemographic or lifestyle data in their business.

3.2 The data in question were supplied by:

A supplier of GIS/computer mapping	30.5%
The data vendor in question	27.8%
A market research agency	14.6%
An advertising agency	9.9%

Notes: Other sources accounted for less than 8% each, total 21.2%.
Figures add to more than 100% because of multiple supply.

3.3 **Spontaneous awareness** of suppliers of geodemographic or lifestyle data gave the following numbers of mentions:

		Per cent of Total Respondents
CACI/ACORN	106	70.2%
CCN/MOSAIC	93	61.6%
NDL Lifestyle	46	30.5%
ICD	42	27.8%
CMT/Behaviourbank/NSS	34	22.5%
CDMS/Superprofiles	32	21.2%
Pinpoint/FiNPiN	31	21.2%
Infolink/PORTRAIT/DEFINE	29	19.2%

Note: Other mentions amounted to less than 20 each.

3.4 **Prompted awareness** of suppliers of **geodemographics** gave the following responses:

	Per cent of total respondents
CACI	85.4%
CCN	71.5%
Infolink	60.9%
GMAP	49.0%
CDMS	40.4%
Market Profiles/GEOPLAN	35.1%
Equifax	34.4%
Data Consultancy	27.1%
Dunn-Humby	23.2%
SPA	22.5%
Euro Direct	20.5%

Note: Other mentions amounted to less than 20% awareness.

3.5 **Usage of geodemographic suppliers** in respondents' current organisation gave the following responses:

	Per cent of total respondents
CACI	40.4%
CCN	40.4%
Infolink	12.6%
Equifax	11.9%
CDMS	9.9%
Data Consultancy	5.3%
SPA	4.6%
Market Profiles/GEOPLAN	4.0%
Dunn-Humby	3.3%
Euro Direct	3.3%
GMAP	2.6%

Note: Other mentions amounted to less than 2.5% usage.

3.6 **Prompted awareness of suppliers of lifestyle data** gave the following responses:

	Per cent of total respondents
ICD	52.3%
NDL	51.0%
CMT	37.1%

3.7 **Usage of lifestyle data suppliers** in respondents' current organisation gave the following responses:

	Per cent of total respondents
ICD	19.9%
NDL	18.5%
CMT	11.9%

3.8 **Prompted awareness of suppliers of GIS/computer mapping** gave the following responses:

	Per cent of total respondents
MapInfo	38.4%
Tactician	17.2%
Strategic Mapping (Atlas)	15.9%
ESRI(ARC-INFO)	11.9%
LaserScan	9.3%
Smallworld	9.3%
GeoMatrix (Prospex)	7.3%

Note: Other mentions amounted to less than 7% awareness.

3.9　**Usage of these systems** in respondents' current organisations gave the following responses:

	Per cent of total respondents
MapInfo	11.9%
Strategic Mapping (Atlas)	2.6%
Tactician	2.0%
Geomatrix (Prospex)	2.0%
ESRI(ARC-INFO)	1.3%

Note: Other mentions amounted to less than 1% usage.

3.10　**Applications addressed** using geodemographic or lifestyle data in respondents' organisations included:

	Per cent of total respondents
Targeting direct mail	55.6%
Market segmentation	47.0%
Customer database building	41.1%
Media analysis	34.4%
Retail location analysis	29.8%
Sales force organisation	13.2%
Other applications	12.6%

3.11　**Companies providing geodemographic services and/or data** to respondents' organisations in the last two years were:

	Mentions (in order of importance)		
	First	Second	Third
Per cent of all respondents	65.6%	34.4%	11.3%
Geodemographic company used:			
CCN	42	13	3
CACI	30	16	3
CDMS	4	1	–
Data Consultancy	3	1	1
Equifax	2	1	2
TGI	2	-	–
SPA	1	1	2
OPCS	-	2	–
Others (one mention each)	15	17	6
Totals	**99**	**52**	**17**

3.12 **Companies providing lifestyle data** to respondents' organisations in the last two years were:

	Mentions (in order of importance)		
	First	Second	Third
Per cent of all respondents	53.6%	20.5%	8.6%
Lifestyle company used:			
NDL	22	7	2
ICD	14	7	4
CCN	13	3	1
CMT	11	6	4
CACI	7	5	1
BMRB	7	–	1
CDMS	2	–	–
Others (one mention each)	5	3	–
Totals	**81**	**31**	**13**

Note: Some confusion evident in what is meant by 'lifestyle data' in this context!

3.13 **Companies providing PC-based market analysis systems and/or GIS or computer mapping** to respondents in the last two years were:

	Mentions (in order of importance)		
	First	Second	Third
Per cent of all respondents	36.4%	11.3%	4.6%
Company/system used:			
CCN	24	1	1
CACI	9	3	–
MapInfo	5	–	–
Data Consultancy	3	1	–
CDMS	2	–	–
ESRI	2	–	–
Euro Direct	2	–	–
IMS	2	–	–
SPA	2	1	–
Others (one mention each)	4	11	6
Totals	**55**	**17**	**7**

3.14 There were two further questions on the questionnaire, concerned with:

(a) the actual or potential usefulness to respondents' businesses, of the types of data and systems surveyed;

(b) whether respondents' organisations had gained tangible benefits from the use of these services.

Sadly, these two questions were not answered in a sufficient number of cases to provide reliable data for analysis.

4. Conclusions

It is believed that this end-user survey has provided the first publicly available information on usage of data and systems in the geodemographics and lifestyles market. While it cannot be claimed that the 75 per cent penetration of all respondents is necessarily the case for the whole of the marketing and advertising community (respondents having 'selected themselves', probably on the basis of their interest in the market); nevertheless, the market shares revealed in this survey are probably fairly representative. Certainly, all the main 'players' in the marketplace are represented in this research report, and anecdotal evidence supports the orders of magnitude shown here.

SOCIAL GRADE, SOCIAL CLASS, SOCIO-ECONOMIC GROUP

NRS SOCIAL GRADE

Social Grade	Social Status	Occupation
A	Upper middle class	Higher managerial, administrative or professional
B	Middle class	Intermediate managerial, administrative or professional
C1	Lower middle class	Supervisory or clerical, and professional, junior managerial, or administrative
C2	Skilled working class	Skilled manual workers
D	Working class	Semi and unskilled manual workers
E	Those at lowest level of subsistence	State pensioners or widows (no other earner), casual or lowest grade workers

DISTRIBUTION OF ADULT POPULATION (15+) BY SOCIAL GRADE OF CHIEF INCOME EARNER, GREAT BRITAIN, 1996

Social Grade	All Adults 15+ '000s	%
A	1,360	2.9
B	8,540	18.5
C1	12,680	27.5
C2	10,368	22.5
D	7,791	16.9
E	5,361	11.6
Total	46,100	100.0

Source: National Readership Survey.

CENSUS DEFINITIONS OF SOCIAL CLASS

It has been customary for Government purposes to arrange the large number of groups in the classification of occupations into a small number of broad categories called social classes. The census definitions of these social classes focuses on residents of private households as follows:

		1991
Social Class I	Professional occupations	6.9%
Social Class II	Managerial and technical occupations	30.8%
Social Class III(N)	Skilled occupations – non manual	12.2%
Social Class III(M)	Skilled occupations – manual	28.9%
Social Class IV	Partly skilled occupations	13.9%
Social Class V	Unskilled occupations	4.6%
Armed Forces		1.0%
On a government scheme		0.7%
Occupation inadequately described or not stated		1.0%
Total		100.0%

Note: Retired and other inactive heads of households are allocated in line with former occupation, so long as they were occupied in previous ten years.

CENSUS DEFINITIONS OF SOCIO-ECONOMIC GROUPS

Social-economic groups bring together people with jobs of similar social and economic status. This classification is applied to the economically active (including unemployed), *retired and *permanently sick by considering their employment status and occupation.

	Broad description	1991 GB Population (Residents)
SEG 1	Employers and managers in central and local government, industry, commerce, etc. – large establishments	4.6%
SEG 2	Employers and managers in industry, commerce, etc. – small establishments	10.1%
SEG 3	Professional workers – self employed	0.9%
SEG 4	Professional workers – employees	3.7%
SEG 5	Intermediate non-manual workers	
5.1	Ancillary workers and artists	12.0%
5.2	Foremen and supervisors non-manual	1.0%
SEG 6	Junior non-manual workers	20.5%
SEG 7	Personal service workers	4.5%
SEG 8	Foremen and supervisors manual	2.0%
SEG 9	Skilled manual workers	13.1%
SEG 10	Semi-skilled manual workers	10.9%
SEG 11	Unskilled manual workers	5.7%
SEG 12	Own account workers (other than professional)	6.2%
SEG 13	Farmers – employers and managers	0.4%
SEG 14	Farmers – own account	0.4%
SEG 15	Agricultural workers	0.8%
SEG 16	Members of the armed forces	0.8%
SEG 17	Inadequately described or not stated occupation	1.0%
	On a government scheme	1.4%
Total		100.0%

*The retired and permanently sick are allocated on the basis of previous occupation if stated on the census.

CENSUS SOCIO-ECONOMIC GROUPS BY MARKETING DEFINITIONS OF SOCIAL GRADE

Social Grade AB:	**Professional and managerial**
SEG 1	Employers and managers in central and local government, industry, commerce etc. – large
SEG 2	Employers and managers in industry, commerce etc. – small establishments
SEG 3	Professional workers – self employed
SEG 4	Professional workers – employees
SEG 13	Farmers – employers and managers
Social Grade C1:	**Intermediate and junior non-manual**
SEG 5.1	Ancillary workers and artists
SEG 5.2	Foremen and supervisors non-manual
SEG 6	Junior non-manual workers
Social Grade C2:	**Skilled manual**
SEG 8	Foremen and supervisors – manual
SEG 9	Skilled manual workers
SEG 12	Own account workers (other than professional)
SEG 14	Farmers – own account
Social Grade DE:	**Semi-skilled and unskilled manual**
SEG 7	Personal service workers
SEG 10	Semi-skilled manual workers
SEG 11	Unskilled manual workers
SEG 15	Agricultural workers

Notes: The Armed Forces are treated separately in the census, and cannot be allocated in a single grade.
SEG17 can reasonably be allocated to this social grade structure by pro-rata.

1991 CENSUS OUTPUT TABLES – LISTING
INDEX OF LOCAL BASE STATISTICS AND SMALL AREA STATISTICS TABLES

100 Per Cent Tables

Source: From '1991 Census User Guide 3', entitled 'Social Statistics, Small Area Statistics, Prospectus'. Published by OPCS/GRO(S). Crown Copyright.

1991 CENSUS OUTPUT AREAS

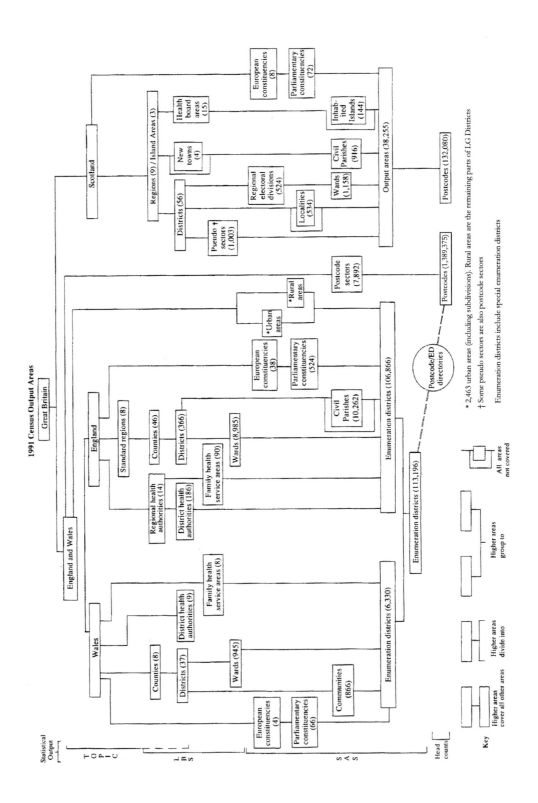

Source: ONS/GRO(S), Crown Copyright.

REFERENCES

Alt, M. 1990, *Exploring Hyperspace – a non-mathematical explanation of multi-variate analysis*, McGraw-Hill.

Bermingham, J., Baker, K. and McDonald, C. 1979, 'ACORN – a classification of residential neighbourhoods', MRS conference 1979.

Binns, S. 1997, 'The use of cluster analysis in evaluating small catchment area potential', MRS Census Interest Group Geodemographics for Business Decisions seminar.

Bond, S. 1997, 'Driving the store development process using geodemographic analysis', MRS Census Interest Group Geodemographics for Business Decisions seminar.

Broom, D. 1996, 'Can a retailer find the right information systems', Admap Targeting Consumers 2000 conference.

Brown, A. and Mackay, A. 1996, 'It's lifestyle – but not as we know it', Admap Targeting Consumers 2000 conference.

Callingham, M. 1996, 'Will the MAU problem defeat turnover estimation modelling?', AGI conference.

Chamberlain, A. 1997, 'Co-operate to accumulate', *New Perspectives*, Issue 7, June 1997.

Charlton, M., Openshaw, S. and Wymer, C. 1985, 'Some new classifications of census Enumeration Districts in Britain: a poor man's ACORN', *Journal of Economic and Social Measurement*, 13.

Cowling, A. 1996, 'New information systems', Admap Targeting Consumers 2000 conference.

Dale, A. and Marsh, C. 1993, *The 1991 Census Users' Guide*, HMSO.

Davies, R. and Rogers, D. (Eds), 1984, *Store Location and Store Assessment Research*, John Wiley.

Department of the Environment, 1987, 'Handling Geographic Information', Report of the Committee of Enquiry Chaired by Lord Chorley', HMSO.

Guy, C. 1994, *The Retail Development Process – Location, Property and Planning*, Routledge & Kegan Paul.

Hallberg, G. 1995, *All Consumers are not Created Equal*, John Wiley.

Hunt, C. 1996, 'Using the power of television: new opportunities for consumer targeting', Admap Targeting Consumers 2000 conference.

Jones, K. and Simmons, J. 1990, *The Retail Environment*, Routledge & Kegan Paul.

Leventhal, B. 1993, 'Birds of a feather? Or, geodemographics – an endangered species?', Market Research Society Annual Conference.

Leventhal, B., Moy, C. and Griffin, J. (Eds), 1993, *An Introductory Guide to the 1991 Census*, NTC Publications Ltd.

Longley, P. and Batty, M. (Eds), 1996, *Spatial Analysis: Modelling in a GIS Environment*, GeoInformation International.

Longley, P. and Clarke, G. (Eds), 1995, *GIS for Business and Service Planning*, GeoInformation International.

Mitchell, V-W. 1992, 'The future of geodemographic information handling', *Logistics Information Management*, Vol. 5, No. 3, MCB University Press.

Openshaw, S. 1983, 'Multivariate analysis of census data: the classification of areas' in *A Census User's Handbook*, Rhind, D (Ed), Methuen.

OPCS/GRO(S), 1992, *1991 Census Definitions: Great Britain*, HMSO.

Peppers, D. and Rogers, M. 1993, *The One to One Future*, Doubleday.

Reynolds, J. 1992, 'Managing the local market: information technology applications in retailing', *Journal of Information Technology*, Vol. 7, No. 4.

Raper, J., Rhind, D. and Shepherd, J. 1992, *Postcodes: The New Geography*, Longman.

Sleight, P. 1990, 'Where are the 55+ target market?' in Buck, S. (Ed) *The 55+ Market: Exploring a Golden Marketing Opportunity*, McGraw-Hill.

Sleight, P. and Leventhal, B. 1989, 'Applications of geodemographics to research and marketing', *Journal of the Market Research Society*, 31, 1, 1989.

Sleight, P. and Leventhal, B. 1993, 'An introduction to multivariate analysis techniques and their application in direct marketing', *Journal of Targeting, Measurement and Analysis for Marketing*, Vol. 1, No. 1, Henry Stewart Publications.

Wilson, G. 1996, 'GIS and statistics in retail insurance marketing', AGI '96 conference.

Wrigley, N. (Ed), 1988, *Store Choice, Store Location and Market Analysis*, Routledge & Kegan Paul.

INDEX